REFERENCE

ED-R

Junior
Worldmark
Encyclopedia of

World Cultures

Junior Worldmark Encyclopedia of

World Cultures

VOLUME 6

Mauritania to Nigeria

AN IMPRINT OF GALE

DETROIT · LONDON

JUNIOR WORLDMARK ENCYCLOPEDIA OF WORLD CULTURES

U•X•L Staff

Jane Hoehner, *U•X•L Senior Editor*
Carol DeKane Nagel, *U•X•L Managing Editor*
Thomas L. Romig, *U•X•L Publisher*
Mary Beth Trimper, *Production Director*
Evi Seoud, *Assistant Production Manager*
Shanna Heilveil, *Production Associate*
Cynthia Baldwin, *Product Design Manager*
Barbara J. Yarrow, *Graphic Services Supervisor*
Pamela A. E. Galbreath, *Senior Art Director*
Margaret Chamberlain, *Permissions Specialist (Pictures)*

Library of Congress Cataloging-in-Publication Data
Junior worldmark encyclopedia of world cultures / Timothy L. Gall and
  Susan Bevan Gall, editors.
      p.   cm.
    Includes bibliographical references and index.
    Summary: Arranges countries around the world alphabetically,
  subdivides these countries into 250 culture groups, and provides
  information about the ethnology and human geography of each group.
    ISBN 0-7876-1756-X (set : alk. paper)
    1. Ethnology--Encyclopedias, Juvenile. 2. Human geography-
  -Encyclopedias, Juvenile. [1. Ethnology--Encyclopedias. 2. Human
  geography--Encyclopedias.]   I. Gall, Timothy L.   II. Gall, Susan B.
  GN307.J85 1999
    306' .03--dc21   98-13810
                                                              CIP
                                                               AC

ISBN 0-7876-1756-X (set)
ISBN 0-7876-1757-1 (vol. 1)   ISBN 0-7876-1758-X (vol. 2)   ISBN 0-7876-1759-8 (vol. 3)
ISBN 0-7876-1760-1 (vol. 4)   ISBN 0-7876-1761-X (vol. 5)   ISBN 0-7876-1762-8 (vol. 6)
ISBN 0-7876-1763-6 (vol. 7)   ISBN 0-7876-1764-4 (vol. 8)   ISBN 0-7876-2761-5 (vol. 9)

Printed in the United States of America
10 9 8 7 6 5 4 3 2

Contents
Volume 6

Cumulative Contents

CUMULATIVE CONTENTS

CUMULATIVE CONTENTS

Volume 5

Volume 6

CUMULATIVE CONTENTS

CUMULATIVE CONTENTS

Contributors

Editors: Timothy L. Gall and Susan Bevan Gall

Senior Editor: Daniel M. Lucas

Contributing Editors: Himanee Gupta, Jim Henry, Kira Silverbird, Elaine Trapp, Rosalie Wieder

Copy Editors: Deborah Baron, Janet Fenn, Jim Henry, Patricia M. Mote, Deborah Ring, Kathy Soltis

Typesetting and Graphics: Cheryl Montagna, Brian Rajewski

Cover Photographs: Cory Langley

Data Input: Janis K. Long, Cheryl Montagna, Melody Penfound

Proofreaders: Deborah Baron, Janet Fenn

Editorial Assistants: Katie Baron, Jennifer A. Spencer, Daniel K. Updegraft

Editorial Advisors

P. Boone, Sixth Grade Teacher, Oak Crest Middle School, San Antonio, Texas

Jean Campbell, Foothill Farms Middle School, Sacramento, California

Kathy Englehart, Librarian, Hathaway Brown School, Shaker Heights, Ohio

Catherine Harris, Librarian, Oak Crest Middle School, San Antonio, Texas

Karen James, Children's Services, Louisville Free Public Library, Louisville, Kentucky

Contributors to the Gale Edition

The articles presented in this encyclopedia are based on entries in the *Worldmark Encyclopedia of Cultures and Daily Life* published in 1997 by Gale. The following authors and reviewers contributed to the Gale edition.

ANDREW J. ABALAHIN. Doctoral candidate, Department of History, Cornell University.

JAMAL ABDULLAH. Doctoral candidate, Department of City and Regional Planning, Cornell University.

SANA ABED-KOTOB. Book Review Editor, Middle East Journal, Middle East Institute.

MAMOUD ABOUD. Charge d'Affaires, a.i., Embassy of the Federal and Islamic Republic of the Comoros.

JUDY ALLEN. Editor, Choctaw Nation of Oklahoma.

HIS EXCELLENCY DENIS G. ANTOINE. Ambassador to the United States, Embassy of Grenada.

LESLEY ANN ASHBAUGH. Instructor, Sociology, Seattle University.

HASHEM ATALLAH. Translator, Editor, Teacher; Fairfax, Virginia.

HECTOR AZEVES. Cultural Attaché, Embassy of Uruguay.

VICTORIA J. BAKER. Associate Professor of Anthropology, Anthropology (Collegium of Comparative Cultures), Eckerd College.

POLINE BALA. Doctoral candidate, Asian Studies, Cornell University.

MARJORIE MANDELSTAM BALZER. Research Professor; Coordinator, Social, Regional, and Ethnic Studies Sociology, and Center for Eurasian, Russian, and East European Studies.

JOSHUA BARKER. Doctoral candidate, Department of Anthropology, Cornell University.

IGOR BARSEGIAN. Department of Sociology, George Washington University.

IRAJ BASHIRI. Professor of Central Asian Studies, Department of Slavic and Central Asian Languages and Literatures, University of Minnesota.

DAN F. BAUER. Department of Anthropology, Lafayette College.

JOYCE BEAR. Historic Preservation Officer, Muscogee Nation of Oklahoma.

SVETLANA BELAIA. Byelorussian-American Cultural Center, Strongsville, Ohio.

HIS EXCELLENCY DR. COURTNEY BLACKMAN. Ambassador to the United States, Embassy of Barbados.

BETTY BLAIR. Executive Editor, Azerbaijan International.

ARVIDS BLODNIEKS. Director, Latvian Institute, American Latvian Association in the USA.

ARASH BORMANSHINOV. University of Maryland, College Park.

HARRIET I. BRADY. Cultural Anthropologist (Pyramid Lake Paiute Tribe), Native Studies Program, Pyramid Lake High School.

MARTIN BROKENLEG. Professor of Sociology, Department of Sociology, Augustana College.

REV. RAYMOND A. BUCKO, S.J. Assistant Professor of Anthropology, LeMoyne College.

JOHN W. BURTON. Department of Anthropology, Connecticut College.

DINEANE BUTTRAM. University of North Carolina-Chapel Hill.

RICARDO CABALLERO. Counselor, Embassy of Paraguay.

CHRISTINA CARPADIS. Researcher/Writer, Cleveland, Ohio.

SALVADOR GARCIA CASTANEDA. Department of Spanish and Portuguese, The Ohio State University.

SUSANA CAVALLO. Graduate Program Director and Professor of Spanish, Department of Modern Languages and Literatures, Loyola University, Chicago.

BRIAN P. CAZA. Doctoral candidate, Political Science, University of Chicago.

VAN CHRISTO. President and Executive Director, Frosina Foundation, Boston.

YURI A. CHUMAKOV. Graduate Student, Department of Sociology, University of Notre Dame.

J. COLARUSSO. Professor of Anthropology, McMaster University.

FRANCESCA COLECCHIA. Modern Language Department, Duquesne University.

DIANNE K. DAEG DE MOTT. Researcher/Writer, Tucson, Arizona.

MICHAEL DE JONGH. Professor, Department of Anthropology, University of South Africa.

GEORGI DERLUGUIAN. Senior Fellow, Ph.D., U. S. Institute of Peace.

CHRISTINE DRAKE. Department of Political Science and Geography, Old Dominion University.

ARTURO DUARTE. Guatemalan Mission to the OAS.

CALEB DUBE. Department of Anthropology, Northwestern University.

BRIAN DU TOIT. Professor, Department of Anthropology, University of Florida.

LEAH ERMARTH. Worldspace Foundation, Washington, DC.

NANCY J. FAIRLEY. Associate Professor of Anthropology, Department of Anthropology/Sociology, Davidson College.

GREGORY A. FINNEGAN, Ph.D. Tozzer Library, Harvard University.

ALLEN J. FRANK, Ph.D.

DAVID P. GAMBLE. Professor Emeritus, Department of Anthropology, San Francisco State University.

FREDERICK GAMST. Professor, Department of Anthropology, University of Massachusetts, Harbor Campus.

PAULA GARB. Associate Director of Global Peace and Conflict Studies and Adjunct Professor of Social Ecology, University of California, Irvine.

HAROLD GASKI. Associate Professor of Sami Literature, School of Languages and Literature, University of Tromsø.

STEPHEN J. GENDZIER.

FLORENCE GERDEL.

ANTHONY P. GLASCOCK. Professor of Anthropology; Department of Anthropology, Psychology, and Sociology; Drexel University.

LUIS GONZALEZ. Researcher/Writer, River Edge, New Jersey.

JENNIFER GRAHAM. Researcher/Writer, Sydney, Australia.

MARIE-CÉCILE GROELSEMA. Doctoral candidate, Comparative Literature, Indiana University.

ROBERT GROELSEMA. MPIA and doctoral candidate, Political Science, Indiana University.

MARIA GROSZ-NGATÉ. Visiting Assistant Professor, Department of Anthropology, Northwestern University.

ELLEN GRUENBAUM. Professor, School of Social Sciences, California State University, Fresno.

N. THOMAS HAKANSSON. University of Kentucky.

ROBERT HALASZ. Researcher/Writer, New York, New York.

MARC HANREZ. Professor, Department of French and Italian, University of Wisconsin-Madison.

ANWAR UL HAQ. Central Asian Studies Department, Indiana University.

LIAM HARTE. Department of Philosophy, Loyola University, Chicago.

FR. VASILE HATEGAN. Author, *Romanian Culture in America*.

BRUCE HEILMAN. Doctoral candidate, Department of Political Science, Indiana University.

JIM HENRY. Researcher/Writer, Cleveland, Ohio.

BARRY HEWLETT. Department of Anthropology, Washington State University.

SUSAN F. HIRSCH. Department of Anthropology, Wesleyan University.

MARIDA HOLLOS. Department of Anthropology, Brown University.

HALYNA HOLUBEC. Researcher/Writer, Cleveland, Ohio.

YVONNE HOOSAVA. Legal Researcher and Cultural Preservation Officer, Hopi Tribal Council.

HUIQIN HUANG, Ph.D. Center for East Asia Studies, University of Montreal.

ASAFA JALATA. Assistant Professor of Sociology and African and African American Studies, Department of Sociology, The University of Tennessee, Knoxville.

STEPHEN F. JONES. Russian Department, Mount Holyoke College.

THOMAS JOVANOVSKI, Ph.D. Lorain County Community College.

A. KEN JULES. Minister Plenipotentiary and Deputy Head of Mission, Embassy of St. Kitts and Nevis.

GENEROSA KAGARUKI-KAKOTI. Economist, Department of Urban and Rural Planning, College of Lands and Architectural Studies, Dar es Salaam, Tanzania.

EZEKIEL KALIPENI. Department of Geography, University of Illinois at Urbana-Champaign.

CONTRIBUTORS

DON KAVANAUGH. Program Director, Lake of the Woods Ojibwa Cultural Centre.

SUSAN M. KENYON. Associate Professor of Anthropology, Department of History and Anthropology, Butler University.

WELILE KHUZWAYO. Department of Anthropology, University of South Africa.

PHILIP L. KILBRIDE. Professor of Anthropology, Mary Hale Chase Chair in the Social Sciences, Department of Anthropology, Bryn Mawr College.

RICHARD O. KISIARA. Doctoral candidate, Department of Anthropology, Washington University in St. Louis.

KAREN KNOWLES. Permanent Mission of Antigua and Barbuda to the United Nations.

IGOR KRUPNIK. Research Anthropologist, Department of Anthropology, Smithsonian Institution.

LEELO LASS. Secretary, Embassy of Estonia.

ROBERT LAUNAY. Professor, Department of Anthropology, Northwestern University.

CHARLES LEBLANC. Professor and Director, Center for East Asia Studies, University of Montreal.

RONALD LEE. Author, *Goddam Gypsy, An Autobiographical Novel.*

PHILIP E. LEIS. Professor and Chair, Department of Anthropology, Brown University.

MARIA JUKIC LESKUR. Croatian Consulate, Cleveland, Ohio.

RICHARD A. LOBBAN, JR. Professor of Anthropology and African Studies, Department of Anthropology, Rhode Island College.

DERYCK O. LODRICK. Visiting Scholar, Center for South Asian Studies, University of California, Berkeley.

NEIL LURSSEN. Intro Communications Inc.

GREGORIO C. MARTIN. Modern Language Department, Duquesne University.

HOWARD J. MARTIN. Independent scholar.

HEITOR MARTINS. Professor, Department of Spanish and Portuguese, Indiana University.

ADELINE MASQUELIER. Assistant Professor, Department of Anthropology, Tulane University.

DOLINA MILLAR.

EDITH MIRANTE. Project Maje, Portland, Oregon.

ROBERT W. MONTGOMERY, Ph.D. Indiana University.

THOMAS D. MORIN. Associate Professor of Hispanic Studies, Department of Modern and Classical Literatures and Languages, University of Rhode Island.

CHARLES MORRILL. Doctoral candidate, Indiana University.

CAROL A. MORTLAND. Crate's Point, The Dalles, Oregon.

FRANCIS A. MOYER. Director, North Carolina Japan Center, North Carolina State University.

MARIE C. MOYER.

NYAGA MWANIKI. Assistant Professor, Department of Anthropology and Sociology, Western Carolina University.

KENNETH NILSON. Celtic Studies Department, Harvard University.

JANE E. ORMROD. Graduate Student, History, University of Chicago.

JUANITA PAHDOPONY. Carl Perkins Program Director, Comanche Tribe of Oklahoma.

TINO PALOTTA. Syracuse University.

ROHAYATI PASENG.

PATRICIA PITCHON. Researcher/Writer, London, England.

STEPHANIE PLATZ. Program Officer, Program on Peace and International Cooperation, The John D. and Catherine T. MacArthur Foundation.

MIHAELA POIATA. Graduate Student, School of Journalism and Mass Communication, University of North Carolina at Chapel Hill.

LEOPOLDINA PRUT-PREGELJ. Author, *Historical Dictionary of Slovenia.*

J. RACKAUSKAS. Director, Lithuanian Research and Studies Center, Chicago.

J. RAKOVICH. Byelorussian-American Cultural Center, Strongsville, Ohio.

HANTA V. RALAY. Promotions, Inc., Montgomery Village, Maryland.

SUSAN J. RASMUSSEN. Associate Professor, Department of Anthropology, University of Houston.

RONALD REMINICK. Department of Anthropology, Cleveland State University.

BRUCE D. ROBERTS. Assistant Professor of Anthropology, Department of Anthropology and Sociology, University of Southern Mississippi.

LAUREL L. ROSE. Philosophy Department, Carnegie-Mellon University.

ROBERT ROTENBERG. Professor of Anthropology, International Studies Program, DePaul University.

CAROLINE SAHLEY, Ph.D. Researcher/Writer, Cleveland, Ohio.

VERONICA SALLES-REESE. Associate Professor, Department of Spanish and Portuguese, Georgetown University.

MAIRA SARYBAEVA. Kazakh-American Studies Center, University of Kentucky.

DEBRA L. SCHINDLER. Institute of Arctic Studies, Dartmouth College.

KYOKO SELDEN, Ph.D. Researcher/Writer, Ithaca, New York.

ENAYATULLAH SHAHRANI. Central Asian Studies Department, Indiana University.

ROBERT SHANAFELT. Adjunct Lecturer, Department of Anthropology, The Florida State University.

TUULIKKI SINKS. Teaching Specialist for Finnish, Department of German, Scandinavian, and Dutch, University of Minnesota.

JAN SJÅVIK. Associate Professor, Scandinavian Studies, University of Washington.

CONTRIBUTORS

MAGDA SOBALVARRO. Press and Cultural Affairs Director, Embassy of Nicaragua.

MICHAEL STAINTON. Researcher, Joint Center for Asia Pacific Studies, York University.

RIANA STEYN. Department of Anthropology, University of South Africa.

PAUL STOLLER. Professor, Department of Anthropology, West Chester University.

CRAIG STRASHOFER. Researcher/Writer, Cleveland, Ohio.

SANDRA B. STRAUBHAAR. Assistant Professor, Nordic Studies, Department of Germanic and Slavic Languages, Brigham Young University.

VUM SON SUANTAK. Author, *Zo History*.

MURAT TAISHIBAEV. Kazakh-American Studies Center, University of Kentucky.

CHRISTOPHER C. TAYLOR. Associate Professor, Anthropology Department, University of Alabama, Birmingham.

EDDIE TSO. Office of Language and Culture, Navajo Division of Education.

DAVID TYSON. Foreign Broadcast Information Service, Washington, D.C.

NICOLAAS G. W. UNLANDT. Assistant Professor of French, Department of French and Italian, Brigham Young University.

GORDON URQUHART. Professor, Department of Economics and Business, Cornell College.

CHRISTOPHER J. VAN VUUREN. Professor, Department of Anthropology, University of South Africa.

DALIA VENTURA-ALCALAY. Journalist, London, England.

CATHERINE VEREECKE. Assistant Director, Center for African Studies, University of Florida.

GREGORY T. WALKER. Associate Director, Office of International Affairs, Duquesne University.

GERHARD WEISS. Department of German, Scandinavian, and Dutch, University of Minnesota.

PATSY WEST. Director, The Seminole/Miccosukee Photographic Archive.

WALTER WHIPPLE. Associate Professor of Polish, Germanic and Slavic Languages, Brigham Young University.

ROSALIE WIEDER. Researcher/Writer, Cleveland, Ohio.

JEFFREY WILLIAMS. Professor, Department of Anthropology, Cleveland State University.

GUANG-HONG YU. Associate Research Fellow, Institute of Ethnology, Academia Sinica.

RUSSELL ZANCA. Department of Anthropology, College of Liberal Arts and Sciences, University of Illinois at Urbana-Champaign.

Reader's Guide

Junior Worldmark Encyclopedia of World Cultures contains articles exploring the ways of life of over 290 culture groups worldwide. Arranged alphabetically by country in nine volumes, this encyclopedia parallels the organization of its sister set, *Junior Worldmark Encyclopedia of the Nations.* Whereas the primary purpose of *Nations* is to provide information on the world's nations, this encyclopedia focuses on the traditions, living conditions, and personalities of many of the world's culture groups.

Defining groups for inclusion was not an easy task. Cultural identity is shaped by such factors as history, geography, nationality, ethnicity, race, language, and religion. Sometimes the distinctions are subtle, but important. Most chapters in this encyclopedia begin with an article on the people of the country as a nationality group. For example, the chapter on Kenya begins with an article entitled "Kenyans." This article explores the national character shared by all people living in Kenya. However, there are separate articles on the Gikuyu, Kalenjin, Luhya, and Luo—four of the largest ethnic groups living in the country. They are all Kenyans, but each group is distinct. Many profiled groups—like the Kazaks—inhabit lands that cross national boundaries. Although profiled in the chapter on Kazakstan, Kazaks are also important minorities in China, Uzbekistan, and Turkmenistan. In such cases, cross-references direct the student to the chapter where the group is profiled.

The photographs that illustrate the articles show a wonderfully diverse world. From the luxury liners docked in the harbor at Monaco to the dwellings made of grass sheltering the inhabitants of the rain forest, people share the struggles and joys of earning a living, bringing children into the world, teaching them to survive, and initiating them into adulthood. Although language, customs, and dress illustrate our differences, the faces of the people pictured in these volumes reinforce our similarities. Whether on the streets of Tokyo or the mountains of Tibet, a smile on the face of a child transcends the boundaries of nationality and cultural identity to reveal something common in us all. Photographer Cory Langley's images on pages 93 and 147 in Volume 6 serve to illustrate this point.

The picture of the world this encyclopedia paints today will certainly differ from the one painted in future editions. Indigenous people like the Jivaro in Ecuador (Volume 3, page 77) are being assimilated into modern society as forest lands are cleared for development and televisions and VCRs are brought to even the most remote villages. As the global economy expands, traditional diets are supplemented with Coke, Pepsi, and fast food; traditional storytellers are replaced by World Cup soccer matches and American television programs; and cultural heroes are overwhelmed by images of Michael Jordan and Michael Jackson. Photographer Cynthia Bassett was fortunate to be among a small group of travelers to visit a part of China only recently opened to Westerners. Her image of Miao dancers (Volume 2, page 161) shows a people far removed from Western culture . . . until one looks a little closer. Behind the dancers, in the upper corner of the photograph, is a basketball hoop and backboard. It turns out that Miao teenagers love basketball!

ORGANIZATION

Within each volume the chapters are arranged alphabetically by country. A cumulative table of contents for all volumes in the set follows the table of contents to each volume.

Each chapter covers a specific country. The contents of the chapter, listing the culture group articles, follows the chapter title. An overview of the composition of the population of the country appears after the contents list. The individual articles follow, and are organized according to a standard twenty-heading outline explained in more detail below. This structure allows for easy comparison between cultures and enhances the accessibility of the information.

Articles begin with the **pronunciation** of the group's name, a listing of **alternate names** by which the group is known, the group's **location** in the world, its **population**, the **languages** spoken, and the **religions** practiced. Articles are illustrated with maps showing the primary location of the group and photographs of the culture group being profiled. The twenty standard headings by which the articles are organized are presented below.

1 ● INTRODUCTION: A description of the group's historical origins provides a useful background for understanding its contemporary affairs. Information relating to migration helps explain how the group arrived at its present location. Political conditions and governmental structure(s) that affect members of the profiled ethnic group are also discussed.

2 ● LOCATION: The population size of the group is listed. This information may include official census data from various countries and/or estimates. Information on the size of a group's population located outside the traditional homeland may also be included, especially for those groups with large scattered populations. A description of the homeland includes information on location, topography, and climate.

3 ● LANGUAGE: Each article lists the name(s) of the primary language(s) spoken by members. Descriptions of linguistic origins, grammar, and similarities to other languages may also be included. Examples of common words, phrases, and proverbs are listed for many of the profiled groups, and some include examples of common personal names and greetings.

4 ● FOLKLORE: Common themes, settings, and characters in the profiled group's traditional oral and/or literary mythology are highlighted. Many entries include a short excerpt or synopsis of one of the group's noteworthy myths, fables, or legends. Some entries describe the accomplishments of famous heroes and heroines or other prominent historical figures.

5 ● RELIGION: The origins of traditional religious beliefs are profiled. Contemporary religious beliefs, customs, and practices are also discussed. Some groups may be closely associated with one particular faith (especially if religious and ethnic identification are interlinked), while others may have members of diverse faiths.

6 ● MAJOR HOLIDAYS: Celebrations and commemorations typically recognized by the group's members are described. These holidays commonly fall into two categories: secular and religious. Secular holidays often include an independence day and/or other days of observance recognizing important dates in history that affected the group as a whole. Religious holidays are typically the same as those honored by people of the same faith worldwide. Some secular and religious holidays are linked to the lunar cycle or to the change of seasons. Some articles describe customs practiced by members of the group on certain holidays.

7 ● RITES OF PASSAGE: Formal and informal events that mark an individual's procession through the stages of life are profiled. These events typically involve rituals, ceremonies, observances, and procedures associated with birth, childhood, the coming of age, milestones in education or religious training, adulthood, and death.

8 ● RELATIONSHIPS: Information on greetings, body language, gestures, visiting customs, and dating practices is included. The extent of formality to which members of a certain ethnic group treat others is also addressed, as some groups may adhere to customs governing interpersonal relationships more or less strictly than others.

9 ● LIVING CONDITIONS: General health conditions typical of the group's members are cited. Such information includes life expectancy, the prevalence of various diseases, and access to medical care. Information on urbanization, housing, and access to utilities is also included. Transportation methods typically utilized by the group's members are also discussed.

10 ● FAMILY LIFE: The size and composition of the family unit is profiled. Gender roles common to the group are also discussed, including the division of rights and responsibilities relegated to male and female group members. The roles that children, adults, and the elderly have within the group as a whole may also be addressed.

11 ● CLOTHING: Many entries include descriptive information (design, color, fabric, etc.) regarding traditional clothing (or national costume) for men and women, and indicate the frequency of its use in contemporary life. A description of typical clothing worn in modern daily life is also provided, especially if traditional clothing is no longer the usual form of dress. Distinctions between formal and work attire and descriptions of clothing preferences of young people are described for many groups as well.

12 ● FOOD: Descriptions of items commonly consumed by members of the group are listed. The frequency and occasion for meals is also described, as are any unique customs regarding eating and drinking, special utensils and furniture, and the role of food and beverages in ritual ceremonies. Many entries include a recipe for a favorite dish.

13 ● EDUCATION: The structure of formal education in the country or countries of residence is discussed, including information on primary, secondary, and higher education. For some groups, the role of informal education is also highlighted. Some articles include information regarding the relevance and importance of education among the group as a whole, along with parental expectations for children.

14 ● CULTURAL HERITAGE: Since many groups express their sense of identity through art, music, literature, and dance, a description of prominent styles is included. Some articles also cite the contributions of famous individual artists, writers, and musicians.

15 ● EMPLOYMENT: The type of labor that typically engages members of the profiled group is discussed. For some groups, the formal wage economy is the primary source of earnings, but for other groups, informal agriculture or trade may be the usual way to earn a living. Working conditions are also highlighted.

16 ● SPORTS: Popular sports that children and adults play are listed, as are typical spectator sports. Some articles include a description and/or rules to a sport or game.

17 ● RECREATION: Listed activities that people enjoy in their leisure time may include structured pastimes (such as public musical and dance performances) or informal get-togethers (such as meeting for conversation). The role of popular culture, movies, theater, and television in everyday life is also discussed where it applies.

18 ● CRAFTS AND HOBBIES: Entries describe arts and crafts commonly fabricated according to traditional methods, materials, and style. Such objects may often have a functional utility for everyday tasks.

19 ● SOCIAL PROBLEMS: Internal and external issues that confront members of the profiled group are described. Such concerns often deal with fundamental problems like war, famine, disease, and poverty. A lack of human rights, civil rights, and political freedom may also adversely affect a group as a whole. Other problems may include crime, unemployment, substance abuse, and domestic violence.

20 ● BIBLIOGRAPHY: References cited include works used to compile the article, benchmark publications often recognized as authoritative by scholars, and other reference sources accessible to middle school researchers. Website addresses are provided for researchers who wish to access the World Wide Web. The website citation includes the author and title of the website (if applicable). The address begins with characters that follow "http://" in the citation; the address ends with the character preceding the comma and date. For example, the citation for the website of the German embassy appears as follows:

German Embassy, Washington, D.C. [Online]
    Available http://www.germany-info.org/, 1998.

To access this site, researchers type:
    www.germany-info.org

A glossary and an index of groups profiled appears at the end of each volume.

ACKNOWLEDGMENTS

The editors express appreciation to the members of the U●X●L staff who were involved in a number of ways at various stages of development of the *Junior Worldmark Encyclopedia of World Cultures.*

SUGGESTIONS ARE WELCOME: We appreciate any suggestions that will enhance future editions. Please send comments to:

Editors
Junior Worldmark Encyclopedia of World Cultures
U●X●L
27500 Drake Road
Farmington Hills, MI 48331-3535
(800) 877-4253

Mauritania

The people of Mauritania are called Mauritanians. Members of the main ethnic group, the Maures (also called Moors or Maurs), speak Hassaniyya Arabic (a dialect of Arabic). They make up about 70 percent of the population.

Mauritanians

PRONUNCIATION: mawr-uh-TAY-nee-uhns
LOCATION: Mauritania
POPULATION: 2.2 million
LANGUAGE: Hassaniyya Arabic; French; Azayr; Fulfulde; Mande-kan; Wolof
RELIGION: Islam (Sunni Muslim)

1 ● INTRODUCTION

Mauritania is part of the west-Saharan region of West Africa. This area is known to have supported a flourishing culture in the centuries preceding Christianity. Waves of immigrants began to flow into Mauritania in the third century AD. People from North Africa entered first during the third and fourth centuries, then again during the seventh and eighth centuries. By the eleventh century AD, traders had spread the Islamic religion throughout the Western Sahara.

Between the twelfth and seventeenth centuries, black Africans from Ghana and-Mali immigrated to Mauritania. By the late seventeenth century, Mauritania had four social groups. The people who spoke Hassaniyya Arabic became known as the Maures.

Early in the twentieth century, French forces occupied and set up a colonial administration in Mauritania, while much of the rest of the Western Sahara was controlled by Spain. After World War II (1939–45), France granted Mauritania some administrative and political freedoms. However, the colony did not become fully independent until November 28, 1960. After independence, there were continuing divisions between the non-Maure black Africans and the Maures, who dominated the political system and armed forces.

In 1976, Spain relinquished control of the Western Sahara (which it had held as a territory), dividing the territory between Morocco and Mauritania. The Polisario guerrillas, a group seeking self-determination for the region, then waged a war against Morocco. Mauritania allied itself with Morocco against the Polisario.

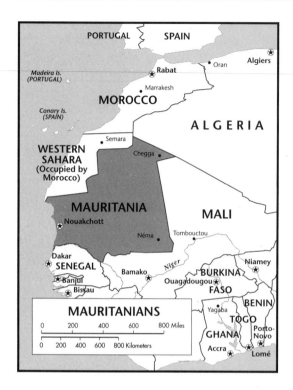

MAURITANIANS

| 0 | 200 | 400 | 600 | 800 Miles |
| 0 | 200 | 400 | 600 | 800 Kilometers |

kilometers). About two-thirds is desert, with an occasional oasis.

Mauritania has four geographic zones: the Saharan, the Sahelian, the Senegal River Valley, and the coastal zones. The topography is generally flat, arid plains. The capital is Nouakchott.

About 40 percent of the country is covered with sand. Some of the sand sits in fixed dunes; other dunes are carried about by the wind.

As of 1995, Mauritania had a population of 2.2 million people. More than half of Mauritanians are urban-dwellers. The greatest numbers live in Nouakchott and Nouadhibou. The remainder live on farms or in small towns.

The Maures are the largest ethnic group in Mauritania.

3 ● LANGUAGE

Mauritania's official languages are French and Hassaniyya Arabic. Hassaniyya is an Arabic language with many other words mixed in. Many people in the larger cities and villages speak French. The other main languages are Azayr, Fulfulde, Mande-kan, and Wolof.

Common boys' names are *Ahmad, Hamadi, Muhammad,* and *'Uthman.* Common girls' names are *Fatima, Bana, Hadia,* and *Safiya.*

4 ● FOLKLORE

Many Mauritanians have faith in the supernatural powers of holy men called *marabouts,* or *murabitun.* It is believed that their *baraka,* or divine grace, allows them to

Growing political conflicts in Mauritania led to a coup d'état (government overthrow) by military officers in July 1978. Another coup took place in December 1984. In July 1991, Mauritania drafted a new constitution that legalized a multiparty system in place of the former one-party system. As soon as the legal restrictions were lifted, sixteen political parties were formed. The constitution makes Islam the state religion, but stresses equality and individual freedoms.

2 ● LOCATION

Mauritania is located in Africa at the intersection of North Africa (the Maghrib) and West Africa. The country is roughly one and a half times the size of Texas. Its area is 398,069 square miles (1,031,000 square perform miracles. They make and distribute amulets and talismans (objects that are thought to bring good luck). These are believed to have mystical powers that provide protection from illness and injury.

5 ● RELIGION

The Mauritanians are Sunni Muslims, and have adhered to Islam since the ninth century AD. Mauritania's Constitutional Charter of 1985 declared Islam to be the state religion.

Islamic Sufi brotherhoods, known as *tariqas,* play an important role in the religious practices of the Mauritanians. Sufism stresses mysticism and the needs of the human spirit. The Qadiriyya brotherhood stresses Islamic learning, humility, generosity, and respect for one's neighbors. The Tijaniyya brotherhood is largely a missionary order that denounces theft, lying, cheating, and killing, and emphasizes continual reflection on God.

6 ● MAJOR HOLIDAYS

Mauritania's major national holiday is Independence Day (November 28). It is celebrated with a military parade that passes in front of a stage on which the president and his advisors are seated. The president addresses the nation in a speech.

Young people celebrate New Year's with parties that include a New Year's Eve countdown.

There are two major Islamic holidays observed in Mauritania. One is *Eid al-Fitr,* which comes at the end of the month of fasting called Ramadan. It is celebrated for three days. The other major Muslim holiday is *Eid al-Adha,* which commemorates the willingness of the Prophet Abraham to obey God's command, even when it meant sacrificing his own son. Traditionally, Islamic holidays are celebrated by wearing new clothes and cooking grilled meat. Girls color their hands with henna (a natural dye).

7 ● RITES OF PASSAGE

Every Mauritanian is expected to marry and have children. In the wedding ceremony, the bride and groom pledge themselves to the marriage with an Islamic marriage contract called an *aqd.* There are also two parties, beginning with the aqd party. Next comes the *marwah* party, a reception to send the bride off to her new family.

8 ● RELATIONSHIPS

A practice known as *essahwa* requires the young to treat the elderly with respect. For example, a young Mauritanian would not smoke in front of an elderly one. Also, the young are careful to use appropriate language in the presence of their elders. They also avoid displays of affection and loud conversation.

9 ● LIVING CONDITIONS

In the desert valleys of the countryside, or *badiya,* people live in cotton tents. These are light-colored on the outside, so as not to absorb the sunlight. They are draped with brightly colored fabrics inside. The ground inside the tent is covered with large woven mats known as *hasira*s.

In the southern regions, homes are built of cement. They are rectangular, with flat roofs and small windows. City homes are

Jason Laure

Mauritanian extended family is not related by blood, but by clan. It consists of a group of related males, with their wives, sons, and unmarried daughters.

furnished with carpets, mattresses, and floor pillows.

The drought of the 1970s and 1980s forced northerners to migrate southward. The result was a housing crisis in the towns of southern Mauritania. Shantytowns known as *kebe*s went up in and around the towns. The migrants set up homes of wood and scrap metal, sun-dried bricks, or tents. In the late 1980s, half the population in Nouakchott, the capital, lived in shanty-towns and slums.

10 ● FAMILY LIFE

The Mauritanian extended family consists of a group of related males, with their wives, sons, and unmarried daughters. The family is part of a larger kinship unit known as the descent, or lineage, group. A group of related lineages that maintain social ties is known as a clan. Marriage within the clan is preferred. First cousins are the traditional marriage partners.

Most daughters are given much training in raising a family and taking care of the house. Often, they are educated at home instead of at school. Traditionally, girls became engaged at ages as young as eight or ten years. Today many girls wait until they graduate from high school or college.

Mauritanian men are permitted to marry more than one wife. While some choose to do so, most do not. Often, however, they have several wives in a row, divorcing one and then marrying another.

11 ● CLOTHING

Mauritanian attire is influenced by the desert heat and Islamic norms. Women wear a *malaffa,* a long cloak wrapped loosely around the body from head to toe. The men wear a *dara,* a long, loose robe over baggy pants known as *sirwal.* Some men wear head-coverings, predominantly turbans or *hawli,* for protection from the winter cold and summer heat. Normal office attire for men is Western-style pants and shirts. In the south, women wear dresses, or skirts and blouses. They also wear long robes called *boubous.*

12 ● FOOD

Lunch is the biggest meal of the day in Mauritania. Commonly, villagers eat a spicy fish-and-vegetable stew with rice for lunch. Another popular Mauritanian lunch is spicy rice mixed with *tishtar,* or small pieces of dried meat. A common dinner meal is *couscous.* This consists of semolina wheat sprinkled with oil and water and rolled into tiny grains. Couscous can be mixed with a number of sauces. In some parts of Mauritania, couscous is known as *lachiri.*

A favorite desert drink is *zrig,* a cool drink made from goat's milk, water, and sugar. And, despite the heat of the desert, tea is common throughout the country.

13 ● EDUCATION

Elementary school lasts for six years and is followed by two stages of secondary school. The first lasts for four years, and the second

for three years. It is not mandatory for children to attend school. Attendance is far from universal. Only 35 percent of young children attend elementary schools. Even fewer (less than 10 percent) attend secondary school. Once girls have completed elementary school, it is common for them to stay home.

There are also numerous traditional schools that provide an Islamic education. They often develop around a learned Islamic leader known as a *marabout.* Boys generally attend religious schools for seven years, and girls attend for two years. The major emphasis is placed on religious learning. However, there is also emphasis on secular academic skills.

Mauritania has one major secular university, one Islamic institute of higher education, and some vocational institutes.

14 ● CULTURAL HERITAGE

Much of the literary work of Mauritanian writers focuses on Islamic affairs. There is also a love of imaginative literature, including poetry. Stories and poems are passed down through the generations in musical form, recited by storytellers known as *ighyuwn.* Tales are accompanied by a drum, a Mauritanian guitar *(tidinit),* or with a harp-like instrument *(ardin).* Poetry is often sung by minstrels and ballad singers. At social events, poetry praising the host or the guests is commonly sung.

15 ● EMPLOYMENT

In the past, 80 to 90 percent of Mauritanians led nomadic lifestyles (moving from one place to another), raising cattle, sheep, and goats. Between 1983 and 1985, a devastating drought struck Mauritania. Since then tens of thousands of animals have died. By the mid-1980s, about 85 percent of herders had moved to the cities to find other employment.

The largest employers in Mauritania are the government and the mining industry. Another major employer is the fishing and fish-processing industry.

16 ● SPORTS

Soccer is the most popular sport in Mauritania.

17 ● RECREATION

Because of the desert heat, desert dwellers rest after lunch, waiting for the sun to descend. In the evenings, families gather outside of the tent, sitting on a light mat called a *hasira*.

Children make many of their own toys from wire and tin cans. They also play games requiring no toys or equipment. One of these is a variation of tug-of-war known as *ligum*.

18 ● CRAFTS AND HOBBIES

Mauritanian craftspeople and artisans are known for their woodwork, jewelry, leatherwork, pottery, weaving, tailoring, and ironwork. Handwoven rugs and handcrafted silver and gold jewelry and cutlery are popular with tourists.

19 ● SOCIAL PROBLEMS

Mauritania's low standards of health care constitute a serious social problem. There are shortages of medical equipment and personnel. Infectious diseases such as malaria are prevalent.

A major political problem is ethnic tension between the Maures and non-Maure black Africans. The Maures (who are both black and white) dominate the country in terms of politics, education, and land ownership. Their most visible opposition comes from the Forces de Liberation Africaine de Mauritanie (FLAM). This is an illegal anti-government organization based south of Mauritania, in Senegal. The group has been accused of trying to overthrow the Mauritanian government. Some FLAM members have been executed, resulting in demonstrations and violent clashes between supporters and opponents of the government.

20 ● BIBLIOGRAPHY

Calderini, Simonetta. *Mauritania.* Santa Barbara, Calif.: Clio Press, 1992.

Goodsmith, Lauren. *The Children of Mauritania: Days in the Desert and by the River Shore.* Minneapolis, Minn.: Carolrhoda Books, 1993.

Handloff, Robert E. (ed.) *Mauritania: A Country Study.* Washington, D.C.: Federal Research Division, Library of Congress, 1990.

Hudson, Peter. *Travels in Mauritania.* London: Virgin, 1990.

WEBSITES

Arabnet. Mauritania. [Online] Available http://www.arab.net/mauritania/mauritania_contents.html, 1998.

Embassy of Mauritania. [Online] Available http://embassy.org/mauritania/, 1998.

World Travel Guide. Mauritania. [Online] Available http://www.wtgonline.com/country/mr/gen.html, 1998.

Mexico

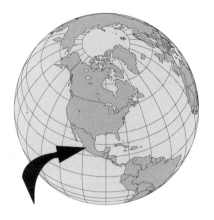

The people of Mexico are called Mexicans. About 75 percent are mestizoes, a mixture of Amerindian (native people) and Spanish heritage. Another 10 percent are pure Amerindian, 15 percent are pure white, and 1 percent fall into some other category, including black.

Mexicans

PRONUNCIATION: MECK-sih-kuhns
LOCATION: Mexico
POPULATION: 95 million
LANGUAGE: Spanish; over 30 Amerindian languages
RELIGION: Roman Catholicism (with Amerindian elements); various Protestant churches

1 ● INTRODUCTION

Mexico was the home of several native American civilizations before the arrival of the Spanish in 1519. The Maya, Olmecs, Toltecs, and Aztecs built cities and pyramids. Cuahtémoc, the last Aztec emperor, is a national hero. Under Spanish rule these peoples were converted to Christianity. European customs were added to their traditional way of life.

Mexico won its independence from Spain in 1821. However, it had lost the northern half of its territory to the United States in 1818. The Institutional Revolutionary Party (PRI) has remained has been in power for much of the twentieth century. Mexico has made great economic progress in the second half of the twentieth century. However, severe recessions resulted when the value of its currency fell in 1982 and 1994.

2 ● LOCATION

Mexico lies between the Pacific Ocean on the west and south, and the Gulf of Mexico and Caribbean Sea to the east. It is bordered on the north by California, Arizona, New Mexico, and Texas, and on the east by the Central American countries of Guatemala and Belize. Most of the country is a highland plateau with little rainfall for most of the year. The plateau is enclosed by two mountain chains, the Sierra Madre Oriental to the east and Sierra Madre Occidental to the west. There is tropical rain forest in parts of the South and the Gulf coast.

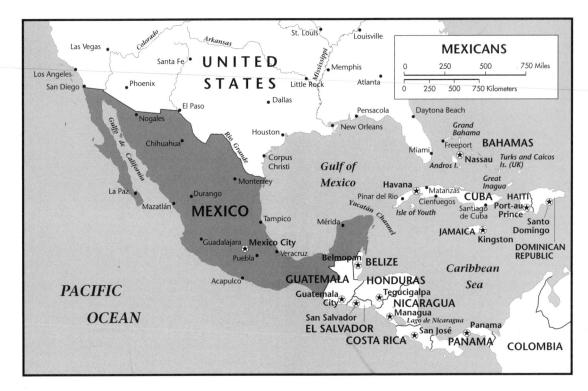

Some 75 to 90 percent of Mexico's 95 million people are of mixed European (mostly Spanish) and Amerindian descent.

3 ● LANGUAGE

Mexico is the world's largest Spanish-speaking nation. Almost all Mexicans speak at least some Spanish. About 7 or 8 percent also speak an Amerindian language as their native tongue. There are more than thirty Amerindian language groups. The largest is Náhuatl; others include Mayan, Zapotec, Otomí, and Mixtec.

4 ● FOLKLORE

Particularly in Amerindian communities, *curanderos* function as healers who communicate with nature gods and spirits.

Christian saints are often credited with the supernatural powers attributed to the gods of native Amerindian religions. Practices at many Christian feasts parallel those associated with the worship of gods dating back to the pre-European past. Traditional masks represent animals, spirits, and religious or mythical figures.

5 ● RELIGION

Between 90 and 95 percent of the Mexican people are Roman Catholics. However, Mexican Catholicism includes folklore and practices of the pre-European religions. The Virgin of Guadalupe was proclaimed patron saint of Mexico in 1737. Similarly, many other Christian saints are identified with gods and goddesses of the Amerindian past.

6 ● MAJOR HOLIDAYS

Holy Week commemorates the events leading up to and including the crucifixion and resurrection of Jesus. Christmas celebrations have been influenced by American customs such as gift giving and Christmas trees (sometimes even in churches). Preceding Christmas are the colorful *posadas*, nightly celebrations that begin December 16 and commemorate Mary and Joseph's search for an inn in Bethlehem before Jesus was born.

On November 2, the Day of the Dead, people visit the graves of their loved ones and leave behind fruits and flowers. December 12 commemorates of the appearance of the Virgin of Guadalupe in 1531.

Secular holidays include national independence day on September 16 and the birthday of revolutionary and statesman Benito Juárez (1806–72) on March 21.

7 ● RITES OF PASSAGE

Infant baptism is practiced even in Amerindian communities where the other Roman Catholic sacraments are not observed. Most Mexican children also are confirmed.

A suitor must court his future in-laws as well as his intended bride. In Amerindian communities, marriages may still be arranged and sealed with an exchange of gifts.

Most Mexicans marry young. Only civil marriages are legally valid. However, more than 70 percent of all couples also marry in church. Many poor couples live together, however, without benefit of clergy or legal license.

The dead are not usually embalmed. Burial takes place twenty-four hours after death. Wakes are held, with the relatives and friends bringing food, drink, and other gifts to the bereaved.

8 ● RELATIONSHIPS

Even brief exchanges and questions call for an introductory *buenos días* (good day) or *buenas tardes* (good afternoon). Male friends show their affection openly. Often they will embrace heartily on meeting and stroll arm in arm.

Government employees, including police officers, sometimes will accept or even ask for the *mordida* (literally "bite" or bribe).

In contrast with Americans, Mexicans set little store on punctuality. In fact, arriving at a dinner or party on time is considered rude.

9 ● LIVING CONDITIONS

About two-thirds of Mexicans are poorly housed. The poorest peasants and urban dwellers build their own adobe huts or wooden shanties. Only half of all dwellings have piped water and flush toilets. However, almost 90 percent have electric lighting. Improvised settlements, or shantytowns, cover the fringes of Mexico City and other cities.

10 ● FAMILY LIFE

Widespread poverty forces households to stay together for economic as well as social reasons. The household in many cases includes grandparents, aunts, and uncles as well as parents and children. Married children and their spouses also remain part of

Andrea Henderson

The more traditional forms of women's dress include a wraparound skirt, sometimes flounced and embroidered.

this unit until they can afford to set up their own households.

Family solidarity extends even beyond blood ties. *Compadrazgo,* or godparenthood, plays a very important part in Mexican life. One study of a Mexico City shantytown found eighteen different occasions for involving godparents in celebrations. In return for his or her aid, a godparent expects loyalty, affection, and respect from the child and parents.

11 ● CLOTHING

The more traditional forms of women's dress include a wraparound skirt, sometimes flounced and embroidered. Also included

are the *huipil,* a sleeveless garment with holes for the head and arms; and the *quechquemitl,* an upper outer garment with an opening for the head only. The *china poblana* costume consists of a richly embroidered white blouse and black shawl, a flounced and spangled red-and-green skirt, high-heeled colored slippers, bracelets, earrings, strings of beads, and ribbons or flowers in the hair. Traditional peasant attire for men consisted of pajama-like trousers and tunic of unbleached cotton, a *serape* (used as both a blanket and a cloak), sandals, and wide *sombrero.* This attire has mostly given way to jeans, shirt, shoes or boots, and a straw cowboy-type hat.

12 ● FOOD

The staple of Mexican food is corn, supplemented by beans, squash, and chili peppers. Cornmeal is patted into a thin pancake called a tortilla. Together with any of a variety of fillings, it forms a soft sandwich-like taco. (The crisp-fried "taco" known in the U.S. is a *tostada*). Fried in chili sauce, the taco becomes an enchilada. The tamale is cornmeal dough wrapped around a filling of meat and chilies, then wrapped in paper, corn husks, or banana leaves for cooking. Tacos made with a tortilla of wheat flour are called burritos. *Mole* is a rich chili sauce that sometimes contains chocolate, which is native to Mexico. *Mole poblano,* traditionally the national dish, consists of turkey (a native bird) topped with a spicy mole.

13 ● EDUCATION

Six years of education are free and compulsory for children from ages six through fourteen. However, many—a majority in rural areas—do not complete the required

Corel Corporation

Weaver in Mexico City, Mexico. Weaving in cotton and other plant fibers on hand looms is thousands of years old; wool was introduced by the Spanish.

six years. About one out of ten Mexicans cannot read or write.

Enrollment in secondary schools has increased greatly in recent years. About four out of every five elementary-school graduates now enter high school. Some receive vocational training, while others continue on to one of the nation's 260 institutions of higher learning. The most important of these is the National Autonomous University of Mexico, in Mexico City.

14 ● CULTURAL HERITAGE

Mexico's rich cultural life draws on both its Spanish and its Amerindian heritage. Oil paintings by twentieth-century artists Diego Rivera, his wife Frida Kahlo, Rufino Tamayo, and others are admired for their vibrant colors.

The most popular stringed instrument in Mexico is the guitar. In *mariachi* (Mexican band) music, stringed instruments are combined with trumpets. The marimba (similar to the xylophone) is popular in southern Mexico. Twentieth-century composer Carlos Chávez drew on traditional musical forms in his works. The Ballet Folklórico mounts productions of traditional dance and tours internationally.

Noted Mexican writers of the twentieth century include the poet and essayist Octavio Paz and the novelists Mariano Azuela, Carlos Fuentes, Juan Rulfo, and Laura Esquivel.

15 ● EMPLOYMENT

Workers are protected by laws guaranteeing minimum wages, legal holidays, paid vacations, collective bargaining, and the right to strike. The minimum wage, however, was under $3 a day in 1995. Many Mexicans work as subsistence farmers or small-scale artisans and merchants. Their hours are long, and the income is generally meager.

16 ● SPORTS

Fútbol (soccer) is by far the most popular sport in Mexico. The top professional teams draw as many as 100,000 spectators to their matches. There is a professional baseball league. Other sports include golf, tennis, swimming, bicycling, track and field, and jai alai. Bullfighting and the *jaripeo*, or rodeo, are also popular, with about thirty-five arenas in Mexico.

17 ● RECREATION

Television now dominates popular culture. Telenovelas (soap operas) and variety shows especially popular. Rock and roll, international-style pop, and even Spanish-language rap are popular. Comic books and magazine-style *fotonovelas* are more common reading material than newspapers and books.

18 ● CRAFTS AND HOBBIES

The most important form of folk painting is the *retablo*, which depicts a miraculous event. Other works of art include murals and yarn and bark paintings. Folk sculptures include masks, papier-mâché skeletons, and candle-bearing trees of life made of clay.

The variety of Mexican handicrafts is almost endless. Silver objects include bracelets, rings, necklaces, and earrings. Objects are also carved out of onyx, jade, and other types of stone. There are many regional styles of pottery. Other crafts include hand-blown glass, tile making, leather work, and lacquering. Weaving and embroidery are age-old crafts that are still practiced.

19 ● SOCIAL PROBLEMS

Many Mexicans are poorly fed and housed and do not receive adequate health care. Alcoholism is also a serious health problem. About 30 percent of the population is not served by a sewage system. Air pollution is a health hazard in urban centers, which are becoming increasingly overcrowded. In the late 1990s, Mexico City was considered one of the world's most dangerous cities in which to conduct business.

20 ● BIBLIOGRAPHY

Frye, David. *Amerindians Into Mexicans: History and Identity in a Mexican Town.* Austin: University of Texas Press, 1996.

Ganeri, Anita, and Rachel Wright. *Mexico,* Country Topics for Craft Projects. New York: Franklin Watts, 1994.

Meyer, Michael C. *The Course of Mexican History.* 5th ed. New York: Oxford University Press, 1995.

WEBSITES

Columbus Group. [Online] Available http://www.quicklink.com/mexico/, 1998.

Embassy of Mexico in Canada. [Online] Available http://www.docuweb.ca/Mexico/, 1998.

World Travel Guide. [Online] Available http://www.wtgonline.com/country/mx/gen.html, 1998.

Maya

PRONUNCIATION: MY-yuh
LOCATION: Southeastern Mexico; Guatemala;
   Belize; Honduras; El Salvador
POPULATION: About 8–10 million
LANGUAGE: Spanish; English; various Mayan
   dialects
RELIGION: "Folk Catholicism"; evangelical
   Christianity

1 ● INTRODUCTION

Today's Maya are descended from one of the great civilizations of the Americas. They live in the same regions of Mexico, Guatemala, Belize, El Salvador, and Honduras as their ancestors and retain many of their ancient traditions. Mayan history reaches back some 4,000 years to what is called the Preclassic period, when civilization first began in Central America. However, it was during what came to be known as the Classic period—from roughly AD 250 to 900—that Mayan culture reached its peak and the Maya achieved their celebrated advances in architecture, mathematics, agriculture, astronomy, art, and other areas.

They built spectacular temples and palaces, developed several calendars—including one reaching back to 13 August, 3114 BC—and evolved a numerical system capable of recording a number that today would be expressed as 142 followed by 36 zeros. They developed a complex system of writing and, beginning in 50 BC, were the first people in the Western hemisphere to keep written historical records. Around AD 900 the construction of buildings and stelae—stone slabs inscribed with names and dates—ceased abruptly, and the advanced lowland civilization of the Maya collapsed, creating a mystery that has fascinated scholars for many years. Possible causes that have been proposed include warfare, drought, famine, and disease.

The Spanish campaign to subdue the Maya and conquer their lands began around 1520 and ended nearly 200 years later when Tayasal, the last remaining Mayan region (in present-day Guatemala), fell to the conquistadors in 1697. The Spanish seized Mayan lands and enslaved their populations, sending many to labor in the mines of northern Mexico. In addition, thousands of Maya died of diseases spread by the Europeans, especially smallpox. During the first half of the nineteenth century, the Central American lands won their independence from Spain, but the lives of the Maya did not improve. They labored on vast tobacco, sugarcane, and henequen plantations, in virtual slavery enforced by their continuing debt to the landowners. In the Yucatán, many joined in a protracted rebellion called the Caste War that lasted from 1847 to 1901.

After the revolution of 1910, the Maya in Mexico gained increased legal rights and better educational and job opportunities. However, a steep drop in world prices for henequen—the "green gold" from which twine was made—turned the Yucatán from one of Mexico's richest regions to one of its poorest. In Guatemala, the disenfranchisement and poverty of the Maya—comprising roughly half the population—continued unchanged into the twentieth century. Since the 1970s, political violence has forced many Maya to flee to Mexico, where they remain as refugees. In Chiapas, Maya of the

Tzeltal and Tzotzil tribes took part in the Zapatista uprising of January 1994.

2 ● LOCATION

The modern Maya live in southeastern Mexico and northern Central America, including Guatemala, Belize, Honduras, and El Salvador. Altogether, their homelands cover an area of approximately 125,000 square miles (323,750 square kilometers) with a varied terrain that encompasses both northern lowlands and southern highlands. Volcanic mountains dominate the highlands. The fertile soil of the highland valleys supports the largest segment of the Maya population. While many Maya have settled in cities—particularly Merida and Cancún—and adopted an urban lifestyle, most remain rural dwellers.

Reliable figures for the total number of Maya are unavailable. Estimates range upward from 4 million. The true figure is probably between 8 and 10 million, including about half of Guatemala's total population of 10 million, close to 2 million Maya in the Mexican Yucatán, and additional numbers in Mexico's Chiapas state, as well as Belize, Honduras, and El Salvador. Among the larger individual groups are about 750,000 Quiché (K'iche') in the midwestern highlands of Guatemala; 445,000 or more Cakchiquel in several Guatemalan departments (provinces); and over 500,000 Mam in southwestern Guatemala and southeastern Chiapas.

3 ● LANGUAGE

Most Maya today speak Spanish. The two Mayan languages of the Classic period, Yucatecan and Cholan, have subdivided into about thirty separate languages, some of which are not mutually intelligible. The most widely spoken are Mam, Quiché, Kekchí, and Cakchiquel. Advocates of Mayan cultural autonomy protest against the relegation of their indigenous languages to limited use, often in remote rural areas, while Spanish remains the language of government, education, the church, and the media. The following example is drawn from a creation myth in the *Popol Vuh,* the Mayan holy book:

Keje k'ut xax k'o wi ri kaj nay puch, u K'ux Kaj.

Are ub'i ri k'ab'awil, chuch'axik.

Translation:

And of course there is the sky, and there is also the Heart of Sky.

This is the name of the god, as it is spoken.

4 ● FOLKLORE

The greatest body of Mayan tradition is contained in the *Popol Vuh,* an ancient text first transcribed into Latin and later translated into Spanish that preserves both sacred and secular lore. According to its creation myth, the gods made three different attempts at creating human beings before they had a version they were satisfied with. The first beings, which were made of mud, were destroyed because they had no brains. The next ones were made of wood and proved deficient because they were without emotions and thus could not properly praise their makers. Finally the correct material—maize (corn)—was found, and perfect beings were fashioned. Ultimately deciding to protect them by limiting the extent of their knowledge, the gods decided to damage their eyes so they could not see too much, and the resulting beings were the first Maya.

5 ● RELIGION

The traditional religions of the Maya, in which astrology and ancestor worship both played a role, were based on a system of beliefs that included the world, the heavens, and an unseen underworld called Xibalba. When Spanish missionaries introduced Catholicism to their regions, the Maya tended to add it onto their existing religion, creating a unique brand of "folk Catholicism." Their traditional gods that belonged to the natural world, such as corn, rain, and the sun, became associated with Christian saints, and various rituals and festivals were transmuted into forms approved by the church.

Since the 1960s, evangelical Christianity, mostly promoted by churches in the southern United States, has been adopted by large segments of the Mayan population. Entire towns have embraced conservative forms of Protestantism, which have not proven as amenable as Catholicism to the retention of customs related to traditional folk religions, such as the use of alcohol in association with religious rituals or the retention of the sacred brotherhoods—known as *cofradias* in Guatemala and as *cargos* in Chiapas—which traditionally oversee village festivals and other aspects of civic life.

6 ● MAJOR HOLIDAYS

Most holidays currently observed by the Maya are the holy days of the Christian calendar. Many of their observances, however, still have characteristics of the traditional nature worship of their ancestors. The most important celebrations are generally Holy Week (the week leading up to Easter in late March or early April) and Christmas (December 25). The Maya living in the Chamula region of Chiapas are known for their five-day Carnival celebration, called Crazy February, whose Christian significance (the period preceding Lent) coincides with the older observance of the five "Lost Days" at the end of the Maya solar calendar. Religious societies called *cargos* sponsor the festivities, which include ceremonial dances, feasting, processions, and ritual reenactments of both religious and historic events.

7 ● RITES OF PASSAGE

Major life transitions (such as birth, puberty, and death) are marked by religious ceremonies, many of which combine Christian and ancestral traditions.

8 ● RELATIONSHIPS

The religious societies known as *cargos* in Chiapas and *cofradias* in Guatemala have been an important vehicle of social cohesion among the Maya. Charged since colonial times with organizing Catholic religious festivals, they provided the means for the Maya to conform to the customs of their colonizers while privately preserving their own religion, traditions, and worldview. Mayan villages today have both civil and religious cargos, whose officials may ascend through a hierarchy of positions to ultimately become respected village elders, or *principales*.

9 ● LIVING CONDITIONS

Housing varies among the different regions and groups of Maya. The Mam, who live in southwestern Guatemala and southeastern Chiapas, live in houses with adobe walls, small shuttered windows, roofs of tile or corrugated metal, and a floor of hard-packed dirt. The K'iche' in the Guatemalan highlands build rectangular houses with double-pitched tile roofs and walls of adobe, thatch supported by boards or poles, or other materials. Increasing numbers live in more modern homes built from brick or lumber with tin roofs.

Maya folk medicine includes the ministrations of ritual healers called *curanderos* and female herbalists who may double as midwives. Common cures include prayers, offerings, herbal remedies, and sweat-baths.

The main means of transport for most Maya is the bus. Buses in Maya areas may be crowded as early as 4:00 or 5:00 AM, often with people traveling from remote villages to the larger market towns. By late afternoon and evening there are fewer travelers on the road. Trains in the Maya regions—like those in many parts of Central and South America—are generally slow, old, and unreliable. In some areas, boats are used for public transportation.

10 ● FAMILY LIFE

Both nuclear and extended families are found among the Maya. Couples generally marry in their late teens or early twenties. Traditionally, all marriages were arranged, but since the 1950s it has become increasingly common among some groups for young people to choose their own mates. In arranged marriages, contact may be initiated by the couple, followed by negotiation between the two families. Gifts are generally exchanged, and in some cases the bride's parents receive a payment to compensate them for having raised her. Couples often have both civil and religious ceremonies, and they may live with the groom's parents until their first child is born.

Family structure may alternate between nuclear and extended, with the addition of newly married couples who will eventually leave to establish their own homes, or elderly parents who come to live with the family when it becomes hard for them to manage on their own.

11 ● CLOTHING

The Maya wear both modern Western-style clothing and traditional garb (although the latter is more commonly worn by women). Men generally wear trousers and sport shirts or *guayaberas*—dress shirts with decorative tucks worn outside the belt in place of a jacket. Women wear either traditional woven and embroidered clothing, or stylish dresses and skirt-and-blouse outfits. Traditional women's attire includes the *huipil* (plural: *huipiles),* a long, sleeveless tunic; the *quechquémitl,* a shoulder cape; and the *enredo,* a wrap-around skirt. Maya garments are commonly decorated with elaborate and colorful embroidery. The designs, which include humans, animals, and plants, often have some religious significance, and every Maya group and village has its own distinctive patterns of decoration. The decorative designs for huipiles are often said to appear to women in their dreams. Men often wear the traditional tunics over store-bought

Many Maya live in rural communities in southern Mexico like the one pictured here.

shirts. *Fajas* are sashes that hold garments in place and also serve as pockets.

12 ● FOOD

The Maya generally eat three meals a day: breakfast *(el desayuno),* lunch *(la comida),* and supper *(la cena).* Corn, the most important food of their ancestors, remains the central ingredient in their diet today and is used to make tortillas or tamales. After corn, beans *(frijoles)* are the most basic staple, served boiled, fried, or refried. Soups—many of them actually thick stews—form a large part of the Mayan diet. One of the most popular is lime soup *(sopa de lima),* made from chicken, limes, and a variety of spices.

Poultry forms the basis of many meals—either turkey, which is native to the region, or chicken, which was introduced by the Spanish. Plentiful seafood caught on the coasts of the Caribbean and Gulf of Mexico is also an important part of the diet. The Yucatán is known for its *ceviche,* a cold dish made with fish prepared with an acidic marinade (usually lime juice), served with onions, chiles, and cilantro. Popular desserts include flan (a custard introduced by the Spanish) and *Torta del Cielo* (Heavenly Cake), a cake made with rum, almonds, and ten eggs that is served at weddings and other special occasions.

One of the best-known foods of the Maya is *Cochinita Pibil*, a pork dish that dates back to pre-Columbian times, when it was made from wild boar cooked in a coal-filled pit. Domesticated pigs, introduced by the Spanish, have replaced the boar, but the dish is prepared with the same seasonings as it was in the past. A recipe for Cochinita Pibil is included in this entry.

13 ● EDUCATION

The Maya are educated at either public or Catholic schools. In Guatemala, a half-dozen Catholic-run boarding schools are the main source of education for those wishing to progress beyond the basic education available in the villages. Maya concerned with preserving their traditions believe that the formal education available to them has caused them to lose touch with their own culture. The Guatemalan Academy of Maya Languages (*Academia de Lenguas Mayas*) leads a movement to preserve the languages of the Guatemalan Maya.

14 ● CULTURAL HERITAGE

The Maya have preserved many aspects of their ancient culture, including their traditional clothing, folklore, agricultural techniques, family structure, language, and dance. Many elements of their ancient religions have also survived for centuries under the guise of Catholic religious observances.

15 ● EMPLOYMENT

In rural areas, the Maya farm their maize fields, or *milpas,* much as their ancestors did thousands of years ago. Forested sites

---

Recipe

Cochinita Pibil (Pork Marinade)

Ingredients

¼ teaspoon ground pepper
¼ teaspoon ground cumin
5 cloves garlic, minced
⅓ cup lime juice
2 pounds lean pork, cut in 2-inch cubes
Banana leaves or aluminum foil
1 small can chopped hot chilies
1 teaspoon dried oregano
Sliced purple raw onions
2 bay leaves, crushed
String

Directions

1. Combine the pepper and the cumin with the minced garlic.
2. Combine the garlic mixture with the lime juice, bay leaves, and oregano.
3. Put the pork cubes in a large plastic bag and add the spice mixture. Seal and turn and shake the bag until the pork is well coated with the mixture. Marinate for at least 3 hours or overnight.
4. Place banana leaves or aluminum foil on the bottom of a roasting pan. (Leaves or foil should drape over the sides of the pan.) Pour the pork cubes and the marinade onto the leaves (or foil).
5. Top with chopped onions and chiles. Fold the leaves (or foil) over the meat. If using banana leaves, tie with string to secure. Preheat oven to 325°F. Cover the pan and bake for 1½ hours.

Serve with beans, salsa, and heated corn tortillas.

Adapted from Gerlach, Nancy, et al. *Foods of the Maya.* Freedom, Calif.: The Crossing Press, 1994.

---

are converted into new fields by felling the trees and burning the brush (today known as "slash-and-burn" agriculture). Maize kernels are then planted into holes made with digging sticks. Where the ancient Maya used stone tools for clearing and hardened the end of the digging stick with fire, today's farmer uses a steel machete and metal-tipped stick. Because this type of agriculture rapidly depletes the soil, fields must be left fallow for periods ranging from seven to as many as twenty years. Besides farming, Maya also work as laborers and artisans or own small shops. In urban areas, they work in jobs involving textiles or computers, for example.

16 ● SPORTS

The ancient Maya played hip-ball, a game that involved keeping a hard rubber ball aloft with any part of the body other than the hands, head, or feet. In some regions, the ball had to be hit through a set of stone rings. Soccer is popular among the Maya of today.

17 ● RECREATION

Sunday afternoons after church are the most popular time for recreation. Most businesses are closed, and many people stroll the village streets or relax in local parks. Popular forms of musical entertainment include marimba teams and mariachi bands.

18 ● CRAFTS AND HOBBIES

Maya women are famous for their weaving, often using locally handspun yarn and natural vegetable dyes. Using the pre-Columbian back-strap loom of their ancestors, they produce striped and plain white cloth for shawls, shirts, and children's clothes,

some with designs that are over 1,200 years old. Colorful hammocks are woven from fine cotton string. Other craft items include both glazed and unglazed pottery, ceremonial wooden masks, and goods woven from palm, straw, reeds, and sisal.

For centuries, traditional Maya dances have been preserved by the religious men's fraternities called *cofradias*. These dances were performed for both ceremonial and entertainment purposes. The *Pop Wuj* dance depicts the four stages of humankind's development: the Man of Mud, who is destroyed because he does not recognize the gods; the Man of Wood, who is too rigid and ultimately burns; the Monkey Man, who is too silly; and the Human Being, who respects and prays to the gods. The K'iche' Maya of Chichicastenango have a dance that centers around Sijolaj, a harvest king whom the Spaniards identified with St. Thomas.

19 ● SOCIAL PROBLEMS

The Maya of Yucatán, like many other Mexicans, suffer from overpopulation, unemployment, and periods of political unrest. In Guatemala, Mayan farmers have been crowded onto mountainous areas with poor land, and laborers must work for extremely low wages. The most serious problem for the Maya in that country has been over two decades of violent political repression by the military and right- and left-wing death squads. Thousands have been murdered or "disappeared," and many have fled the country for Mexico or the United States.

The health of the Tzotzil and Tzeltal Maya of Chiapas has been compromised by their inadequate diet, which consists of fewer than 500 calories a day—one-fifth of the minimum standard set by the United Nations. Life expectancy is only forty-four years, and the infant mortality rate is 150 deaths per 1,000 live births.

20 ● BIBLIOGRAPHY

Brosnahan, Tom. *Guatemala, Belize and Yucatan: La Ruta Maya.* Hawthorn, Australia: Lonely Planet Publications, 1994.

Canby, Peter. *The Heart of the Sky: Travels Among the Maya.* New York: HarperCollins, 1992.

Gerlach, Nancy, and Jeffrey Gerlach. *Foods of the Maya: A Taste of the Yucatan.* Freedom, Calif.: The Crossing Press, 1994.

Olson, James S. *The Indians of Central and South America: An Ethnohistorical Dictionary.* New York: Greenwood Press, 1991.

Trout, Lawana Hooper. *The Maya.* New York: Chelsea House, 1991.

WEBSITES

Columbus Group. [Online] Available http://www.quicklink.com/mexico/, 1998.

Embassy of Mexico in Canada. [Online] Available http://www.docuweb.ca/Mexico/, 1998.

Science Museum of Minnesota. Maya Adventure. [Online] Available http://www.sci.mus.mn.us/sln/ma/, 1998.

World Travel Guide. [Online] Available http://www.wtgonline.com/country/mx/gen.html, 1998.

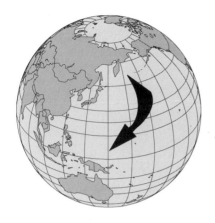

Micronesia

The islanders of Micronesia are called Micronesians. A small number are of Polynesian descent.

Micronesians

PRONUNCIATION: mye-cro-NEE-zhuns
LOCATION: Federated States of Micronesia (also Guam, Republic of Belau, Kiribati, Marshall Islands, Republic of Nauru, the Northern Mariana Islands, and thousands of smaller islands)
POPULATION: 100,000
LANGUAGE: Indigenous languages of the islands; English
RELIGION: Catholicism; Protestantism

1 ● INTRODUCTION

The name Micronesia comes from Greek, meaning "small islands." The Micronesian cultures are located in the northern Pacific Ocean. Most of the nearly 2,500 islands that make up Micronesia were administered by the United States until 1986 as the Trust Territory of the Pacific Islands. In 1986, the territory was dissolved into four constitutional governments: the Federated States of Micronesia, the Republic of Belau (Palau), the Republic of the Marshall Islands, and the Commonwealth of the Northern Mariana Islands. All four have continuing politi-cal and economic relationships with the United States.

2 ● LOCATION

The Micronesian region is shaped like a parallelogram. Its corners are formed by the Republic of Belau in the southwest; Kiribati, formerly the Gilbert Islands, in the southeast; Guam in the northwest; and the Marshall Islands in the northeast.

Volcanic and coral islands make up Micronesia. Almost all of the islands within the region of Micronesia are located north of the equator. The largest island is Guam, with 225 square miles and about half of the total population. The Republic of Nauru (not previously administered by the U.S.) is one of the smallest countries in the world, with a total area of 9 square miles. It is also one of the least densely populated, with only about 9,000 people.

3 ● LANGUAGE

The languages of the Micronesian region belong to the large family of Austronesian languages. Austronesian is widely spread

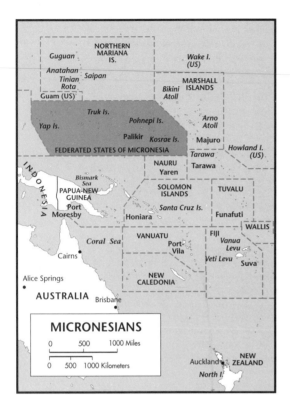

MICRONESIANS

0   500   1000 Miles

0   500   1000 Kilometers

throughout the Pacific Basin. Micronesian languages are related to other Austronesian languages such as Javanese, Tagalog (Pilipino), Balinese, Hawaiian, and Malay. English is also spoken.

4 ● FOLKLORE

One Palauan myth recounts the story of a magical breadfruit tree that the child of the sun provided for his human mother. In order to provide fish for her to eat, the son cut a hole in the center of a breadfruit tree growing outside her house. Fish were thrown through the hole by the waves of the sea. The mother just had to walk out her door to collect fish. Her neighbors became jealous and cut down the breadfruit tree. This caused a catastrophic flood that engulfed

the whole island. Only the mother was saved; her son flew her through the sky on a raft.

5 ● RELIGION

Christian missionaries in Micronesia have converted most of the people to either Catholicism or Protestant faiths. Traditional religion in Micronesian cultures involved belief in ghosts and ancestor worship. People also believed in spirits associated with specific places, objects, and activities. Chants and offerings were directed to these patron spirits.

6 ● MAJOR HOLIDAYS

Major religious holidays in Micronesia now are based on the Christian calendar. Many Micronesian states celebrate Ash Wednesday (in February), Easter (in March or April), All Saints' Day (in November), and Christmas (December 25). American secular holidays, including Thanksgiving, are observed in many parts of Micronesia. A major event for the display of traditional culture is the South Pacific Arts Festival. Performing groups from a number of different Pacific Island nations participate in it.

7 ● RITES OF PASSAGE

Many of the traditional celebrations that accompany events like birth, the start of adolescence, marriage, and death have been replaced by Christian rituals. On the island of Yap, however, male adolescence is still marked by a hair-cutting ceremony.

8 ● RELATIONSHIPS

Traditionally, there were specific rules of etiquette for Micronesians to follow when

Economic self-sufficiency and cultural survival are two of the major problems facing Micronesian countries. The challenge of creating compromises between various factions on each island and between islands will likely continue for many years to come.

they visited another island. Most societies had three distinct social classes. Social status still determines etiquette in Micronesian societies.

Greetings among many Micronesians are equivalent to the English "welcome." In the Chamorro language of the Northern Marianas, the greeting is *hafa adai.*

9 ● LIVING CONDITIONS

Western-style housing has become common in Micronesia. Some houses, however, are still constructed out of traditional materials, with the addition of a corrugated tin roof.

Electricity and running water are available on those islands where there has been an American or European presence. Some families own gasoline-powered generators to run their appliances.

10 ● FAMILY LIFE

Households in traditional Micronesian societies include a husband, a wife, and their unmarried children. Women's councils play an important role in village decision-making in Belau.

11 ● CLOTHING

Micronesians wear Western-style clothing most of the time. However, for ceremonial occasions they often return to traditional styles of dress. Before European colonization, typical clothing was a loincloth for men and a skirt of natural fibers for women.

12 ● FOOD

The Micronesian diet is pretty much the same across the region. There are some local differences due to climate patterns and geographic features. Foods including taro root, breadfruit, coconuts, and yams are staples in many households throughout the region. Europeans introduced corn, sweet potatoes, and manioc (cassava). Fish is the most important source of protein in all parts of Micronesia.

Western foods have become important, especially to younger people. Packaged American foods such as breakfast cereals are part of many Micronesian daily meals.

13 ● EDUCATION

Western-style education has been introduced throughout Micronesia. There are a number of American-run schools where residents from the United States send their children. Opportunities for a college education must be found in the U.S. or in other developed countries.

14 ● CULTURAL HERITAGE

Micronesian music is mainly vocal. Very few musical instruments are produced by Micronesian cultures. The shell trumpet and the nose flute are the most common instruments in the region.

Polynesian-style music from Hawaii has become popular in parts of Micronesia. American music and dance have been introduced by television and by Americans living on the islands.

15 ● EMPLOYMENT

Traditionally, men have engaged in fishing and harvesting. Women were responsible for gardening and household chores. Wage labor is now common for both men and women in Micronesia. Many states have set minimum-wage standards. In the Northern Marianas Islands, the minimum hourly wage for 1996 was $3.05.

16 ● SPORTS

Traditional forms of competitive sports have all but disappeared from most parts of Micronesia. Sports introduced from foreign nations (such as the United States and Japan), have become popular.

17 ● RECREATION

Television and video have become popular in many Micronesian societies. The programming is mostly foreign—usually from the U.S. or Japan—and often out of date.

Movie theaters on many of the islands run current American and other foreign films.

Traditional forms of entertainment in Nauru consisted of singing and dancing contests and kite flying. The competing "teams" were organized along family lines.

18 ● CRAFTS AND HOBBIES

Belau, in western Micronesia, is well known for the elaborately carved and painted wooden fronts of the houses known as *bai*. Every plank of the panels at either end of the house front was illustrated with scenes from a historical or mythological story. In the 1930s, the Palauans began to create copies of these planks, as well as new "storyboards," for sale to tourists. Carved bowls of various shapes and sizes and finely braided mats for sleeping and sitting on are also produced for the tourist industry.

19 ● SOCIAL PROBLEMS

Economic self-sufficiency (independence) and the survival of the many cultures are two of the major problems facing Micronesian countries. Tensions must be resolved between factions, both on each island and also between islands.

20 ● BIBLIOGRAPHY

Ashby, Gene, ed. *Some Things of Value: Micronesian Customs and Beliefs.* Eugene, Ore.: Rainy Day Press, 1985.

Kluge, P. F. *The Edge of Paradise: America in Micronesia.* New York: Random House, 1991.

WEBSITES

World Travel Guide. Micronesia. [Online] Available http://www.wtgonline.com/country/fm/gen.html, 1998.

Moldova

The people of Moldova are called Moldovans. About 65 percent are ethnic Moldovans. Other groups include Ukrainians (about 14 percent) and Russians (about 13 percent). For more information on Ukrainians, see the chapter on Ukraine in Volume 9; on the Russians, see the chapter on Russia in Volume 7.

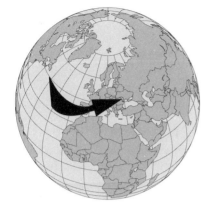

Moldovans

PRONUNCIATION: mole-DOE-vuhns
LOCATION: Moldova
POPULATION: 4.4 million (about 65 percent, or about 2.8 million, are ethnic Moldovans)
LANGUAGE: Moldovan (Romanian); Russian
RELIGION: Russian Orthodox Church; Judaism

1 ● INTRODUCTION

The area now known as Moldova was occupied as far back as 2000 BC. Over the centuries Moldova has been under the rule of many Eastern European groups as well as the Mongols. In 1349, Prince Bogdan of Hungary established Moldova as an independent principality (state ruled by a prince) under Hungarian rule. The area occupied by Moldova consists of the land between the Prut and Dnestr rivers, formerly known as Bessarabia.

Moldova fell to the Ottoman Turk Empire in 1512 and remained an Ottoman territory for the next three centuries. During the 1700s and 1800s, the Russian Empire battled the Ottomans for control over the region. In 1878, Russia claimed the territory and held onto it until the collapse of the Russian imperial government in 1917. The Bessarabian government voted for a total union with Romania. However, in 1924 the Soviet Union established it as a Soviet republic. One of the worst consequences of Soviet rule was the forced collectivization of agriculture (changing small, private farming into large, state-run agricultural enterprises). Farmers who refused to cooperate with collectivization were deported to Siberia. The ones who stayed in Moldova had to cope with severe famine from 1945 to 1947 caused by drought, crop failure, and poor government policies.

The Soviet authorities changed the name of the Romanian language, spoken by the majority of the population, to Moldavian. They also changed the alphabet from Latin to Cyrillic (the alphabet of Russia). For approximately forty-five years, Moldovans had limited access to their history and culture.

At the end of the 1980s, an independence movement called the Popular Front of Moldavia (PFM) arose. The PFM demanded the end of Communist rule, began the revival of the Romanian language and culture, and wanted to again unite the Moldavian republic with Romania. In 1989, the government restored the use of the Latin alphabet and officially changed the name to the Republic of Moldova.

The movement for territorial unification with Romania has lost most of its momentum. Moldova is gradually building a democratic society and a market economy (an economy based on supply and demand).

2 ● LOCATION

The Moldovan homeland is historic Bessarabia—the land between the Prut and Dnestr rivers in the southwestern corner of the former Soviet Union. One of the smallest of the former Soviet republics, Moldova is only slightly larger than the state of Maryland. Most of the terrain consists of hilly plains with many rivers and streams.

Today, about 65 percent of Moldova's 4.4 million inhabitants are ethnic Moldovans. Moldova has historically been home to a large number of ethnic groups, including Russians, Ukrainians, Gagauz (a Turkish group of the Christian faith), Gypsies (Roma), Jews, Poles, and Germans. Although Moldova was the most densely populated of all the former Soviet republics, since its people are traditionally rural, there are few large cities.

3 ● LANGUAGE

The language spoken in Moldova is Romanian. By a recent amendment to the Moldovan Constitution, it is called Moldovan in order to stop the movement toward unification with Romania. Romanian is a Romance language of the Indo-European family. It is similar to Italian, Spanish, French, and Portuguese. Moldovan was temporarily written in the Cyrillic (Russian) alphabet during the Soviet era, but is now written in the Latin alphabet again. Opinions continue to differ on whether to call the language Moldovan or Romanian.

Mihai, Ion, Mircea, Octavian, and Andrei are common boys' names. Elena, Angela, Diana, Christina, and Liliana are common girls' names. Examples of everyday Romanian words include *noroc* (hello), *buna ziua* (good afternoon), *da* (yes), *nu* (no), *poftim* (please), *multumesc* (thank you), and *la revedere* (goodbye).

4 ● FOLKLORE

Moldova has a long history of folklore, consisting of ballads, songs, tales, jokes, riddles, dances, and games. The ancient folk ballad "Miorita" is the favorite of all ballads in traditional Moldovan culture. Its rhyme reveals the melodiousness and beauty of the Romanian language.

Ileana Cosinzeana and Fat Frumos are the romantic couple present in a number of fairy tales. The brave Fat Frumos frees the beautiful and kind Ileana Cosinzeana from the evil dragon, and they live happily ever after. Pacala and Tindala are two funny men who are the characters of hundreds of jokes.

5 ● RELIGION

Because of the influence of Romanian culture, almost all Moldovans belong to the Orthodox Church. In 1992, the Moldovan government guaranteed freedom of religion but required that all religious groups be officially registered with the government.

A pogrom (an organized persecution or massacre) against Moldovan Jews in 1903 severely reduced the urban Jewish population. Jews in Moldova were also harassed during the Soviet era. In the early 1990s, many Jewish newspapers were started, and a synagogue and Jewish high school opened in Chisinau. Also, the Chisinau State University created a Department of Jewish Studies.

6 ● MAJOR HOLIDAYS

The major holidays celebrated widely in Moldova are the traditional Christian holidays, such as Christmas (December 25) and Easter. Christmas is celebrated in much the same way as in Western countries, although it is less commercialized. Easter is a family holiday, when women bake a special kind of bread called *pasca* and paint eggs red.

Each village has its own holiday once a year, called *hram* (church). It celebrates the establishment of the village church. In modern times it has lost some of its religious character. It is now a special day when each family prepares delicious food and receives guests from other villages or towns.

Independence Day is on August 27, when Moldova declared its independence from the Soviet Union. It is a national holiday. *Sarbatoarea Limbii Noastre* (National Language Day) is on August 31. It marks the day when Romanian became the state language of Moldova and was changed back to the Latin alphabet. During this day, people attend outside concerts and book fairs.

7 ● RITES OF PASSAGE

Christian baptism is an important rite of passage for Moldovan children and their parents. High school graduation usually presents a young Moldovan with the choice of either going to work or continuing school in preparation for the university. Many also begin to consider marriage after graduation, because the completion of high school marks the end of childhood and the beginning of adulthood. As with many other cultures, the wedding ceremony formally recognizes the union of the couple and the joining of their families.

8 ● RELATIONSHIPS

Social relations in urban and rural areas differ from each other. In villages, even strangers are supposed to say "Buna ziua" (Good day) to each other. In big towns and cities, only acquaintances greet each other. In formal settings, adults greet each other with "Buna ziua." Men shake hands and may also kiss the women's hands.

Young people usually greet each other with "Salut" or "Noroc," which are the Romanian equivalents of "Hi" and "Hello." Close friends may hug and kiss each other on the cheek. Family and relatives greet each other with hugs and kisses. It is very common for parents to kiss and hug their children.

9 ● LIVING CONDITIONS

The rural culture of Moldova has always placed a high value on private housing. In the 1990s, private builders were responsible for 95 percent of construction in rural areas. As of 1994, about 90 percent of the rural, and 36 percent of the urban, apartments were privately owned. Most of the urban housing units were built in the years immediately following World War II (1939–45), because the cities had been heavily bombed during the war. When Moldova became independent in 1991, there was a severe shortage of building materials.

10 ● FAMILY LIFE

At the beginning of the twentieth century, families with between five and nine children were common in Moldova. Nowadays, most couples have only one or two children. This may be due to financial concerns as well as the fact that usually both parents work full-time and are not able to take care of more children. Family connections are quite strong due to long-standing traditions, and also because of financial dependence. Children depend on the support of their parents for a long time, even after they get married. Parents count on the help of their children when they retire. Quite often grandparents dedicate themselves to babysitting.

The distribution of family duties between men and women is uneven. Most women work full-time, take care of their children, and do most of the shopping, cooking, laundry, and cleaning. Men usually spend most of their time at work. It is not common for men to cook or do the dishes or the laundry.

11 ● CLOTHING

The traditional national costume is now only found in museums and in some family collections. The female's traditional garment consists of a white embroidered blouse, an embroidered vest trimmed with sheep fleece, and a white skirt with lace on the hem, usually covered by a black embroidered overskirt. The male costume consists of a white embroidered shirt, a vest similar to the women's, white pants, a hat decorated with peacock feathers or flowers, or a sheep fleece cap, and a wide belt. Both men and women wear *opinci,* leather shoes with leather laces that tie around the ankles

The costumes used to be entirely handmade. Every young girl was supposed to be able to weave cloth and do elaborate embroidery. Now only folk music and dance groups wear national costumes, but most of these are mass-produced.

People who live in cities and towns dress like other Eastern or Western Europeans. Jeans and T-shirts are popular with teenagers and young people. Villagers wear everyday clothing fit for farming work: women wear flowery cotton or flannel dresses, and kerchiefs on their heads; men wear shirts and pants made of durable cloth, and caps or hats.

12 ● FOOD.

Traditional Moldovan dishes resemble those of neighboring countries. Stuffed cabbage or grape leaves are considered part of the national cuisine. So is *placinte,* a special pastry filled with cheese, potatoes, cherries, cabbage, and other ingredients. A typical breakfast may consist of a sandwich, a piece of cake, an omelet, or porridge, with tea, coffee, or milk. Lunch is an important meal. It consists of a starter (appetizer), soup, and a hot dish. Dinner may also be a hot meal, or may be lighter than lunch. Fresh fruits and vegetables can be found at the local bazaar (market). The availability of fruit and vegetables depends on the season. Moldovans take great pride in their tradition of wine-making.

13 ● EDUCATION

Moldova has an extensive system of primary and secondary schools. The educational system requires students to complete ten years of basic education. After that, students may choose either a technical school or a university preparation track. In the early 1990s, about 96 percent of the adult

Recipe

Placinte (Filled pastry)

Ingredients

Dough:
3¾ cups of flour
2 packages of yeast
2 eggs, slightly beaten
1 Tablespoon butter, melted
1 Tablespoon oil
1 teaspoon sugar
Filling:
1 cup ricotta cheese
1 Tablespoon butter
1 egg
1 teaspoon flour
2 Tablespoons milk
1 teaspoon sugar

Directions

1. Dissolve the yeast in a bowl in about ¼ cup warm water. Add flour, ½ cup at a time, until the batter is the consistency of thick sour cream. Dust the surface of the batter with flour. Set it aside to rise.
2. Put remaining flour into a large bowl, indenting the center of it to make a well. Add eggs, melted butter, and oil. Combine with yeast mixture.
3. Using very clean hands, knead the dough in the bowl, adding more flour a little at a time, until the dough no longer sticks to the bowl.
4. Make the filling. Combine ricotta cheese, butter, egg, milk, flour, sugar, and a dash of salt. Mix well.
5. Roll out the dough and cut it into 3-inch squares. Place a spoonful of cheese in the middle and fold the corners to make an envelope.
6. Brush with beaten egg and bake at 350°F 15 to 20 minutes. Serve warm.

Valerii Corcimari

Moldovan students in class. Moldova has over fifty technical and vocational schools, and ten universities.

population was literate (able to read and write). About 15 percent of all Moldovans age fifteen or older have completed a secondary education.

Since independence, the Moldovan government has restored the Romanian language as the language of instruction. In addition, classes in Romanian literature and history have been added to the curriculum. Ethnic minorities have the right to education in their own languages. Moldova has over fifty technical and vocational schools, and ten universities. Perhaps the most unique educational institution in Moldova is the 150-year-old College of Wine Culture,

which graduates about three hundred students from all over Eastern Europe each year.

14 ● CULTURAL HERITAGE

Moldovan music, dance, and arts share many traits with their Romanian counterparts. Moldovans often play the *cobza,* a wooden stringed instrument similar to the lute that is common in traditional Romanian music.

The Moldovan government promotes folk culture through Joc, the national dance company, and Doina, the national folk choir. There are numerous semiprofessional and amateur dance and music groups that perform around the country as well. There are also twelve professional theaters.

Moldova shares most of its literary heritage with Romania. Sometimes it is difficult to draw a dividing line between Romanian and Moldovan literature. The nineteenth century produced many outstanding Romanian authors, such as the poet Mihai Eminescu; the storyteller Ion Creanga; the linguist, writer, and historian Bogdan Petriceicu Hasdeu; the literary critic Titu Maiorescu; and many others. World-famous Romanian writers and philosophers such as Mircea Eliade and Lucian Blaga are widely studied and respected by Moldovans.

15 ● EMPLOYMENT

Although Moldova has been independent for several years, the condition of the labor force has not changed much since the Soviet years. In the early 1990s, about 75 percent of all employment was in the government sector. Private businesses employed only about 9 percent of the Moldovan labor force in 1995. Unemployment, rated low by official estimates, was probably actually between 10 and 15 percent.

In villages, children begin to help their parents around the house, or on the farm, at an early age. In the city, high school graduates start working when they are around seventeen years old, and college graduates begin working at around twenty-two. Many students have part-time jobs.

During Soviet rule, there was an extensive system of social welfare that provided good pensions for retirees. Due to recent

Valerii Corcimari

A young Moldovan engaged in the sport of rock climbing.

inflation, the pensions are now barely enough to meet basic needs.

16 ● SPORTS

Soccer is popular with youths and adults, both for playing and watching as spectators.

17 ● RECREATION

Attending family and friends' reunions, the theater, concerts, movies, and discos are typical forms of recreation. The numerous public parks of Chisinau are wonderful recreation spots. On vacations many people travel to the Romanian or the Ukrainian seaside or mountains. Traveling abroad, however, is affordable only to a small percentage of the population.

18 ● CRAFTS AND HOBBIES

Pottery, woodcarving, carpet-weaving, and metalwork are the most famous Moldovan handicrafts.

19 ● SOCIAL PROBLEMS

Moldovans face many of the same economic problems as other former Soviet republics in the transition to a market-oriented economy. These include inflation, price deregulation, unemployment, and the weakening of the social welfare system. Wages have not kept up with the increase in prices. Many Moldovans have been plunged into poverty. Retirees, single parents, and the unemployed have been the most vulnerable groups.

There is also some division among Moldovans over whether or not their country (or parts of it) should pursue a political merger with Romania. Tension continues to exist with two regions within the country that have declared their independence from Moldova: the Gagauz region and the Transdnister.

There are many environmental problems in Moldova. Pesticides, herbicides, and artificial fertilizers were used in the past to increase crop output. Because of this, Moldova's ground water and soil are contaminated with chemicals. Deforestation has also contributed to the ongoing soil deterioration problem.

Crimes motivated by money or drugs have become the most common.

20 ● BIBLIOGRAPHY

Fedor, Helen, ed. *Belarus and Moldova: Country Studies*. Lanham, Md.: Federal Research Division, Library of Congress, 1995.

Moldova. Minneapolis, Minn.: Lerner Publications Co., 1993.

WEBSITES

Embassy of Moldova, Washington, D.C. [Online] Available http://www.moldova.org/, 1998.

World Travel Guide. Moldova. [Online] Available http://www.wtgonline.com/country/md/gen.html, 1998.

Monaco

The people of Monaco are called Monégasques. The native-born population is about 15 percent of the total. Foreign-born residents include French (more than 50 percent) and Italians (about 17 percent).

Monégasques

PRONUNCIATION: mah-neh-GASKS
LOCATION: Monaco
POPULATION: 30,000
LANGUAGE: French; Italian; English; Monégasque
RELIGION: Roman Catholicism; small number of Church of England members

1 ● INTRODUCTION

Aside from Vatican City, Monaco is the world's smallest independent state. It is a principality—a state ruled by a prince. In 1997, the Grimaldi family celebrated 700 years of rule in Monaco. Located on the French Riviera (the region including southern France and its neighbors along the Mediterranean Sea), Monaco borders the Mediterranean Sea. It shares its remaining borders with France. Since the establishment of its famous casino at Monte Carlo in 1861, Monaco has been a mecca (a sought-after location) for the rich and famous. Its glamorous image increased when its reign-

ing monarch (ruler), Prince Rainier III (b.1923), married American film star Grace Kelly (1929–82) in 1956.

Today, Monaco is a model of order and civility. However, it had its troubled times as the ruling family struggled to keep their tiny country independent of its large and powerful European neighbors. The principality was occupied by Germany during World War II (1939–45).

In the 1970s, Prince Rainier began encouraging the development of light, non-polluting industries. He aimed to prevent Monaco from becoming overly dependent on casino revenue. In the 1980s, new beaches were developed from reclaimed land, and luxury high-rise apartment buildings and condominiums were constructed to appeal to wealthy residents and investors.

Princess Grace was killed in a car accident in 1982. She was mourned in Monaco and throughout the world. Princess Caroline (b.1957), eldest daughter of Princess Grace and Prince Rainier, has taken on her mother's official duties. Her brother, Prince

MONÉGASQUES

0   .5   1 Miles

0   .5   1 Kilometers

FRANCE

Beausoleíl

Monte-Carlo

La Condamine

Port of Monaco

Monaco-Ville ☆

Fontvieille

Capd'ail

Port of Fontvieille

MEDITERRANEAN SEA

The people of Monaco are called Monégasques. Of Monaco's estimated population of 30,000 people, only about 5,000 are citizens. The remainder are foreigners attracted by Monaco's glamorous lifestyle and, more practically, by the absence of income and inheritance taxes. Native Monégasques come mainly from an area of central Europe once called Rhaetia and now part of Switzerland and Austria. More than half (over 50 percent) of Monaco's foreign residents are French, and about 17 percent are Italian. The rest belong to diverse nationalities including Belgian, British, and American.

3 ● LANGUAGE

French is Monaco's official language. Residents also speak Italian, English, and Monégasque, a local dialect derived from both Genoese Italian (a variation on Italian spoken in Genoa) and Provençal French (a variation on French spoken in southern France).

4 ● FOLKLORE

A colorful legend surrounds Monaco's patron saint, St. Dévote. She was born in Corsica (an island in the Mediterranean Sea) in the third century AD. Persecuted by the Romans for her religious beliefs, she died a martyr's death before the age of twenty. Witnesses heard the voice of the Lord answer her dying prayer and saw a white dove fly from her mouth. Following instructions they had received in a vision, two priests put St. Dévote's body in a boat with them and set out to sea. The boatmen followed the flight of the dove and landed in Monaco. The saint's body was buried there at a chapel that is still dedicated to her. Her martyrdom is commemorated every year on January 26, a national holiday. As part of

Albert (b.1958), is heir to the throne. (Monaco's constitution dictates that the succession to the throne will be to male heirs only.) Monaco became a member of the United Nations in 1993, with Prince Albert serving as the head of the Monaco delegation.

2 ● LOCATION

Monaco is situated at France's southeastern corner, near the Italian border. With an area of 1.9 square miles (0.73 square kilometers), it is smaller than New York City's Central Park. The principality is composed of four distinct areas: the royal palace, the gambling casino and hotel area, the port and business district, and an industrial zone. Its population is entirely urban.

the observance, Prince Rainier's family (the Grimaldis) and other government officials set fire to a wooden boat in front of the church of St. Dévote near the harbor.

On a darker note, another legend claims that Rainier I, an ancestor of the current monarch, wronged a woman. She then placed a curse on his family, casting a shadow on any happiness they might enjoy. The Grimaldi family has had its share of unhappy events in the past few decades. In 1982, Princess Grace was killed in a car accident. In 1990 Stefano Casiraghi, the husband of Princess Caroline (the eldest daughter of Prince Rainier III and Princess Grace), died while competing in a boating race. Princess Caroline was thus widowed with three small children.

5 ● RELIGION

About 95 percent of Monaco's population are Roman Catholics. Roman Catholicism is the state religion. Monaco also belongs to the Church of England's Gibraltar diocese.

6 ● MAJOR HOLIDAYS

Most national holidays are holy days of the Christian calendar. These include Easter (in March or April), Ascension Day (forty days after Easter), Pentecost Monday (the seventh Monday after Easter), the feasts of the Assumption (August 15), Fête-Dieu (All Saints' Day—November 1), the Immaculate Conception (December 8), and Christmas (December 25). The martyrdom of the country's patron saint, St. Dévote, is commemorated on January 26. Other holidays include New Year's Day (January 1) and Labor Day (May 1).

7 ● RITES OF PASSAGE

Monégasques live in a modern, industrialized, Christian country. Hence, many of the rites of passage that young people undergo are religious rituals. These include baptism, first communion, confirmation, and marriage. In addition, many families mark a student's progress through the education system with graduation parties.

8 ● RELATIONSHIPS

The people of Monaco interact with each other in ways similar to those of people in sophisticated cities worldwide. Men and women greet each other with handshakes, or may kiss each other on both cheeks.

9 ● LIVING CONDITIONS

Monaco's residents enjoy a high standard of living. They have both the greatest per capita (per person) income and the highest level of car ownership in the world. The demand for housing is so great that in order to have lawns they are put on the roofs of some new apartment buildings. Architectural styles range from ornate, nineteenth-century villas to modern, high-rise apartment buildings. Meeting the high demand for luxury housing is a priority for both the government and the construction industry. In the late 1990s, rent for a small apartment was $20,000 a month or more, and the purchase price of a one-bedroom apartment was likely to be $600,000.

10 ● FAMILY LIFE

The typical family in Monaco, as in most of Monaco's western European neighbors, is the nuclear family composed of parents and their children. Most Monégasque families have one or two children. Due to the small size of their country, the residents of Monaco have an unusually personal relationship with their royal family. All adult Monégasques are invited to the palace to celebrate major events of the royal family, such as engagements, weddings, and christenings. All Monégasque children under the age of twelve are invited to an annual palace Christmas party that includes refreshments, entertainment, and a gift for every child.

11 ● CLOTHING

Monégasques wear modern Western-style clothing typical of developed countries. Its many wealthy residents can be seen wearing the latest in high fashion, especially in the evening, at Monaco's restaurants, casinos, and other entertainment spots. Topless bathing is common and accepted on the beaches in Monaco (as in other parts of the French Riviera). However, dress standards off the beach are much more conservative.

12 ● FOOD

Monaco's cuisine is Mediterranean, featuring plenty of olive oil, fresh tomatoes, onions, garlic, black olives, and anchovies. Fresh fish—including sea bass, red mullet, and *daurade*—are plentiful and widely eaten, as is the famous fish stew, *bouillabaisse*. The region is also known for its abundance of fresh vegetables. Salads are popular, as well as dishes such as ratatouille, a vegetable stew made from tomatoes, onions, peppers, and eggplant (called aubergine on the Mediterranean coast). Champagne has the status of a national beverage in Monaco. (A single glass can cost as much as $40 at a fashionable restaurant.)

Recipe

Mediterranean Fresh Tomato and Onion Salad

Ingredients

6 to 8 fresh, ripe tomatoes, sliced crosswise
1 sweet red onion (or ½ Spanish onion), sliced crosswise into thin rings
¼ cup olive oil
1 Tablespoon vinegar
1 clove garlic, peeled and crushed
½ cup fresh parsley, chopped
salt and pepper to taste
dash of ground cumin (optional)
dash of paprika (optional)

Directions

1. Combine the tomato and onion slices in a wooden salad bowl or other serving bowl.
2. Combine remaining ingredients to make a dressing.
3. Pour dressing over tomatoes and onions. Toss gently and serve.

13 ● EDUCATION

Education in Monaco is required between the ages of six and sixteen, and literacy (the ability to read and write) is practically universal. The school curriculum is based on that of France. Students are also taught the history of Monaco and given some formal instruction in Monégasque, one of the dialects spoken in the principality.

14 ● CULTURAL HERITAGE

Monaco's national orchestra has performed with many leading conductors and soloists.

© Corel Corporation

Monaco's 5,000 citizens are guaranteed lifetime employment by Prince Rainier III. Many citizens work in the tourist industry, which attracts over 600,000 visitors from abroad every year.

Monte Carlo's historic theater, the Salle Garnier, is a world-famous venue (site) for opera, ballet, and orchestral concerts. Monaco also has its own ballet company, established in 1975. The Oceanographic Museum houses an impressive aquarium and a display of whale skeletons, and reflects the interest of Prince Albert (1848–1922) who once ruled Monaco.

Under Prince Rainier III, Monaco established an annual literary prize awarded to a Monégasque author writing in French. The Princess Caroline Library specializes in literature for children.

15 ● EMPLOYMENT

Monaco has practically no unemployment. Its 5,000 citizens are guaranteed lifetime employment by Prince Rainier III. Over two-thirds of its labor force commutes to work from France or Italy. Tourism is a major employer since over 600,000 visitors come from abroad every year. Monte Carlo's casino enterprise provides numerous jobs in its restaurants, hotel, and theater, as well as in the casino itself. Many workers—especially those who commute from neighboring countries—are employed in the nonpolluting light industries that have been established in Monaco since the 1970s.

Products include perfumes and cosmetics, pharmaceutical goods, precision instruments, jewelry, leather goods, and radio parts.

16 ● SPORTS

Monaco is famous for two auto racing events: the Monaco Grand Prix and the Monte Carlo Rally. Many consider the Grand Prix to be the world championship of Formula One auto racing. The race course lies totally within Monaco's modest borders. Residents gather at strategic spots throughout the principality to view the race. Other well-known sporting events include the Monte Carlo Golf Open and the prestigious Monte Carlo Tennis Open.

Golf and tennis are popular spectator and participation sports in Monaco. Overlooking the Mediterranean Ocean, the Monte Carlo Country Club's tennis courts are some of the most scenic in Europe. Monégasques also enjoy a variety of water sports, including sailing and big-game fishing.

17 ● RECREATION

Monaco has been known as a gambling mecca since the opening of the casino at Monte Carlo in the mid-1800s. Residents and visitors alike enjoy Monaco's beaches, its numerous museums and other cultural venues, and its beautiful gardens. The Princess Grace Rose Garden boasts 150 different varieties of roses. Monaco's residents receive both foreign and locally produced radio and television programs.

18 ● CRAFTS AND HOBBIES

Princess Grace established shops in Monte Carlo and Monaco-Ville where potters and other local artisans can sell their work.

19 ● SOCIAL PROBLEMS

A watchful police force sees to it that street crime is virtually nonexistent. There are nearly 500 police officers who patrol the streets of the tiny principality. Eighty-one surveillance cameras allow officers at police headquarters to further monitor any suspicious activity. Some residents are concerned that industrial development and residential construction are detracting from the quality of daily life.

20 ● BIBLIOGRAPHY

Bailey, Rosemary, ed. *Côte d'Azur and Monaco. Insight Guides.* Boston: Houghton Mifflin, 1993.

Black, Loraine. *Let's Visit Monaco.* London: Pegasus House, 1984.

Hopkins, Adam. *Essential French Riviera.* Lincolnwood, Ill.: Passport Books, 1994.

WEBSITES

European Travel Commission. Monaco. [Online] Available http://www.visiteurope.com/Monaco/Monaco01.htm, 1998.

Monaco Tourist Office, New York. [Online] Available http://www.monaco.mc/usa/, 1998.

World Travel Guide. Monaco. [Online] Available http://www.wtgonline.com/country/mc/gen.html, 1998.

Mongolia

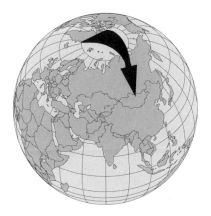

Almost 90 percent of the population of Mongolia are Mongols. The Kazaks are the leading minority group, making up about 6 percent of the population. People of Russian and Chinese origin are about 2 percent each. For more information on the Kazaks, see the chapter on Kazakstan in Volume 5; on the Russians, the chapter on Russia in Volume 7; and on the Chinese, the chapter on China in Volume 2.

Mongols

PRONUNCIATION: MAHN-guhls
ALTERNATE NAMES: Mengwushiwei
LOCATION: China (primarily Inner Mongolia Autonomous Region)
POPULATION: 4.8 million
LANGUAGE: Mongol
RELIGION: Lamaism

1 ● INTRODUCTION

The term "Mongol" originated from a tribe called Mengwushiwei in the Chinese book *Jiu Tang Shu (The Ancient History of the Tang Dynasty),* written in the tenth century. Mengwushiwei was changed to "Mongol" for the first time during the Yuan Dynasty (1271–1368). It gradually became the common name of many tribes. The Mongol people originally lived along the east bank of the Erguna River in central Inner Mongolia. Around the seventh century, they started to migrate toward the grassland in the west. In the twelfth century, they lived in the upper reaches of Onon River, Kerulen River, and Tola River, east to the Kente Mountains. Their tribal leader, Temujin, was a powerful man whose strength came from his ability to command his loyal army. He conquered other tribes and set up the Mongol empire. He took the title of Genghis Khan. From 1211 to 1215, Genghis Khan expanded his territory to Central Asia and to the southern part of Russia. His successors swept west as far as Vienna and deep into the Middle East. The occupied territory soon split into numerous independent countries. In 1260, Kublai (grandson of Genghis Khan) became the fifth supreme Khan and founder of the Yuan Dynasty (1271–1368). He destroyed the Southern Song Dynasty in 1279 and established China as the center of his huge empire. After the fall of the Yuan Dynasty in 1368, the Mongols suffered from internal division and conflict for many years.

In the 1920s, a large part of the traditional homeland of the Mongols became the People's Republic of Mongolia, established with the support of Soviet Russia. The other portion of the former Mongolian homeland remained within the Chinese border and was called Inner Mongolia. After 1949, it became the Inner Mongolia Autonomous Region.

2 ● LOCATION

The Mongols living in China numbered 4.8 million in 1990. They are mainly concentrated in the Inner Mongolia Autonomous Region. Many also live in autonomous regions in Xinjiang, Qinghai, Gansu, Heilongjiang, Jilin, and Liaoning. There are also Mongol communities scattered in Ningxia, Hebei, Sichuan, Yunnan, and Beijing. The territory of the Inner Mongolia Autonomous Region covers some 460,000 square miles (1,191,300 square kilometers), mostly hilly grassland and desert.

3 ● LANGUAGE

The Mongol language belongs to the Altaic family, Mongolian group. There are three dialects. The writing system was created in the thirteenth century AD. Kublai Khan ordered a Buddhist monk from Tibet to reform an ancient writing system. The system had been used to record oral literature but had ultimately been abandoned. The Mongolian writing system was later revised several times by native Mongol linguists so as to conform to the spoken language.

4 ● FOLKLORE

A large number of Mongolian myths are related to the origins of the Mongol people.

One of their more important myths describes a tribe called Mongu fighting with other tribes for many years. Finally, the Mongu were defeated. All their people were killed except two men and two women who, by sheer luck, escaped death. They went through many hardships and ultimately took refuge in a remote, thickly forested mountain. Only a narrow winding trail led to the outside world. This was a place with plenty of water and lush grass. They married. Many years later, the population grew so large that the land could not produce enough grain to feed all the people. They had to move but, unfortunately, the narrow trail was blocked. However, an iron mine was discovered. They cut down the trees, killed bulls and horses, and made a number of bellows to use in making iron into tools. Then they began to work the mine. They not only opened an outlet to the outside world, but they also got plenty of iron. They are the ancestors of the Mongols. To commemorate their heroic undertakings, the Mongols used to smelt iron at the end of every year.

5 ● RELIGION

Originally, the Mongols believed in shamanism. The shaman is a witch doctor, a dream reader, and an intermediary (go-between) between the living and the spirit world. He is also skilled in divination (predicting the future or reading signs in nature) and astrology. Remnants of shamanism still exist, including sacrificial offerings to ancestors, and reverence for the Sun, Moon, and nature.

Lamaism, the Tibetan form of Buddhism, entered the Mongolian society in the sixteenth century. It had a strong impact on

the Mongolian culture for centuries. Mongols sought the counsel and help of the *lama* (priest or monk) for every aspect of their life: migration, marriage, childbirth, disease, and death. Since 1949, Lamaist beliefs and practices have decreased drastically.

6 ● MAJOR HOLIDAYS

The Spring Festival (or lunar New Year, on the Western calendar, between January 21 and February 20) is an important holiday for the Mongols, as it is for the other nationalities of China. In preparation for this holiday, the Mongols make new clothes and store large amounts of mutton, wine, and dairy products. On the eve of the lunar New Year, all members of the family sit cross-legged in the center of the *ger* or *yurt* (a framed tent made of felt or hide) and begin their dinner at midnight. They offer toasts to the elders, eat and drink a great deal, and listen to storytelling all night long. Early the next morning, they dress up and call on relatives and friends at their homes. Dancing and singing are part of the celebration.

The Feast of Genghis Khan is on April 23 on the lunar calendar, set according to the phases of the moon. On the Western calendar, it falls between May 17 and June 16. On this occasion, there are activities to commemorate Genghis Khan, exchanges of goods, theatrical performances, and sports games.

In June or July of each year, the Mongols celebrate a special ritual, called *Aobao*. This holiday seems to go back to an ancient shamanistic practice. Aobao is a kind of altar or shrine made of a pile of stone, adobe bricks, and straw. The Aobao is believed to be the dwelling of the gods. During the ritual, tree branches are tossed into the Aobao, which is surrounded by lit joss sticks (similar to incense). Wine and horse milk are sprinkled over the mound, and mutton and cheese are placed on it as sacrificial offerings. While performing the ritual, the shaman (witch doctor) dances and enters into a trance. Wrestling and horse racing follow the religious ceremony.

The Nadam Rally is a traditional holiday of the Mongols. *Nadam* means recreation and play. It is a happy festival of the herders, held annually on a selected day in the summer or in the fall.

7 ● RITES OF PASSAGE

Depending on local custom, the Mongols practice cremation, burial in the ground, or hold a funeral in the wilderness. In the western region (where herders travel in search of pasture), the last form of burial is the most common. The body of the dead is placed in an open, horse-drawn cart and carried over rough terrain until the corpse falls off the cart due to the bumps. Then the body is laid in the wild. It is believed that when it is eaten by wolves or vultures, the soul of the dead rises to heaven. If the body is still there after a week, it is regarded as unlucky: the soul was not accepted in heaven. A lama (priest) is then invited to recite the scriptures and pray for the dead.

8 ● RELATIONSHIPS

There are no inns or hotels in the boundless grasslands, but one can always count on the Mongols for help. Their hospitality displays the generosity that is characteristic of nomadic peoples. The master of a *ger* or *yurt* (house) will put up a stranger for the night. He offers milk tea, mutton, and wine. The whole family shows concern by asking detailed questions. Upon leaving, the guest will be accompanied for quite a distance, then told the direction of his destination.

The Mongols in Yunnan have a special custom called "to meet the firewood-cutter." When it is about time for someone to return home after cutting firewood for a whole day, one member of the family will go ahead to meet the tired person halfway. In this manner they express loving care for the family member engaged in hard labor.

9 ● LIVING CONDITIONS

The *ger* or *yurt* is the traditional housing of the Mongols. It can be taken apart and carried on horseback, thus being suitable for nomadic life. The yurt is round with an

Jeannine Davis-Kimball

A Mongolian family poses outside their home, a traditional yurt.

umbrella-like cover. The *qana* (walls) are made of lattice similar to an expandable baby gate used in Western homes. The wall sections are held together with leather lacing. The roof ring is a usually a large hoop to which the wall sections and roof poles are attached. The door is usually constructed of wood, and is always positioned to face the southwest. The threshold is believed to hold the spirit of the household, and it is considered a great insult to the owner of the house to step on the threshold.

The exterior is covered with large pieces of felt tied together by ropes. Only a round skylight and a doorframe toward the southwest are left open. The yurt may be small as 4 yards (3.6 meters) in diameter, but much larger ones may house hundreds of people. Stationary yurts are common in seminomadic districts. Most of them are made of wood and adobe.

In agricultural areas, the Mongols usually dwell in one-story houses like the Chinese, within the boundaries of a village. Mongols living in towns and cities have, to a large extent, adopted the Chinese way of life.

Horseback riding is the traditional mode of transportation. Recently, however, bicycles, motorcycles, and cars have become more common in Mongol towns and villages.

10 ● FAMILY LIFE

A Mongolian family generally consists of a husband, a wife, and their young children. The sons, after marrying, move out of their parents' home. However, they live nearby and may travel with their parents in search of new pastures. In seminomadic districts, families often include parents, sons, and daughters-in-law.

The Mongols are monogamous. The family is dominated by the man, but herders usually consult their wives about major decisions. Furniture, clothes, and ornaments brought to the family by the wife during the wedding ceremony remain her own property.

A custom of "denying entrance on marrying" has been common among the nomadic and seminomadic Mongols. The bridegroom, accompanied by relatives, rides to the bride's yurt (house). He finds the door slammed in his face. After repeated requests, the door is finally opened. He presents a *hada* (ceremonial silk scarf) to his parents-in-law on entering and is given a banquet with a whole lamb. After the meal, the bride sits with her back to the others. The bridegroom kneels behind her and asks what her nickname was in childhood. He drinks at her house all night long. The following day, the bride leaves the yurt first. She circles the yurt on horseback three times, then speeds along to the bridegroom's house. The bridegroom and his relatives ride after her. The door is also slammed in her face and is only opened after repeated requests.

11 ● CLOTHING

Mongol dress varies with the environment and the seasons. In winter the Mongols living in pastoral areas (where domesticated animals are herded) usually wear a sheep fur coat with silk or cloth on the outside. In summer, they wear loose robes, usually in red, yellow, or dark navy, with long sleeves and silk waistbands called *bus*. Knives with beautiful sheaths, snuff-bottles, and flint are worn as pendants at the waist. (Snuff, a tobacco product, is either powdered and inhaled, or ground up and held between the cheek and gums. Flint is a hard stone used for striking a spark to start a fire.) High leather boots with the toes turned up are often worn.

Mongolian peasants wear a cloth shirt and robes, or cotton-padded clothes and trousers, along with a waistband. Felt boots are worn in winter. Men wear black or brown pointed hats, and some of them wrap their heads with silk. Women wrap red or blue cloth on their heads and wear a cone-shaped hat in winter.

12 ● FOOD

The main traditional foods of the Mongols include beef, mutton, and milk products, supplemented by grain and vegetables. Roasted mutton and yogurt are popular. Breakfast usually consists of stir-fried millet tea with milk. Beef, mutton, and noodle soup are eaten for lunch and dinner. Mongols drink the milk of horses, cows, and sheep, as well as tea and wine. Rice and flour are the staple foods of the peasants. Common dishes include dumplings, steamed stuffed buns, and meat pie.

13 ● EDUCATION

There are more than a dozen universities and colleges, more than 80 technical schools, about 5,000 middle (junior and senior) schools, and 30,000 primary schools in Inner Mongolia. The cultural and educational level of the Mongols is higher than average among the national minorities of China.

14 ● CULTURAL HERITAGE

There are quite a number of Mongolian folk songs. They may be divided into two different groups. One is common in pastoral areas, slow in tempo and free in rhythm. The other is popular in seminomadic districts, with quicker tempo and regular rhythm. *Haolibao* is a popular style of singing performance. The melody is rather fixed, but the words are impromptu (spontaneous), usually inspired by a sudden event that touches the singer. *Matouqin* ("horsehead stringed instrument") is a traditional instrument of the Mongols. The Chopstick Dance and Winecup Dance, soft and gentle, are frequently seen during festivities. The Horse Dance and Saber Dance, bold and generous, reflect the nomadic styles.

Literature in Mongolian includes the heroic epic "Life of Jiangger," which was written in the fifteenth century, and "Historical Romance," written in the nineteenth century.

15 ● EMPLOYMENT

Most Mongols are engaged in livestock husbandry, raising mainly sheep, cows, and horses. Mongolian horses, small and tough, are used for transport and as a source of milk, and they are the subject of dance and

Jeannine Davis-Kimball

Archery has been a popular sport in Mongolia since the eleventh century.

songs. The Mongols develop a reverence for horses from childhood. Most children love horseback riding, and participate in games and races on horseback.

16 ● SPORTS

The three main sports in Mongolia are horse racing, arrow shooting (archery), and wrestling. After a day of work, children, teenage boys, and male adults under the age of fifty frequently gather before the yurt (house) and wrestle. For a match, they wear a black vest, heavy boots, and sing as they wrestle.

There are no weight classes, and the object is to knock the opponent off balance, causing his to touch one knee and one elbow to the ground.

In archery, the Mongolian target is made of a row of small woven leather rings about 10 feet (3 meters) long. Some of the rings are painted red. In the last few decades, women have joined in the competition. Men shoot 40 arrows from about 215 feet (75 meters), and women shoot 20 arrows from about 180 feet (60 meters).

17 ● RECREATION

Movies and television have become popular and widespread over the last decades of the twentieth century. Publications, broadcasts, drama, and films in the Mongolian language are flourishing. The Inner Mongolia Autonomous Region boasts a state-of-the-art film studio. Cultural centers and libraries promote the Mongolian language and cultural productions in cities, towns, and even in the pastoral areas.

18 ● CRAFTS AND HOBBIES

Snuff-bottles are treasured among the Mongolians. They are made of gold, silver, copper, agate, jade, coral, or amber, with fine relief (raised carving) of horses, dragons, rare birds, and other animals. Another artifact is the pipe bowl, made of five metals, with delicate figures and designs. Supplemented by a sandalwood pole and red agate holder, the pipe bowl is considered precious. According to a Mongolian saying, "A pipe bowl is worth a sheep."

19 ● SOCIAL PROBLEMS

Urgent problems facing the Mongols are how to stabilize livestock husbandry and how to introduce scientific methods to breed the livestock. Breeding livestock is the mainstay of the Mongolian society. The modernization of their traditional way of making a living is one of the keys to economic success.

20 ● BIBLIOGRAPHY

Dreyer, June Teufel. *China's Forty Millions.* Cambridge, Mass.: Harvard University Press, 1976.

Eberhard, Wolfram. *China's Minorities: Yesterday and Today.* Belmont, Calif.: Wadsworth Publishing Company, 1982.

Lebar, Frank, et al. *Ethnic Groups of Mainland Southeast Asia.* New Haven, Conn.: Human Relations Area Files Press, 1964.

Schwarz, Henry G. *The Minorities of Northern China: A Survey.* Bellingham, Wash.: Western Washington University Press, 1989.

WEBSITES

World Travel Guide. Mongolia. [Online] Available http://www.wtgonline.com/country/mn/gen.html, 1998.

Ewenki

PRONUNCIATION: ee-WEHN-kee
ALTERNATE NAMES: Kamonikan; Suolun; Tongusi; Yakute
LOCATION: China; Mongolia
POPULATION: 30,000
LANGUAGE: Ewenki; Chinese
RELIGION: Traditional beliefs; Lamaism; Eastern Orthodox Christianity

1 ● INTRODUCTION

Until the mid-twentieth century, the Ewenki living in different areas were called by various names: Suolun, Tongusi, Yakute, and others. In 1957, they chose a unified name: Ewenki, which means "people living in the wooded mountains." The ancestors of the Ewenki lived northeast of Lake Baikal and in the forest bordering the Shilka River. They survived by hunting, fishing, and raising reindeer. In the early 1600s, the Manchus of northeast China conquered the Ewenki (known by a different name then). In the early 1700s, the Qing of China sent Ewenkis to a military post in a grassland region that would later become Mongolia. The Ewenki were allowed to bring their wives and children along, so the ended up settling there, becoming the direct ancestors of the present-day Ewenki. Modern Ewenki are hunters, farmers, or nomadic pastoralists—those who raise domesticated animals and wander with their herds in search of pasture and water.

2 ●LOCATION

The Ewenki number over 30,000 people. They are mainly scattered in Inner Mongolia, living together with the Mongols and Chinese. The region where they live in small, tight communities is called Ewenki Autonomous Qi County. It is a hilly grassland with more than 600 lakes, as well as a large number of rivers flowing in all directions.

3 ●LANGUAGE

The Ewenki language belongs to the Altaic linguistic family. There are three dialects but there is no writing system. Ewenki children are educated in schools set up in pastoral (rural) areas. Schools use the Mongolian language, both oral and written. In agricultural and mountainous areas, however, Chi-

nese language and characters are widely used.

4 ●FOLKLORE

The origin of humankind is explained in the following Ewenki myth: After the creation of the sky and the earth, the god Enduli made ten men and ten women from the skeletons of birds. Encouraged by his success, he planned to make more men and women, one hundred of each. He made men first, but in the process of his great work, he nearly ran out of bird skeletons. He had to use soil as an extra material to make the women. As a result, the women were weaker, a part of their body being made of soil.

The Ewenki have a special reverence for fire. This may be related to the severe cold of their environment and is reflected in one of their main myths. A woman was injured by a shower of sparks from the household hearth (fireplace). Angered by her pain, she drew her sword and stabbed violently at the hearth until the fire died out. The following day, she tried but could not light a fire. She had to ask for a burning charcoal from her neighbor. Leaving her house, she found an old woman crying miserably, with a bleeding eye. She asked the old woman what had happened to her. The old woman said: "It was you who stabbed me blind yesterday." The woman, suddenly realizing what had happened, asked the Fire God for forgiveness. The Fire God finally pardoned her. From then on, she never failed in lighting a fire. Up to the present, the Ewenki throw a piece of food or a small cup of wine into the fire as an offering to the Fire God before meals. Sprinkling water on a fire or poking a fire with a sword while roasting meat is taboo (forbidden).

5 ● RELIGION

The traditional beliefs of the Ewenki are rooted in shamanism (the belief in good and evil spirits that can be influenced by the shaman or holy person) and totemism (the practice of having animals or natural objects as personal and clan symbols). Ewenki religion stresses the worship of ancestors, animals, and nature. Special rituals are performed for Jiya (the livestock god), and fire. Fire should never be allowed to die out, even when Ewenki families migrate.

In some areas, all the clans of the Ewenki have a bird totem, such as the eagle, swan, or duck. Whenever a bird flies overhead, they sprinkle a little milk in the air. Killing or doing harm to a bird is considered taboo, especially if the bird is one's own totem. Almost every clan has a shaman, who explains the cause of disease, predicts and explains fortune and misfortune, exorcises (drives out) ghosts, and dances in a trance.

In some pastoral areas, the Ewenki believe in Lamaism, the Tibetan form of Buddhism adopted by the majority of Mongols. In some areas, one finds communities belonging to the Eastern Orthodox Church, a remnant of Russia's influence in the region in earlier centuries.

6 ● MAJOR HOLIDAYS

Some Ewenki holidays are the same as those celebrated by the Chinese. Unique Ewenki festivals include Aobao Gathering and the Mikuole Festival.

Aobao is a Mongolian term meaning "a pile." It consists of a pile of stones and adobe bricks, surrounded by a particular number of poles from which multicolored silk streamers are hung. Some streamers are covered with sacred Buddhist inscriptions. According to Ewenki shamanic beliefs, the Aobao is regarded as the dwelling of God. In some areas, the Aoboa is a large tree. The Aobao Gathering is one of the most important festivals of the Ewenki. It is held around June or July on the lunar calendar (between June 22 and August 21 on the Western calendar). Oxen and sheep are slaughtered as sacrificial offerings. The festival includes popular sporting events such as horse racing and wrestling.

The Mikuole Festival is essentially a fair of the livestock raisers. It is held in the last ten days of lunar May (between June 11 and July 21 on the Western calendar). Horses are branded and their long manes are shaved; sheep's ears are tattooed with the owner's mark. This is a special occasion for villagers to call on each other and to gather for dinner parties. The Ewenki also celebrate the Spring Festival (lunar New Year; between January 21 and February 20 on the Western calendar), which is a common holiday for all the nationalities of China.

7 ● RITES OF PASSAGE

Regardless of gender, the young pastoral Ewenki start to look after calves at age six or seven. Boys learn to ride a horse by age seven, and are taught how to lasso and break in a horse shortly afterward. Girls learn to milk cows at age ten. The children pay due respect to their elders, saluting them by bending at the knee and cupping the hands

Jeannine Davis-Kimball

Ewenki boys and girls learn to ride a horse at age six or seven.

in front of the chest. The seats and beds in a room are assigned on the basis of generation. Traditionally the Ewenki practiced tree burial (or wind burial). The corpse was placed in a coffin, or wrapped with bark or willow twigs and then hung high in a tree. The blowing of the wind, drenching of the rain, scorching of the sun, and beaming of the moon were believed to transform the dead into a star. Ground burial is now more common under the influence of the neighboring nationalities.

8 ● RELATIONSHIPS

The visit of a guest is always a happy event. A fur cushion is offered by the host. The guest sits on the cushion wherever it is; any shift of its place is considered impolite behavior. The hostess serves deer milk, deer meat, toasted cake, and homemade wild fruit wine. The host pours a few drops of wine on the fire, takes a sip for himself, and then hands the cup over to the guest.

Hunters store their food, clothes, and tools in their storehouse in the forest, which is never locked. Any hunter is allowed to take food from the storehouse as needed without prior agreement with the owner. When he meets the owner, he should, however, return the amount of food taken.

9 ● LIVING CONDITIONS

The traditional Ewenki house resembles an umbrella framed by twenty-five to thirty

Jeannine Davis-Kimball

The arrival of a visitor is always a happy event. The guest sits on a fur cushion that the host has positioned; any shift of its place is considered impolite.

poles covered with birch bark and deerskin. One side with a door is used as the living room. The other three sides are all platforms for sleeping. In the center is a fiery pit with a pan hanging over it. An opening at the top allows for ventilation. The tablet of the ancestors is attached to the top of the central wooden column.

In hunting areas, the house is a wooden cube. The walls are built by piling up logs, and the roof is made of birch bark. In some areas, Ewenki live in a Mongolian-style *yurt* or *ger*—a framed tent made of felt or hide. Construction of a ger is described in the section on Living Conditions in the "Mongols" article in this chapter.

10 ● FAMILY LIFE

The Ewenki live in small families that are patrilineal (tracing ancestry through the father's bloodline). Since they need to help each other hunt and search for pastures, they form nomadic villages. Villages, whether nomadic or sedentary (agricultural), have a clan structure in which each family has blood ties with the other families.

Ewenki families are monogamous. In the past, arranged marriage was common. Nowadays, the custom of "elopement marriage" is common. A young man and woman pretend to elope with the participation of both families. (The young man's family even prepares a new house for the couple ahead of time.) The couple enact a sequence of rituals with each family, honoring ancestors, asking forgiveness, and begging both sets of parents to accept their marriage. Afterward, all members of the clan congratulate the couple. A huge banquet follows, with dancing and singing.

11 ● CLOTHING

In former times, both sexes wore a long fur robe covering the ankles, and a long coat down to the knees. The cuffs and the bottom of the women's robes were embroidered with multicolored figures and designs. They all wore fur hats. Today, Ewenki mostly wear cloth robes, and padded cotton garments in winter. The dress of urban Ewenki is similar to that of the Chinese.

12 ● FOOD

The Ewenki's staple food is animal meat, including deer meat, mutton (sheep), beef, and pork of wild hog. They also eat grains such as Chinese sorghum, corn, millet, oats, and buckwheat. On account of the cold climate, vegetables are scarce. "Cooked meat held in hand" is very popular during festivals. The meat, attached to the bone, is chopped in big pieces and is half-cooked with a little salt. Gruel (hot cereal) with milk, another popular food, is also a sacrificial offering to the gods.

13 ● EDUCATION

Most of the Ewenki were illiterate (unable to read or write) in the past. Today, primary school education in the Ewenki Autonomous Qi County has become popular. Eighteen middle schools (junior and senior) have been set up. A growing number of students enroll in the university. Compared to other nationalities, however, education is at a low level.

14 ● CULTURAL HERITAGE

Ewenki folk songs, slow and loose, evoke the vast expanses of the grassland. Dancing styles vary according to region and occasion. A dance called *Ahanba* is performed by women at wedding ceremonies. There are no accompanying instruments; the tempo (speed) is set by the singers' voices. Each group consists of two to four dancers. In the beginning, they cry softly, "A-Han-Ba, A-Han-Ba," while swinging their arms. Then they turn face to face, and bend their knees. The tempo is gradually increased and the rhythm is intensified by the movement of their feet until they are dancing in full swing. Another dance, performed by two young men, acts out a confrontation between a hunter and a wild hog.

Ewenki literature has been handed down orally; it includes myths, tales, folk songs, and riddles.

15 ● EMPLOYMENT

The frequent migrations of the Ewenki over the course of history have resulted in scattered communities. Due to the significant difference of natural environments in which they lived, their lifestyle varied a great deal. There are four major lifestyles: livestock husbandry (raising domesticated animals), mixed economy (half farming and half hunting), farming, and hunting. Hunters ride deer and are thus called "deer-back-riding Ewenki."

16 ● SPORTS

The Ewenki start to ride, lasso, and break in horses early in their childhood. Later, they frequently gather to learn arrow shooting, high jumping, pole vaulting, long jumping, and skiing. Brave hunters and capable herders have mastered these skills by the time they are adults. Horse lassoing is a popular competition, and is a part of many festivals.

As early as 1,300 years ago, the ancestors of the Ewenki, called Shiwei, made a primitive form of skis. The skis used nowadays by the Ewenki for hunting are just an improved version of the Shiwei "snow-sliding boards."

17 ● RECREATION

Most of the areas where the Ewenki live have a movie theater and a television station. Film studios and television broadcasting stations have been set up in Inner Mongolia and Heilongjiang Province. Therefore, most Ewenki have access to television on a daily basis.

In remote hunting areas, old hunters are master storytellers, spinning tales about ancient and modern heroes in their fight against the harsh environment and wild animals. This is still the preferred form of entertainment.

Children enjoy outdoor activities. They use pieces of sheep ankle bone, dyed different colors, to play a kind of horse racing game. This could be compared to a homemade board game.

18 ● CRAFTS AND HOBBIES

The Ewenki excel in designing and producing tools for daily use. They also make toys from birch bark. Painting on birch bark is a common and well-known art of the Ewenki. Canoes made of birch bark, besides their unique design, provide swift and easy transport on the many lakes and rivers of the Ewenki land.

19 ● SOCIAL PROBLEMS

Poverty and isolation are serious problems confronting the Ewenki. Their scattered communities, harsh environment, illiteracy, and the absence of a market economy make these problems difficult to solve.

20 ● BIBLIOGRAPHY

Eberhard, Wolfram. *China's Minorities: Yesterday and Today.* Belmont, Calif.: Wadsworth Publishing Company, 1982.

Heberer, Thomas. *China and Its National Minorities: Autonomy or Assimilation?* Armonk, N.Y.: M. E. Sharpe, 1989.

Ma Yin, ed. *China's Minority Nationalities.* Beijing: Foreign Languages Press, 1989.

Ramsey, S. Robert. *The Languages of China.* Princeton: Princeton University Press, 1987.

WEBSITES

World Travel Guide. Mongolia. [Online] Available http://www.wtgonline.com/country/mn/gen.html, 1998.

Morocco

Berbers make up about 34 percent of the population, and Arabs, 66 percent. In the past, the Jewish community played a significant role in the economic life of Morocco, but its numbers have decreased as many have emigrated to Israel since it was established in 1948. In 1992, some 60,000 foreign citizens, mostly French, Spanish, Italian, and Algerians, were living in Morocco.

Moroccans

PRONUNCIATION: muh-RAHK-uhns
LOCATION: Morocco
POPULATION: 29 million
LANGUAGE: Arabic (official); French; English; Berber; Spanish
RELIGION: Islam (99 percent); Christianity; Judaism

1 ● INTRODUCTION

Morocco has been invaded many times throughout its history. Arab invaders brought Islam to Morocco during the seventh century. They later brought art, architecture, and universities. From the fifteenth to the nineteenth century, European nations gained control of Morocco. In the twentieth century, France made Morocco a protectorate. However, the people did not want to be ruled by others, so they revolted against any conqueror. Morocco finally gained independence on March 2, 1956. The government is now a constitutional monarchy. It is ruled by a king who is a descendant of the Prophet Muhammad, the seventh-century messenger of Islam. The king appoints a cabinet, known as the Council of Ministers. He also appoints a prime minister as head of the government. The people elect the *majlis al-nuab,* or Council of Representatives.

2 ● LOCATION

Morocco has an area of 172,368 square miles (446,550 square kilometers). Its coastline is more than 1,000 miles (1,600 kilometers) long. The population of Morocco is estimated to be 29 million.

The Moroccan landscape consists of desert, rivers, plains, and four major mountain ranges. The northwestern part of the Sahara Desert covers almost half of Morocco. Morocco's rivers are not navigable, but they are a major source of water for irrigation. Morocco's plains are cultivated with a variety of crops, such as oranges, figs, olives, almonds, barley, and wheat.

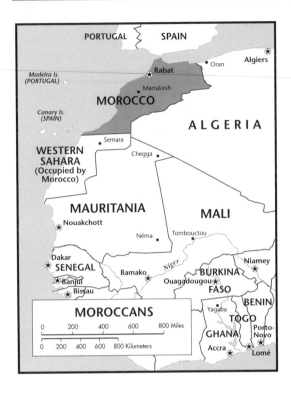

The country has a variety of weather patterns. The desert is hot and dry. The coastal plains have mild temperatures. In the summer the mountains are hot and dry. In the winter they are cold, rainy, and often snowy.

3 ● LANGUAGE

Modern standard Arabic is the official state language of Morocco and Arabic is the most common language spoken. When pledging to do something, a Moroccan Muslim says *insha Allah,* or "if God wills it." Before doing something, a Muslim should say *Bismillah,* or "In the name of God." Common female Arabic names are Fatima, Aisha, and Khadija. Common male Arabic names are Muhammad, Hasan, and Ali. All of these are also names of famous people in Islamic history.

Titles of respect are often attached to names. An older woman may be referred to as *Lalla,* which is similar to "Ma'am." A man may be referred to as *Sidi,* or *Si* for short, which is similar to "Mr."

4 ● FOLKLORE

Morocco has many legends based on the exploits of Muslim holy men called *murabitin* in Arabic. Murabitin were believed to have *baraka,* or divine grace, that let them perform miracles. Their burial sites are visited by people hoping for blessings and favors. The murabitin are more common in the countryside than in the urban areas.

Some Moroccans believe in spiritual beings called *jinn.* Jinn are said to take on the forms of animals. To ward off these spirits, Moroccans wear verses from the Quran (Koran) on an amulet. The Quran is the Muslim holy book. They also wear the "hand of Fatima," a charm in the shape of the right hand, to protect against the evil eye.

Often, women in the countryside believe in (and might practice) *sihr,* or witchcraft. Sihr is given orally, usually as a potion mixed with food or drink. A potion might make someone fall in love, or it might invoke a curse to take revenge.

Most folklore in Muslim countries tells stories of important people in religious history. According to the tale, *al-Isra wa al-Mi'raj,* on the twenty-sixth day of the Islamic month of Rajab, the Prophet Muhammad traveled at night from Mecca (a city in what is now Saudi Arabia, then known as Hijaz) to Jerusalem. From Jerusa-

Cory Langley

A sign near Marrakesh, Morocco, written in Arabic and French marking the direction and distance to the city of Tombouctou in the country of Mali. According to the sign, it would take someone traveling by camel 52 days to reach Tombouctou.

lem, he rode his wondrous horse, al-Burak, on a nighttime visit to heaven. This legend is celebrated every year throughout the Islamic world.

5 ● RELIGION

Almost all Moroccans are Muslim. Islam is the state religion. The largest mosque in Africa is the Karaouine Mosque, built in AD 862 and located in the city of Fez. This mosque has enough room for more than 20,000 worshipers. A small number of people—about 70,000 are Christian (mainly Roman Catholic). An even smaller minority (6,000–7,000) are Jewish.

6 ● MAJOR HOLIDAYS

Moroccans celebrate secular and Muslim religious holidays. One major Muslim holiday is *Eid al-Fitr*. It is observed the last three days of the month of fasting called Ramadan. The other major Muslim holiday is *Eid al-Adha*. It commemorates the willingness of the Prophet Abraham to obey God's command. Eid al-Adha signals the end of the Muslim pilgrimage to Mecca, or *hajj*. Every Muslim must make this pilgrimage at least once during his or her lifetime.

Secular holidays include King Hassan II's Coronation Day (March 3); Labor Day

Cory Langley

The traditional attire of Moroccans is a one-piece, floor-length, hooded dress, known as a jellaba.

gather for three days to mourn and recite from the Quran (Koran). On the fortieth day after the death, friends and relatives gather again to mourn and have a feast, known as *sadaqa.*

8 ● RELATIONSHIPS

Moroccans shake hands during greetings and farewells. Close friends of the same sex commonly hug and exchange kisses on the cheeks. People of the opposite sex just shake hands. The most common greeting among Moroccans is the phrase *Al-salamu alaykum,* which means "May peace be upon you." The response is *Wa alaykum al-salam,* or "May peace be upon you also."

Family members are very courteous to one another and to their guests. However, in public each person hopes to advance his or her own interests, so they might not show the same courtesy.

Boys and girls are kept apart until they grow old enough to understand sexuality. It is considered inappropriate and shameful for unmarried males and females to socialize. Premarital sex is strictly forbidden. A girl who loses her virginity outside of marriage brings great shame to her family's reputation. Moroccan males can socialize outside of the home, often at the cafe. Women are rarely seen at cafes.

(May 1); Independence Day (November 18); and New Year's Day (January 1).

7 ● RITES OF PASSAGE

All Moroccans are expected to get married. Weddings take several days, and involve elaborate parties with food and dancing. Every wife is expected to have children. Circumcision of males is required by Islam. In Morocco, it is usually done when the boy is young, sometime before his sixth birthday. People who die are buried within twenty-four hours. Relatives and neighbors

9 ● LIVING CONDITIONS

Moroccan neighborhoods have different types of homes, some new and some centuries old. The older towns, known as *medinas,* are usually surrounded by high, thick walls. The newer towns have houses with Western conveniences.

Modern high-rise apartment buildings can be found in Morroco's major cities.

All Moroccans have access to clean water, and to cooking and heating fuel. Most homes also have electricity. Some homes have central heating and telephones. Most urban areas have public phones. Most toilets are porcelain-covered holes in the ground. Modern homes have Western-style toilets.

The streets are well developed. Most cities are connected by two-lane roads, railroads, and buses. The country has six major seaports and seven international airports.

More than half of the population is under the age of nineteen. Nearly one-third is under the age of ten. Casablanca is the largest city. It has about 3 million inhabitants. The life expectancy is sixty-three years for males and sixty-five for females. Morocco has a high rate of infant mortality—seventy-six deaths in every 1,000 live births. Moroccans have only one doctor for every 5,200 people, and one dentist for every 100,000 people.

10 ● FAMILY LIFE

The family is the center of every Moroccan's life. Children live with their families until they get married or go away to school. It is common for Moroccan women to live with their husband's family. Women are expected to take care of the home. The elderly are highly respected and are cared for by their families. Both men and women play a strong role in decision-making. Women have more freedom in the cities. More restrictions are placed on rural women.

Every Moroccan is expected to marry. For many women, marriage and childbearing are the ultimate goals in life. Most women want to get married before their mid-twenties, and most men before their thirties. Not all marriages are arranged by the parents, but parents have a say in the choices made by their children.

11 ● CLOTHING

The traditional attire of Moroccans is a one-piece, floor-length, hooded dress, known as a *jellaba*. It is worn by both men and women. Western attire is often worn under the jellaba. In cold weather, many men cover their jellabas with a hooded cloak called a *burnus*. Religious and/or conservative women cover their hair in public. Berber women wear long, colorful dresses, often covering their heads with straw hats. They also often have tattoos on their foreheads, cheeks, or necks. However, this custom is slowly fading away. Rural men often wear turbans. A knitted skullcap is common attire for men going to a mosque.

12 ● FOOD

Moroccans generally have three meals per day. Breakfast might consist of bread, olive oil, butter, and preserves, or a pancake-like food known as *baghrir*. Lunch is the largest meal of the day. It consists typically of *couscous* and *tajin*. Dinner ranges from light to heavy meals, with soup, known as *harira,* and bread being common. Moroc-

---

> ## *Recipe*
>
> ### Moroccan Oranges
>
> **Ingredients**
>
> 6 oranges, peeled and sliced
> 3 Tablespoons powdered sugar
> ½ teaspoon cinnamon
> water or orange soda
>
> **Directions**
>
> 1. Place the orange slices in a shallow dish.
> 2. Drizzle lightly with water or orange soda.
> 3. Sprinkle with the sugar and cinnamon.
> 4. Chill for 1½ hours, turning the slices occasionally.

---

cans are serious tea-drinkers, although coffee, with much milk and sugar, is also very popular. Moroccans, being Muslim, are prohibited from consuming pork or alcoholic beverages. However, alcohol is served in bars and cafes throughout the country.

Moroccans eat at a low, round table and often are served from one platter. Morocco's national dish is couscous, a kind of wheat pasta that looks like rice. Couscous is combined with meat, lamb, and other ingredients to make a main course. Another favorite Moroccan dish is *tajin,* which is a stew of vegetables and meat baked in earthenware pots.

13 ● EDUCATION

Public schools are free and children between the ages of seven and thirteen are required to attend. This law, however, is not enforced. In 1992, only two-thirds of this age group attended school. In 1995, more than half of adults were illiterate (unable to read and write). French is taught in all public schools from the third grade through the completion of secondary school. English is taught in public schools at the secondary level. The school year is similar to that in Western countries: classes begin in September and end in June.

14 ● CULTURAL HERITAGE

Moroccans enjoy rhythmic music and dancing. Most music on the radio and television is traditional Arab entertainment. However, more Western music is being broadcast, and MTV is now available by satellite. Traditional Arabic music uses string instruments, such as the *rebec, lotar, ud,* and *kamanja.* It is common to see girls and women dancing at an informal gathering. Sometimes the dancer seems to go into a trance-like state that may cause her to faint.

At festivals held in honor of local saints, horsemen, wearing white robes and white turbans, gallop toward the audience and then fire their guns into the air.

15 ● EMPLOYMENT

Morocco's upper class is made up mostly of wealthy merchants and of the Prophet Muhammad's descendents, who are known as the *Sherfa.* The middle class is made up of educated professionals such as university professors, civil servants, doctors, lawyers, and high school teachers. The less-educated are employed mostly in factories and/or farms. Morocco has high unemployment, so many Moroccans find work in France, Bel-

gium, Canada, Italy, Libya, and the Netherlands.

Most Moroccans work in agriculture, either as laborers or vendors. The plains of Morocco are cultivated with barley, corn, wheat, tobacco, citrus fruits, olives, tomatoes, and other fruits and vegetables. Morocco's chief export is the mineral phosphate. Morocco's third-most-important industry is fishing. Tourism is also important. In 1994, three million tourists visited Morocco.

16 ● SPORTS

Soccer is popular in Morocco, as it is throughout the Middle East and North Africa. It is viewed weekly on television and played by men and boys throughout the country.

17 ● RECREATION

Moroccan men spend much leisure time socializing at outdoor cafes. Most women's socializing is done in the home or on the rooftop. Here they might knit, crotchet, or embroider with other women. Men often go to movie theaters, but few theaters are open to women. Men and women both attend movies in "cineclubs," which are private clubs that show films for a small fee. Morocco has two television stations. About half the programs are in French, and the other half are in Arabic. Satellite dishes have made more programming available, including MTV and the Middle East Broadcasting Company (MBC).

18 ● CRAFTS AND HOBBIES

Women weave rugs and carpets by hand, using a loom. These have intricate patterns and can take months to complete. Handbags and clothing are crafted from animal skins. In some villages in Morocco, women tattoo their hands and feet in very detailed patterns that cover virtually the entire limb. These henna tattoos fade away within a few weeks.

19 ● SOCIAL PROBLEMS

The Moroccan government has made claims over the Western Sahara. It now spends a substantial amount of its resources fighting a war against the Western Sahara's guerrilla movement, the *Polisario*. The government often arrests people and groups that it considers threatening. Human-rights organizations have criticized this practice. As a result, between June 1989 and April 1990 the government released 2,163 political prisoners.

Morocco's major problem is the lack of opportunities available to the people. Unemployment is widespread, and people have sometimes rioted over inflation. Slums are filled with people who moved to the cities in hopes of finding jobs. Crime is common in Morocco, but very little of it is violent. While hard drugs are rare, hashish and marijuana are common, but nevertheless illegal.

20 ● BIBLIOGRAPHY

Hargraves, Orin. *Culture Shock! Morocco: A Guide to Customs and Etiquette*. Portland, Ore.: Graphic Arts Center Publishing Co., 1995.

Nelson, Harold D., ed. *Morocco: A Country Study*. Washington, D.C.: American University, 1985.

Park, Thomas K. *Historical Dictionary of Morocco*. London: Scarecrow Press, 1996.

Wilkins, Frances. *Morocco*. New York: Chelsea House Publishers, 1987.

WEBSITES

ArabNet. [Online] Available http://www.arab.net/morocco/morocco_contents.html, 1998.

Interknowledge. Morocco. [Online] Available http://www.geographia.com/morocco/, 1998.

Moroccan Ministry of Communications. Morocco. [Online] Available http://www.mincom.gov.ma/, 1998.

Mozambique

The people of Mozambique are called Mozambicans. There are ten major ethnic groups. The largest, residing north of the Zambezi River, is the Makua-Lomwé group, representing about 37 percent of the total population. Others include the Yao (Ajawa), Makonde, Nguni, Maravi, Tsonga, Chopi, and Shona (or Karanga).

Mozambicans

PRONUNCIATION: mo-zam-BEE-kuhns

LOCATION: Mozambique

POPULATION: 18 million

LANGUAGE: Portuguese (official); 33 African languages; English (trade)

RELIGION: Traditional African religions; Islam; Christianity

1 ● INTRODUCTION

Mozambicans inhabit primarily Mozambique, a nation in southern Africa that was colonized by Portugal. However, Mozambicans cannot be described as a single distinct cultural group. When Europeans scrambled to colonize Africa, they drew country boundaries that often enclosed many different ethnic groups. The first inhabitants of Mozambique were hunters and gatherers, ancestors of the Khoisan (Bushmen) now found in South Africa, Botswana, and Namibia.

Mozambicans are a people in transition. They fought for and won their independence from Portugal in 1975. From 1975 until the late 1990s, however, opposing factions continued to fight for control of the government. A peace agreement was signed between the two main warring factions on October 4, 1992, and a general cease-fire began.

Natural disasters have also plagued the country. Mozambique has experienced recurrent drought, flooding, cyclones, water pollution, and desertification (the process by which land loses its nutrients and becomes desert). Mozambique remains one of Africa's poorest countries.

2 ● LOCATION

Mozambique is located in southern Africa between South Africa and Tanzania. The

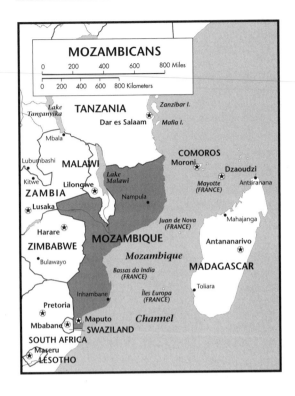

MOZAMBICANS

0 200 400 600 800 Miles

0 200 400 600 800 Kilometers

only an estimated 30,000 people in Mozambique speak the language, and 27 percent of those speak it as a second language. In urban centers, particularly in Maputo, English is becoming popular because many neighboring countries use English as their official language.

4 ● FOLKLORE

The various ethnic groups of Mozambique contribute to a rich variety of myths and legends in the country. Traditional African religions generally place great emphasis on the importance of ancestors. The long-standing use of storytelling to preserve history has resulted in a wealth of folk traditions and stories.

One such legend from the Makonde people demonstrates the importance of folklore. The Makonde, who live in northern Mozambique and southern Tanzania, believe that they descended from one man who lived alone like a wild pig in the forest. The man wanted a family, so he carved a wife out of wood and eventually had children. The first two children were born near the river and both died. The third was born on the plateau and survived. This was taken as a sign that the Makonde should live on high ground. The Makonde are world-famous for their woodcarvings, of both human figures for family worship and masks for initiation ceremonies. Traditionally, they believed that their carving abilities proved they could control the world of nature and communicate with ancestors and spirits.

country is almost twice the size of California. The climate is tropical to subtropical, and most of the country is coastal lowlands. The capital city is Maputo.

Mozambique's population is nearly 18 million people, and experts estimate 3 million more Mozambicans were forced to leave their homes during the fight for independence and internal fighting that followed. Some refugees were still living in Malawi, Zimbabwe, and South Africa in the late 1990s, although 1.6 million refugees had returned to Mozambique.

3 ● LANGUAGE

There are thirty-three languages spoken in Mozambique. The official language adopted by the government is Portuguese. However,

5 ● RELIGION

Roughly 60 percent of the population practice traditional African religions, 30 percent

Jason Lauré

Mozambicans on a ferry.

are Christian, and 10 percent are Muslim (practice the religion of Islam). Most traditional African religions believe in one supreme being who acts through spirits and ancestors. Traditional religions are not necessarily viewed as incompatible with religions imported from Europe and northern Africa such as Christianity and Islam. Many Mozambican Christians continue to practice the witchcraft, sorcery, spells, and magic associated with traditional religions.

6 ● MAJOR HOLIDAYS

In addition to the national holiday, Independence Day on June 25, many major religious holidays are celebrated in Mozambique. The Portuguese Catholic influence is very heavy among the 30 percent who are Christians. Consequently, holidays such as Christmas and Easter are celebrated much as they are in Western cultures. Similarly, the Muslim population observes Islamic holy days.

7 ● RITES OF PASSAGE

As with most traditional African societies, rites of passage are very important to the Mozambicans. Such practices vary from one ethnic group to another. Some groups practice circumcision of boys aged ten to twelve to mark their passage into manhood. Others do not practice initiation or circumcision for boys. The Makonde practice initiation ceremonies that integrate young people into the adult world through links with ancestors and supernatural beings. Makonde rites of passage ceremonies include the use of masks.

8 ● RELATIONSHIPS

Customs concerning greetings, visiting, body language, and dating vary from one ethnic group to another. Portuguese and English greetings are common in urban areas.

9 ● LIVING CONDITIONS

Mozambique has not yet emerged from the heavy influence of its more than thirty-year struggle for independence. The influence of colonialism also remains in many aspects of life, including housing. "Cement town" describes European-style settlements once occupied by colonists. "Cane towns" are the African settlements that surround them. Mozambican homes are often constructed of cane and mud. In the cities, high-rise apartments are crowded, with twenty people sometimes living in three-room apartments. Electricity and plumbing are often unreliable in the cities and are nonexistent in rural areas.

The war left nearly half of the country's primary health care network destroyed. This resulted in many children dying from preventable diseases like measles. Starvation was widespread. An estimated one million land mines remain in the country. From 1995 to 1997, in the Maputo province alone, ninety-eight people stepped on landmines—sixty-eight of whom were children.

© Corel Corporation

Maize (corn) is an important element of the Mozambican diet. Mealie pie, for example, is a cornmeal mush that is a southern African staple.

10 ● FAMILY LIFE

Most African cultures emphasize one side of the family tree—father's or mother's—more heavily than the other. In matrilineal groups, for example, the family tree is traced through the mother's side of the family. In addition, property passes from one generation to the next based on matrilineal ties. Kinship ties are more important in African societies than in Western societies. This is so in part because land is usually owned by and passed down within the extended family group. Both matrilineal and patrilineal descent groups exist in Mozambique. However, it is common for men to control issues related to ownership of land.

Mozambicans continue to practice subsistence farming (farming that provides for the family's needs with little left over for marketing) as a means of survival. Men traditionally perform the initial plowing or hoeing to prepare the land for planting. Women maintain the farm and are responsible for most of the harvesting. Women are also responsible for the traditional roles of taking care of children, food preparation, and homemaking.

11 ● CLOTHING

During the war, *deslacados*—people dislocated by the war—often had no clothes and covered themselves with tree bark. Clothing became a precious commodity and was more valued than currency in many areas. In Maputo, guards were posted at clotheslines. A shirt cost as much as a laborer could earn in a month. Western-style clothing is common, but traditional clothing such as capulanas and headscarves are still in use. *Capulanas* are squares of colorful cloth that can be worn as a wraparound skirt or on the upper body. They can also serve as baby slings.

12 ● FOOD

In parts of Mozambique, meat is scarce, but pork and wild pig are favorite dishes and are usually prepared in a sauce. The Portuguese influence can be found in Mozambique cuisine in the use of spicy sauces. Products of the fishing industry, especially shrimp and shellfish, are popular in the coastal region. The mainstay, however, in Mozambique as well as other parts of southern Africa, is maize (corn). Mealie pie, for example, is a cornmeal mush that is a southern African staple. During periods of violent conflict, Mozambicans depended on food from relief agencies; some scavenged for wild berries, nuts, and caterpillars; and many others starved.

13 ● EDUCATION

During the war, school was often conducted under trees, without books or supplies. By 1989, 52 percent of first-level primary schools in Mozambique had been destroyed or forced to close. In addition, families often cannot afford the loss of farm labor to allow children to attend school. In 1988, conflict had so disrupted education that most students in Zambezia Province had not progressed beyond the first grade. People forced to leave their homes—*deslocados*—were often too hungry to attend school.

Perhaps one-third of Mozambicans over the age of fifteen are literate (able to read and write). Primary education is free, and 40 percent of primary school age children enroll. Secondary education is not free. Only a tiny percentage of primary school students go on to secondary, professional, technical, or university education.

14 ● CULTURAL HERITAGE

Mozambicans practice various forms of music, dance, and storytelling. African art is used to communicate spiritual messages, historical information, and other truths to society. Distinctive cultural heritage plays an important role among the various ethnic groups. The Chope, for example, are masters of the African piano, the *mbila*. The Makonde are world-famous for their woodcarvings.

Many writers and artists are natives of Mozambique. Poet and artist Rui de

Noronha is considered the father of modern Mozambican writers. Other influential writers and artists include poet Albuquerque Freire; short-story writer and journalist Luis Bernardo Honwana (also known as Augusto Manuel); and poet and painter Malagatana Gowenha Valente. Noemia Carolina Abranches de Sousa (also known as Vera Micaia) is considered to be the first Mozambican woman writer. Much Mozambique literature, like other African literature written in Portuguese, is anticolonial and promotes traditional African themes.

15 ● EMPLOYMENT

Most Mozambicans rely on *machambas,* family garden plots, for survival. As much as 80 to 90 percent of the population practices some agricultural activity, primarily subsistence farming. The annual per capita income for Mozambicans is $90 per year. Unemployment registers at about 50 percent.

16 ● SPORTS

Soccer is the most popular organized spectator sport in Mozambique. One of the leading soccer players for Portugal in the 1960s was Eusobio from Mozambique. Many other Western sports are played by children and adults, particularly in the urban centers.

17 ● RECREATION

In Mozambique's urban centers, theater and television are popular. The government tried to promote rural village theater, but the effort was disrupted during the war years and has not been reestablished. Children enjoy playing games such as hopscotch and hide-and-seek.

18 ● CRAFTS AND HOBBIES

The Makonde of Mozambique are known for their woodcarvings. In the Shetani style (*Shetani* is a Swahili word meaning "devil"), the carvings are tall and gracefully curved with stylized and abstracted faces and symbols. Most are carved in heavy ebony. Another style of woodcarvings (called *Ujamaa* or tree of life) are totem-type structures. They show lifelike people and faces (representative of family members), huts, and everyday articles like pots and agricultural tools. The Makonde are also known for their water pots, as well as masks used in initiation ceremonies.

19 ● SOCIAL PROBLEMS

A vast array of social problems afflict a country so recently traumatized by war. While Mozambique adopted a democratic constitution in 1990, human rights violations continue to be reported. These include a pattern of abusive behavior by security forces and an ineffective judicial system. The transition to better economic conditions, improved health care and education, and the guarantee of human rights will take time.

20 ● BIBLIOGRAPHY

Azevedo, Mario. *Historical Dictionary of Mozambique.* London: Scarecrow Press, 1991.

Dillon, Diane, and Leo Dillon. *The African Cookbook.* New York: Carol Publishing, 1993.

WEBSITES

Government of Mozambique. [Online] Available http://www.mozambique.mz/, 1998.

World Travel Guide. [Online] Available http://www.wtgonline.com/country/mz/gen.html, 1998.

Myanmar

The people of Myanmar are called Burmese. The population is comprised of a number of ethnic groups. The Burman, related to the Tibetans, make up almost 70 percent of Myanmar's total population. Other ethnic groups remain distinct, and have sought to preserve their independence, sometimes by violent means. These groups include the Shans, making up about 7 percent of the population; the Karens, representing about 6 percent of the population; and other smaller groups, representing less than 5 percent of the population each.

Burman

PRONUNCIATION: BUR-muhn
ALTERNATE NAMES: Myanmar
LOCATION: Myanmar (Burma)
POPULATION: 30 million
LANGUAGE: Burmese
RELIGION: Buddhism

1 ● INTRODUCTION

The country, Union of Myanmar, is known by two names: Myanmar and Burma. The Burman people pronounce the name of their country as "Bamah." In 1990, the military government of the Union of Burma named the country "Myanmar" (which the people pronounce as "Myanmah"). Outside Myanmar, people refer to the country as both Burma and Myanmar, mainly depending on whether they support the military government or not.

The Burman people originally came from western China. In the Myanmar capital city of Rangoon, at least half of the population is of mixed descent from China, India, and Europe.

In 1885, the British annexed Burma and colonized the region. In 1947, the Burmese leaders negotiated with the British for Burma's independence. The neighboring areas of Chin, Kachin, and Shan became part of independent Burma. Burma functioned as a democracy until 1962, when a military dictatorship took over. This started a decline in the country's economy. By the late 1990s, Myanmar had become one of the ten poorest countries in the world.

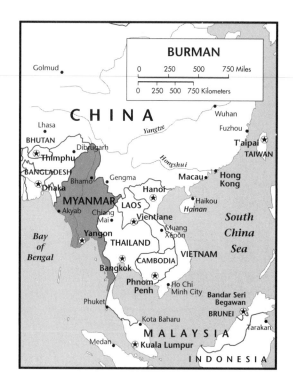

BURMAN

COMMON PHRASES

English	Burmese	Script
hello	byou	၍
goodbye	thwa ba-do	သွား ၍ တော
how are you?	nei kaun ye la?	နေ ကောင်း လား
how do you do?	ma-ye la?	ဘာ ရဲ့ လား
never mind	nei-bazei	နေ ၀ါ စေ

same way as "Mr." in English. *Ma* is equivalent to "Miss." *Daw* means "aunt" and is used to refer to women in the same was as "Mrs." or "Miss."

The Burmans stress age in social and human relations. An elder must be addressed as "uncle." If the ages are not far apart, as with an elder brother, then *ako* is used; for an elder sister, *ama* is used. Most Burman names consist of two or three words (for example, *Ne Win* or *Khin Maung Gyi*).

2 ● LOCATION

There are an estimated 30 million people in Myanmar. Myanmar is bordered by India, Bangladesh, China, Laos, Thailand, and the Indian Ocean.

3 ● LANGUAGE

The Burman language is similar to Tibetan and tribal languages in China. The Burman script was taken from the Sanskrit and is similar to Urdu, Hindi, Thai, and Cambodian.

Burman people have only a first name, and all names have meanings. Burmans have no family names. It is impossible to trace one's ancestors by name. For example, *U Nu* means "uncle young" or "uncle tender." *U* means "uncle" but is used in the

4 ● FOLKLORE

The Burman revere spiritual beings called the *Nat*, which they celebrate in their ceremonial plays, prayers, sacrifices, and dances. The *Nat* or *Nathami* (female) are believed to be very clever and possess immense power. They inhabit human bodies and exist in the trees, on top of mountains, in the ocean, and everywhere else. The Burman cannot imagine what the Nat look like, but they fear them. The people give offerings to the Nat so that they will protect them. Thagyamin, a Nat considered to be a god, hears all and knows all, and is usually honored during the New Year Festival.

The Burman also honor the *Naga*, spirits that live at the bottom of rivers, seas, and oceans in places built from precious stones and pearls. They are the protectors of the water and land. The Naga have the advantage of being able to take the form of human beings, whereby the female Naga become beautiful women and marry powerful men in order to influence them. The Burman also believe in *Bilus*, the loner cannibals who are said to live in hidden places.

5 ● RELIGION

The Burman people are almost all Buddhists. To promote Buddhism, Burman kings invaded their neighboring countries and brought back slaves to build pagodas or temples. They also brought back religious teachers. Myanmar has over one million Buddhist temples. Despite being devoted Buddhists, the Burmans still believe in their traditional spirit beings.

6 ● MAJOR HOLIDAYS

The Burman have two major religious holidays. The Burman New Year, combined with the *Thakyan* (Water Festival) takes place April 13 to 16; April 17 is the New Year. During the Water Festival, loved ones splash each other with water from cups or buckets. Young Burmans take this opportunity to express their secret love to girls or boys by throwing water on them.

Another Burman holiday takes place on the full moon in November and is called the Light Festival, which is celebrated like Christmas in the Western world. The Burman decorate their houses with lights (mostly candles because electricity is not widely available). Wearing their best cloth-

Cory Langley

Myanmar has over 1 million Buddhist temples.

ing, young men and women walk the town streets which are filled with people.

The Burman celebrate Independence Day on January 4 with military parades, speeches, and gun salutes. Union Day, observed on February 12, celebrates the signing of the Panglong agreement, in which the Shan, Kachin, and Chin agreed to join the Burman to form the Union of Burma in 1947. Union Day is usually celebrated with sporting competitions among the ethnic nationalities. Each ethnic group has its own costumes, making the Union Day celebrations very colorful. *Arjani nih* or Martyr's Day (August 12) commemorates Aung San (1914?–47), the father of the Union of Burma, who was assassinated.

Myanmar has many more holidays, far outnumbering the usual holidays celebrated in the United States.

7 ● RITES OF PASSAGE

The birth of a child is not a particularly important event because the Burman usually have many children. As soon as a baby is born, the mother avoids eating meat and fish. She also does not use soap. From birth, boys and girls are treated differently. Names are usually given immediately after birth, but it is not out of the ordinary for the baby to be unnamed for many months. When a boy is born, a learned man is invited to wash his hair. The learned man places gold and silver coins in the cup that is used to wash the baby's hair so that he will grow up rich. Girls consider ear-piercing an important event to make themselves more beautiful.

One of the most important duties of the parents of a boy is to send him to the Buddhist temple to train as a novice monk. Although it costs money, a parent who sends his child to monkhood is believed to have secured a place in paradise after death. The boy can enter the temple anytime between the ages of nine and thirteen, depending on when he feels ready to go without food from noon until night. The celebration marking the beginning of Buddhist training starts with the boy's dressing up as a prince and being carried on a platform to the temple. He may not touch ground. On reaching the temple, the boy's head is shaved and the parents bring out a special cloth to catch his hair before it drops to the ground. He then officially becomes a novice monk. Prayers and Buddhist chanting celebrate the moment. The duration of a boy's Buddhist training is usually from three days to a week. Some novices stay on to become monks for the rest of their lives.

At death, it is believed the deceased will travel in the afterlife. Therefore, the corpse is buried with a quarter in its mouth to pay for boat and bus fares. The family brings dirt from the funeral ground back home so that the dead know the way home. Seven days after death, a monk is called to tell the deceased that he can go any place he or she wishes to go from that day on.

8 ● RELATIONSHIPS

Burman greet each other by asking "Have you eaten?" They do not have a "good morning" or "good evening" greeting. If the person is visiting and replies in the negative, the host is obligated to serve food. If the answer is in the positive, then the next question will be, "What did you have for your meal?" Meeting on the street, they tend to ask, "Where did you go?" or "From where did you come?" These greetings are more a formality than they are actual questions. In the morning they may say to each other, "Are you up already?"

Burman men and women seldom touch each other in public. They hold hands in public only if they are already engaged or married. However, men often hold hands with each other, and women may hold hands with each other. Burman do not traditionally shake hands. A young man may touch the head of a girl without holding it to express his closeness to her. Hugging is not practiced, although people may hug each other in private. Kissing is regarded as a Western custom, and kissing in public places is not allowed. As in the United States, nodding the head means "yes," and shaking the head means "no." If a Burman is hungry, he may touch his stomach.

Because telephones are rare, people visit each other in their homes whenever they have time. They visit each other in the very early morning or at night, usually unannounced. The Burman are very friendly and are always open to receiving visitors.

Parents play a role arranging their children's marriages. Because the Burman traditionally do not date, it is difficult for young boys and girls to meet. Nowadays, though, a boy and a girl might go to see a movie or have dinner together. Before a boy and a girl go together, they match their birth day of the week according to Burmese superstitions. For example, Burmans believe two people are a good match if they were born on a Wednesday and a Saturday. If a boy likes a girl, he may walk in front of the girl's house a thousand times until the girl and her family notice him. He may also give her a love letter. The girl might refuse the letter or reluctantly accept it. A girl's acceptance of admiration is a serious commitment and indicates that a wedding is not far off.

9 ● LIVING CONDITIONS

Sanitation is very poor because there are no sewer systems and therefore most houses do not have bathrooms. Sewage washes down into streams and rivers, which also serve as the drinking water supply. Therefore, many diseases are common. Malnutrition is also widespread among children.

People have very few material goods. They have only necessities, such as two or three cooking pots, a few plates, wooden spoons, and very few articles of clothing. Because it is a warm climate, they rarely have blankets.

Myanmar is agricultural and about 80 percent of the population lives in the country. Most farmers have two oxen or buffalo for wet rice cultivation, a hoe, and a cart. Burman farmers do not have horses. Rural houses, including the floors and walls, are made mostly of bamboo. The houses are actually small huts and have two partitions; one side is for cooking and storage, and the other half is used for sitting and sleeping. There is no furniture in the houses. In urban areas, brick and concrete buildings offer very small living spaces.

For most Burmans, the only means of transportation is the cart. Public transportation systems are hopelessly overcrowded and are often unsafe and dirty.

10 ● FAMILY LIFE

Usually a Burman family has about five children. The family also consists of grandparents and the extended family members.

Under Buddhism there is no limitation on the number of spouses one can have at the same time. A person can marry as many women or men as they want to, although this practice is rare today.

When a young Burman man marries a young woman, they will live with the wife's family. The brothers and sisters of the wife might also live in the house. The man goes to live with his in-laws because he is expected to go to work all day and be absent from the home. He has very little contact with his mother-in-law. On the other hand, if the couple went to live with the husband's family, the young wife would be in constant contact with her mother-in-law, and they may experience difficulties. In the family, the man is expected to earn a living and the wife's duty is to look after what her husband earns. Thus the man delivers all his paychecks to the wife and she administers the household budget. Grandparents also help the young couple take care of any babies that are born. If a farmer has only a son, the son must stay in the parents' household to take over the farm. Thus the bride must live in the groom's home. Burman are expected to look after their elderly, so it possible that parents may stay with their children their whole lives.

Dogs are the most common pets of the house. Cats are also a common pet. Many families keep cows and buffalo.

11 ● CLOTHING

Both Burman women and men wear *htami* or *longyi*, a long tube of cloth that is wrapped around and tucked in at the waist. No matter how poor a Burman may be, he or she will still own a Burmese jacket and a silk longyi or htami to wear on important occasions. The designs on the longyi and htami are different according to personal tastes. Men wear collarless shirts with their longyis and women wear short, fitted tops. For special occasions they wear silk shirts or blouses. They may own only one or two shirts or blouses. Burmans do not wear underclothing.

Cory Langley

Most Burman are farmers. Both Burman women and men wear htami *or* longyi, *a long tube of cloth that is wrapped around and tucked in at the waist.*

12 ● FOOD

The staple of the Burman diet is usually rice, eaten with a lot of curry (but not as much as in Indian food), garlic, and ginger. Fish sauce and dried shrimp are used for flavor. *Ngapi*, a stong-flavored pickled-fish paste, is eaten at almost every meal. Burman do not eat meat in large quantities. Meat is usually cut into small pieces and fried with oil. Onions, garlic, and spices such as curry and salt are mixed and slowly cooked. The two most common Burman dishes are *Mohinga* and *Ohnnukhaukswe*. Mohinga is slightly fermented rice noodles mixed in a thick, fish soup. Ohnnukhaukswe is a chicken stew cooked in coconut milk, also served with noodles. Underripe mangoes and limes are typically served with meals. Burman eat hot, sour, sweet, salty, bitter, and spicy snacks. The Burman commonly eat with their fingers. Soup is eaten with a spoon shared by two or more people.

Green tea is one of the most common drinks, next to water. Alcohol is frowned upon and very few people drink it regularly. Food is a favorite topic of conversation among the Burman. That is why they greet each other by saying, "Have you eaten?" or "What did you have for lunch?" The Burman normally eat two times a day, once in the morning, which could be considered brunch, and the other meal in the afternoon.

13 ● EDUCATION

The literacy rate (ability to read and write) among the Burman is usually quite high because Buddhist monasteries serve as the center of learning, where the monks function as teachers. Since the introduction of schools by the British, learning in the monasteries is becoming less popular since the British schools offer more subjects. Monastery education only consists of reading and writing. Because Burma was a colony, people looked at the colonial officers with envy, so they encouraged their children to get a good education and become civil servants. Students are, however, allowed to quit public schools at any time.

14 ● CULTURAL HERITAGE

There are different types of Burman music, classical and modern. Classical music is performed at *Pwes*, or concerts, in open-air theaters. A traditional Burmese instrument is the *saung gauk*, a harp-like stringed instrument. Modern Burman music shows strong Western influence, especially from country music.

Burmese dances are very graceful movements of the whole body. Hand gestures are combined with skilled footwork. It is said that Burman dances were copied from Thailand, and indeed, they have many similarities. Burmese dances are performed by learned professionals, and therefore do not offer the average Burman a chance to participate in the dancing.

15 ● EMPLOYMENT

Most Burman are farmers, who go to work early in the morning, long before dawn. When the sun becomes hot they go back to their huts to rest, eat, and possibly sleep. They return to the fields when it cools down and work until dark. People with education are likely to work for the government.

16 ● SPORTS

A typical Burman sport is the *chinlon*, a cane ball that is kicked by people standing in a circle, passing the ball from one to the other. This sport can be played by two or more. There are no losers or winners. This sport can be played on flat ground anywhere—on the streets or in the yards. Soccer is the favorite spectator sport of the Burman, attracting large crowds.

17 ● RECREATION

The most common entertainment for the Burman is the *Pwe*, a comedy drama with music and dance. Puppet shows are also popular. There are no plays in established theaters, as there are in the West. Pwes and puppet shows are street theaters. Movies have become the most popular entertainment.

Television was introduced to Myanmar recently. Videotaped Burman plays are becoming very popular. The most popular recreation is, perhaps, gossiping.

18 ● CRAFTS AND HOBBIES

The dry zone of Myanmar is full of pagodas and monasteries. Prayer pavilions of the pagodas are decorated with elaborate wood carvings. Almost all Burman homes have a Buddhist shrine with beautiful wood carvings of Buddha sitting on an elaborate throne. Lacquerware is a popular Burman craft. Bowls, trays, betelnut and cigarette containers are the most commonly made lacquerware.

News in the papers or on radio or television is controlled by the government. People gossip to such an extent that news about people, especially the ruling elite, reaches everyone.

19 ● SOCIAL PROBLEMS

Myanmar's social problems are the result of political and economic isolation, which have been brought on by the government during the last thirty years. Myanmar is one of the ten poorest countries of the world. Crime is growing, and public corruption and theft are prevalent. Myanmar is also the

EPD Photos

The saung gauk is a graceful harp-like instrument that is played by plucking the silk strings. Courtesy of the Center for the Study of World Musics, Kent State University.

largest opium producer in the world. Opium and heroin are available on every corner of Myanmar and affect a large section of the population, especially young people. Many people are unemployed and seek relief from drugs to forget their daily miseries.

The government demands that each household or family supply laborers to work in the construction of railroads, roads, government buildings, and the like, calling it voluntary work. These people are never paid and must bring their own food for the duration of their assignment, usually two weeks. If a household is unable to supply a laborer, the household is fined a large sum of money, which is impossible for most families to pay. The military also forces villages to supply porters to carry army supplies to their operations. According to the government, these are voluntary works that were common under the colonial administration.

The United Nations has declared Myanmar as among the worst human rights abuses in the world. People are often arrested without any reason and jailed without trial for many years. There is fear in the mind of every citizen. There are no civil or human rights in Myanmar—only the government has rights. Because the Burman are the majority in a multi-ethnic society, they control every branch of the administration and oppress the smaller minority groups.

20 ● BIBLIOGRAPHY

American University. *Burma: A Country Study.* Washington, D.C.: Government Printing Office, 1983.

Herbert, Patricia M. *Burma.* Santa Barbara, Calif.: Clio Press, 1991.

Orwell, George. *Burmese Days.* New York: Harcourt, Brace, 1935.

Silverstein, Josef. *The Political Legacy of Aung San.* Ithaca, N.Y.: Cornell University, 1993.

Steinberg, David J. *The Future of Burma: Crisis and Choice in Myanmar.* New York: Asia Society, 1990.

Wright, D. *Burma.* Chicago: Children's Press, 1991.

WEBSITES

Interknowledge Corp. Myanmar. [Online] Available http://www.interknowledge.com/myanmar/, 1998.

World Travel Guide. Myanmar. [Online] Available http://www.wtgonline.com/country/mm/gen.html, 1998.

Karens

PRONUNCIATION: kuh-RENS
ALTERNATE NAME: Padaung
LOCATION: Southern and eastern Myanmar (Burma); Thailand
POPULATION: 5 million (estimate)
LANGUAGE: Pwo and Sgaw dialects of Karen; Burmese
RELIGION: Buddhism; animism; Christianity (Baptist, Catholicism)

1 ● INTRODUCTION

The Karens are a large ethnic group spread throughout Southeast Asia. They trace their origins to the Gobi Desert, Mongolia, or Tibet. Karens settled in southern and eastern Myanmar as far back as the seventh century. (Myanmar was known as Burma until 1990, when the military government changed the country name.) In the 1700s, Karens also began living in neighboring Siam (now called Thailand).

There are numerous Karen subgroups. These varied people lived mainly in tribal societies, governed by chiefs or princes. They sometimes came into conflict with the Burmese (Burman) dynastic rulers, or with other ethnic groups inclined to wage war.

The advent of British colonization in the mid-to-late nineteenth century brought a new sense of security to the Karens. Contact with American and European Christian missionaries, who brought literacy and education, was welcomed. The British administrators recruited many Karens into their police and armed forces. When World War II (1939–45) came to Burma, those

Karens became loyal guerrilla fighters for the Allies against Japanese occupiers.

As Britain granted Burma independence after the war, Karen politicians hoped for their own nation. The Karen people, who had never recognized Burmese authority, had enjoyed "protectorate" status with the British Empire, and also expected their nationhood to be recognized. Instead Karens, along with other ethnic populations, were absorbed into the new Union of Burma. Problems began almost immediately, when troops of the predominantly Burmese (Burman) government killed Karen villagers. A Karen insurgency sprang up and rapidly gained momentum until it threatened to seize control of the Burmese capital, Rangoon. The Karen rebels were driven back by the government troops, and the military came to dominate the country, eventually taking over power in 1962. The military government pledged to quell rebellion and unify the country by force.

Government forces sent to subdue the rebellion actually drove more Karens into joining the rebels. A consistent pattern of deliberate human rights violations by the government against ethnic minority civilians has continued to this day, driving tens of thousands of Karens to Thailand as refugees and making the Karen conflict the world's longest running rebellion.

2 ● LOCATION

Estimates of the Karen population of Myanmar vary greatly, as there has been no census in decades. Perhaps 5 million Karen tribal members live in Myanmar. Another 300,000 Karen-ethnic peoples have roots in

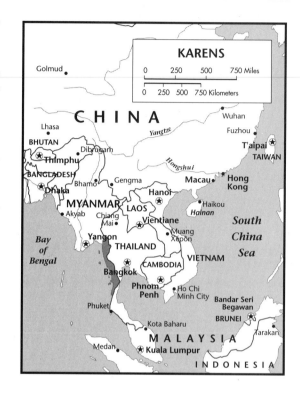

Thailand, and thousands of others live there as refugees.

Karen people live in several parts of southern and eastern Myanmar. The largest Karen population is in the Irrawaddy Delta area, a vast agricultural lowland whose main city is Bassein. Another important region for the Karens is the eastern border with Thailand.

3 ● LANGUAGE

The language of the Karens is generally considered to be of the Tibeto-Burman family, and the main dialects of Karen are Pwo and Sgaw. Many Karen people in isolated hill areas remain illiterate, and those in the Delta region often can speak only Burmese. Their language does, however remain a feature of Karen cultural pride. Baptist missionaries developed scripts based on Burmese for Pwo Karen (with twenty-five letters) and for other Karen languages. An old Pwo script known as "chicken scratch," because of the shapes of its letters, was devised by Karen Buddhists as well.

In Sgaw Karen, an informal greeting (How's it going?) is *Madee leh?* and a farewell is *Leh mu mu* (Go pleasantly). "Thank you" in Sgaw Karen is *Dah bluet.*

4 ● FOLKLORE

Karen folklore impressed early Christian missionaries with its similarity to the book of Genesis in the Bible. The tribal mythology also told of the Karen language being kept in a book, which was lost in the mass migration south from "the river of sand." There is a sense in their old stories of being exploited by other ethnic groups, and of wishing to regain some past glories through miracles or supernaturally gifted leaders. Sometimes Karens have become cult followers of messianic leaders who assure them that special clothing or tattoos will make them impervious to harm. In traditional animist, spirit-worshipping belief systems, the Karens must make offerings to natural forces such as "the lord of land and water." Even Christian Karens still have their skin adorned with tattoos as a form of magical protection. Buddhist Karens often wear amulets (small metal, stone, or clay Buddha images) around their necks.

A Karen subgroup, the Kayan, are known for the neck rings made of brass worn by girls and women. Over time, more and more coils are added to the rings, pushing the collarbone down, giving the appearance of an elongated neck (hence their Burmese name, Padaung, meaning "long-neck"). The Kayan subgroup of Karen is traditionally a matriarchy. The rings around necks, arms, and knees are sometimes explained as a traditional protection against tiger bites. Many Kayans have become refugees in recent years, and women with neck rings have been exploited as "freak show" tourist attractions in Thailand and Myanmar.

5 ● RELIGION

Most Karens are Buddhists or animists (believers in spirits in nature). There are also significant populations of Christians, mainly Baptists and Catholics.

There is considerable interplay between animist rituals and Buddhist practices among the Karens. Animists believe in helpful female guardian spirits called *ther myng khae,* the "lord of land and water," and local spirits, as well as beneficial and malicious ghosts. The Christians emphasize Bible study and prayer services with hymn singing. Villages tend to be predominantly one of the three religions, even though there is a variety of houses of worship in the towns. Christian Karens have tried to convert the Buddhists and animists, and in recent years Myanmar's military government has encouraged conflict between Buddhist Karens and the Christian Karens.

6 ● MAJOR HOLIDAYS

The Karen New Year in January is celebrated as a national holiday in Myanmar and is often the occasion for traditional dances and music. Christian Karens celebrate Christmas with parties and caroling trips from village to village. Buddhist

Karens hold festivals to mark their religious New Year (mid-spring) and the end of Lent (post-monsoon). Animists hold crop-protection festivals during the monsoon season and after the harvest.

7 ● RITES OF PASSAGE

Traditional Karen society has various taboos for pregnant women, such as not drinking liquor and not going to funerals. Births usually take place at home, assisted by family members or a village "midwife" (often a man). After the birth, the mother eats a special diet of rice and chicken, and strings are tied around the baby's wrists to protect it from evil spirits. Deaths in childhood are very common among the Karens. In rural areas there is little understanding of hygiene and nutrition, but Karen medical practitioners are working to spread information that can save lives.

Among Buddhist Karens, young boys often become novice monks for a short period of time. Teenaged Karen boys sometimes get tattooed with magical symbols to show their bravery and protect them from harm. Kayan girls may begin to wear coils of brass around their necks as young as six years old, and keep adding to the coils during their teenage years until the neck piece stretches as long as 10 inches (25 centimeters).

Karens have a variety of funeral customs, according to their religions. The animist Karens believe in an afterlife and dress the corpse to be accepted in the land of *Khu See-du,* the lord of the dead. The body may be cremated or buried. Buddhist Karens hold cremation ceremonies with prayers to ease the deceased person into the next incar-

nation. Christian Karens hold a funeral prayer service and bury the body. Usually a wooden cross marks the grave.

8 ● RELATIONSHIPS

For a polite greeting, a Karen holds his or her right elbow in their left hand, and shakes hands with the right hand. They use the same gesture to give or offer objects to other people. Introductions will include the titles Karens use with their names, usually *Saw* for men and *Naw* for women.

Karens are very hospitable and will expect any guests to eat with them and, if possible, stay overnight or longer. In traditional Karen bamboo houses, sleeping quarters for guests are on the veranda.

Boys and girls usually meet in school, at Buddhist festivals, or in Christian youth groups. In traditional animist villages, funerals have been the scene of boy-girl socializing. When a young couple gets involved, love letters and secret messages are often exchanged. Sometimes a game is played between groups of boys and girls, with the boys asking poetic questions and the girls replying with rhyming answers. The questions and answers are about romance, but are subtle and symbolic.

9 ● LIVING CONDITIONS

Warfare and forced relocation campaigns by the Burmese government have displaced much of Myanmar's Karen population. Many villagers have had to leave their family homes and move to resettlement camps near government army bases (where they are forced into labor). Other villagers have fled to forest areas or across the border to Thailand in order to escape Burmese oppression. When the Karens come into contact with other environments and societies, they often become infected with diseases. Many Karens, especially children, die from such infectious illnesses. Little health care is available, although in Karen rebel strongholds some clinics have been set up by teams of traveling medics. A few foreign aid agencies had been operating in Thailand's Karen refugee camps, but then the entire camps were burned in cross-border raids.

Malnutrition is widespread among the Karens, many of whom subsist on rice with chili pepper, and perhaps some fish sauce and greens gathered from the forests. Anemia and vitamin deficiency are common. In addition to forced relocation, the widespread capture of farmers by the government military for forced labor has made it hard for the Karens to grow their own crops. Rampant deforestation as the Burmese government sells off forests to Thai logging firms has decreased the Karens' sources of wild game and edible plants, as well as causing climate changes and landslides.

For many generations, the Karen people have lived in harmony with the forest. Only if teak trees reached a certain size could they be harvested. They were replanted and the logs were transported by elephants and river rafts. Forest-dwelling Karens build their houses of bamboo with some wood, perched on stilts and with thatched roofs. The stilts are especially high if the house belongs to an elephant-owning family, since the veranda can be used for loading and unloading the animal. In bamboo houses, the family will sit and sleep on woven mats on the floor. In larger houses, which are made of teak or other wood, the family members sit on benches at tables and sleep on raised wooden beds with mosquito netting.

Baths are taken, wearing sarongs, in a river or by pouring water from a village pump or an urn of rainwater. Sections of bamboo or plastic buckets are used to carry water from nearby streams for cooking and washing. Toilets are usually small pit latrines with a bamboo shelter.

The ox-cart is the usual means of transport for goods and people, along with elephants and motorized river long-boats. The Karens are well known for their work with elephants, which they capture, train, and use for hauling and transport. Some Karen tribes often raise ponies or mules for transportation as well.

10 ● FAMILY LIFE

In Karen societies, other than the Kayan subgroup, women have traditionally been considered inferior or subservient to men. They did a great deal of difficult farm work, but had little status or decision-making power. This has been changing as more Karen women have become educated and have taken noteworthy roles in fields such as teaching and health. Dr. Cynthia Maung, a Karen physician, is admired for her brave work in bringing medical care to remote, war-torn regions. Many older women have become village leaders when men have been taken away for forced labor. Underground political and social women's groups have begun, emphasizing self-help programs and economic empowerment.

Traditionally, either a boy or girl can propose marriage, and the whole village is allowed a say whether their marriage would be appropriate and not offensive to any spirits. Weddings are festive occasions when both the bride's and groom's villages come together. The bride changes from her unmarried woman's long dress to a married woman's two-part outfit. Marriage is considered to be for life, and among Karens of all faiths, adultery is considered taboo—an unnatural act that can bring catastrophe on the whole village. Karens have an average of four or five children, but infant and child mortality rates are very high.

Karen families keep dogs for hunting and as pets. Sometimes families keep birds or baby forest animals such as squirrels or gibbons. Karen elephant tamers "adopt" one elephant, train it, and take care of it for life.

11 ● CLOTHING

While many Karens now wear mass-produced shirts, T-shirts, trousers, and sarongs of factory-woven batik cloth, traditional dress is still popular, especially in mountain areas and for special occasions. Traditionally, Karens wear tunics and sarongs of homespun cotton, dyed red, blue, and black. Men and married women wear a loose tunic over a wrapped sarong. The women's tunics are often elaborately embroidered with colored thread and seed-beads. The men's tunics are plain, having only fringed hems. Unmarried girls wear simple, long white dresses called *hsay mo htoo* in Sgaw Karen. Men and women often wear turbans, and Pwo men sometimes have very long hair—worn loose or in sideswept ponytails. Women wear masses of bead necklaces and a great many silver bracelets on their wrists and upper arms.

Among subgoups, Kayans are often known as Karennis ("red Karens") because of their predominantly red homespun clothing. The women wear short sarongs wrapped over one shoulder with a belt or sash and cords of thin black rattan wrapped around their legs.

12 ● FOOD

Karens are known for eating a huge variety of foods, including jungle products such as snake, bat, monkey, grubs, bee larvae, ants, palm sugar, wild honey, forest herbs, frog, and lizard. Many types of birds and fish are consumed, and Karens raise chickens, ducks, pigs, cattle, corn, and pumpkins for food. A favorite dish for Karens in the forest is *takataw,* made by adding a handful of rice and some shreds of dried meat (often venison or wild boar) to boiling water, letting it cook until the meat and rice are soft like porridge, and then adding some chopped vegetables.

Due to deforestation, crop confiscation, and rural dislocation, nowadays many Karens have trouble obtaining enough food for their families. Karen refugees and poor villagers typically live on rice, chili peppers, some fish paste, and whatever greens they can gather. The Karens normally eat several helpings of rice at meals and for snacks. They eat mostly white rice now, which is less nutritious than red or brown rice. For flavoring, many people use monosodium glutamate powder, which comes from Thailand.

Kelly Cross

A young Karen woman in Thailand. Kayan girls may begin to wear coils of brass around their necks as young as six years old, and keep adding to the coils during their teenage years.

Karens often chew betel nut, which comes from a species of palm and is combined with leaves and lime paste; it is a mild stimulant and stains the mouth bright red.

13 ● EDUCATION

During the British colonial period (1885–1947), missionaries helped the Karens start Christian-staffed village schools, which were supported by Buddhist and animist parents as well. The Burmese military government took over those schools in the 1960s, changing them to a national rather than a Karen curriculum. In rebel-held areas, a series of schools up to the secondary level was established, but most of these schools are gone now, as the Karen rebels have lost more and more territory to the government. Even in refugee camps, the Karens try to have formal education for their children, but makeshift schools, like the refugee health clinics, have mostly been destroyed in cross-border raids. Textbooks, often decades old, and school materials are in very short supply, and what schools there are tend to be understaffed. Educators also are faced with schoolchildren who are traumatized by their experience of human rights abuse, who are malnourished, and who are beset by malaria and other diseases.

14 ● CULTURAL HERITAGE

Karen music includes traditional songs (many of which are love songs) and Western-influenced Christian hymns. In the rebel areas there are also political songs and military marching music played by drum and flute corps. Music that uses the repetitive beat of metal gongs accompanies such dances as the rice-planting dance and the bamboo dance, as well as wedding processions. In the bamboo dance, sets of eight to twelve long bamboo poles are placed in a grid. Participants kneel on the ground and bang the poles together in time to the music, while dancers step in and out of the openings in the grid.

The Karens have several musical instruments of importance. The Karen drum is a symbol of the culture. It is round and made of cast bronze, often decorated with figures of frogs and elephants. The Karens play a harp called the *t'na*, which has five or six strings and is tuned with pegs along the neck of the instrument. Another stringed instrument is the large, wooden guitar-like *haw tu*. The *pa ku* is a bamboo xylophone played with hammers, and there are bamboo panpipes and mouth-harps of various sizes. Karens also use imported instruments such as guitars and electric keyboards, especially for Christian church music.

The Karen literary tradition is mostly in oral form. Folktales abound, often about a poor orphan boy who falls in love with a girl of a wealthy family. Books by Karens written since World War II (1939–45) include *Memoirs of the Four-Foot Colonel* by Smith Dun, a high ranking officer in the British Army, and *The Golden Book*, a Christian interpretation of ancient Karen prophetic poems.

15 ● EMPLOYMENT

The Karens have long been rice farmers in wet, irrigated fields in the Delta or in hill fields in the mountains. In the past, to grow rice in the highlands, villagers would selectively burn small plots of forest. This system, called "swidden cultivation," worked well when Karen populations were small and stable. At that time, the Myanmar forests were hardly touched by logging. Now, large timber companies are drastically reducing the size of the forest, and adding "swidden cultivation" to indiscriminate logging contributes to erosion and loss of wildlife habitat. Karen rebels have established wildlife sanctuaries where no hunting or farming is allowed, but even these species-rich preserves are now under threat from the Burmese government's petroleum transport projects and government deals with foreign timber firms.

Karens also make their living by fishing in coastal areas, working in tin or wolfram mines, and gathering forest products like rattan and honey. There are some educated professionals among the Karens, but many of them live overseas as exiles or serve in the Karen National Union.

16 ● SPORTS

Soccer, volleyball, and a type of kickball called *chinlone* are popular with Karen young people. Even in mountainous areas, Karen villages often have one flat open space where such sports can be played. Karens sometimes play a game they call *mahket* in which the large seeds are rolled to knock over other seeds.

17 ● RECREATION

In their free time, Karens enjoy musical activities, movies and video shows, and taking walks around their town or village in the evening when the air cools. People rise at or before dawn and often take an afternoon nap.

18 ● CRAFTS AND HOBBIES

Karen women are known for their fine cotton weaving of clothing, blankets, and shoulderbags. The weaving is usually done on a small loom set up with a strap that wraps around the waist at one end, but in some areas there are large wooden frame looms as well. The thread is dyed with natural or artificial colors, sometimes with a pattern produced by tie-dying. Some woven items are now produced for overseas sale as a means for refugee women to support their families. The Karens also produce etched silver jewelry, baskets, and embroidery.

19 ● SOCIAL PROBLEMS

The Karens feel particularly persecuted after several decades of widespread abuse by military forces of the Burmese government. The consistent pattern of human rights violations includes forced labor as army equipment porters, human mine-sweepers, human shields, and road and railway builders; destruction of entire villages; torture of civilians suspected of rebel sympathies; and massacres and executions without trial. Government military abuse of Karen women, particularly rape of village girls by troops, is especially common. These events have transformed the usually stable Karens into terrified nomads and have turned many into stubborn rebel fighters. Some Karens today are third-generation guerrilla soldiers who have grown up knowing nothing but war.

20 ● BIBLIOGRAPHY

Dun, Smith. *Memoirs of the Four-Foot Colonel.* Ithaca, N.Y.: Cornell University, 1972.

Falla, Jonathan. *Truelove and Bartholomew: Rebels on the Burmese Border.* Cambridge: Cambridge University Press, 1991.

Herbert, Patricia M. *Burma.* Santa Barbara, Calif.: Clio Press, 1991.

Mirante, Edith T. *Burmese Looking Glass: A Human Rights Adventure.* New York: Grove Press, 1993.

Silverstein, Josef. *The Political Legacy of Aung San.* Ithaca, N.Y.: Cornell University, 1993.

Smith, Martin. *Ethnic Groups in Burma.* London: Anti-Slavery International, 1994.

Wright, D. *Burma.* Chicago: Children's Press, 1991.

WEBSITES

Interknowledge Corp. Myanmar. [Online] Available http://www.interknowledge.com/myanmar/, 1998.

World Travel Guide. Myanmar. [Online] Available http://www.wtgonline.com/country/mm/gen.html, 1998.

Shans

PRONUNCIATION: SHAHNS
LOCATION: Myanmar (Shan Plateau); India; China; Laos; Thailand; northern Vietnam
POPULATION: 4 million (estimate)
LANGUAGE: Shan; Chinese; Burmese
RELIGION: Buddhism, with elements of animism

1 ● INTRODUCTION

A people known as the Tai have long inhabited a vast area of Asia, including Thailand, Laos, and northeastern Myanmar. The name for the Tai ethnic group of Myanmar is "Shan." The Shans migrated into Myanmar from China, to the north, many centuries ago, and settled in the valleys. They established kingdoms and expanded their territory, often in conflict with other ethnic groups such as the Burmese (Burman). From the fifteenth century on, the Shan Plateau was their main homeland. The people were governed by hereditary princes called Sao-Phas who ruled in as many as forty different principalities.

When the British Empire annexed Burma in 1885, the Shan princes negotiated protectorate agreements that allowed them to continue to rule their domains, while acknowledging British supremacy. With time, the Sao-Phas became more educated and more willing to work together, and in the 1920s they formed the Federated Shan States. After World War II (1939–45), the

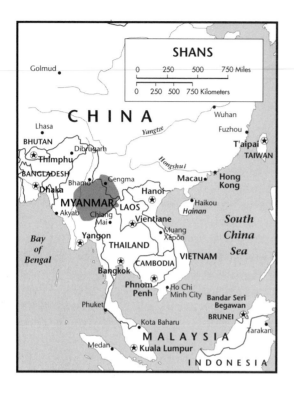

SHANS

0   250   500   750 Miles

0   250   500   750 Kilometers

Armed rebel groups promoting Shan nationalism sprung up throughout the Shan state. The Shan rebellion was characterized by many factional splits and by "warlords" who took advantage of the state's lucrative opium trade to form their own narcotic-trafficking armies. In the 1990s, most of those groups have surrendered to Burma's central government or have reached ceasefire agreements, allowing them to continue in the drug trade.

2 ● LOCATION

Although there are no sure census figures in Myanmar, the Shan population there has been estimated at around 4 million. There are Shan ethnic people in India's Assam region, China's Yunnan province (the Dai people), Laos, Thailand, and northern Vietnam as well. Myanmar's Shan state has a border with Yunnan in the north, Laos to the east, and Thailand to the south. The region is often called the Golden Triangle and is associated with trade in opium, the raw material for heroin. There are thousands of Shan refugees who have fled forced labor and other human rights abuses, seeking shelter in neighboring Thailand. In addition to the Shans, numerous other ethnic groups live in the Shan state, mainly in the hills: Palaungs, Pa-Os, Was, Lahus, Akhas, and other tribal people, as well as the Kokang Chinese.

The Salween River flows from China down through the Shan state, and the Mekong River forms the border with Laos. Major cities include Taunggyi, Keng Tung, and Lashio. In the southeast of the state is Inle Lake, where the Intha people live in stilt houses above the water and grow vege-

British granted independence to Burma, and Shan leaders participated in the Panglong Agreement with Burma's independence hero, General Aung San (1914–47), ensuring a great deal of autonomy for the Shan aristocrats. The independent constitution of Burma created a Shan State and granted it the right to secede after ten years.

Many Shans, including pro-democracy Sao-Phas, became disillusioned with being part of the Union of Burma. They felt that their culture was being suppressed by the majority Burmese. Conflicts with central government troops resulted. A military government took over Burma in 1962, and Burma's president—a Shan—Sao Shwe Thaike, was put in prison, where he died.

tables on floating gardens. The Shan state has been green and fertile, but deforestation in the last ten years, as Myanmar's military government sells off teak wood to neighboring countries, has degraded the terrain.

3 ● LANGUAGE

The Shans speak the Shan language, classified as Sino-Tai. It is distantly related to Cantonese and other Chinese dialects, and closely related to Lao and Thai. There are considerable regional differences in the Shan spoken in various areas. Throughout northeast Myanmar, Shan is used as a common language for trade among various ethnic groups. Many Shans speak some of the Yunnanese dialect of Chinese and some Burmese, as well as Shan. The traditional Shan alphabet has eighteen consonants and twelve vowels; more letters have been added in a modernized version. The letters have a circular shape, like those of the Burmese language.

To say "Thank you very much," Shans say *Yin lii nam nam*. The usual greeting in a Shan village is *Kin khao yao ha*? meaning, "Have you eaten?" The reply is probably yes, so the follow-up question asks what the person had for lunch or dinner. A popular expression is *Am pen tsang*—meaning "No problem," because the Shans value a relaxed lifestyle. Sometimes one will hear the phrase even during a crisis, as Shans try to stay calm to deal with any situation.

4 ● FOLKLORE

Many Shans believe in ghosts and demons who haunt forests, graveyards, and other lonely places. Shamans or Buddhist monks can be called on to exorcise such ill-intentioned spirits. The forest is believed to be inhabited by animals that are considered ferocious human ghosts, such as *were-tigers*.

5 ● RELIGION

Shans, like most Tai peoples, are Buddhists. They practice a religion based on compassion for all beings and the search for enlightenment within a reincarnation cycle of birth and death. Buddhist monks, revered for their learning and self-discipline, are important to Shan communities. The power that stems from keeping precepts (abstaining from violent acts, intoxication, and other negative forms of conduct) can prevent evil and bring good fortune. Shan Buddhism also incorporates many animist elements, such as belief in a fertility goddess known as "the Rice Mother," and local spirits known as "the Lord of the Village."

6 ● MAJOR HOLIDAYS

The Shans observe Buddhist holidays and more animist-related ones such as an annual "repairing the village" ceremony called *mae waan*, meant to drive away dangerous beings. On holy days, everyone is expected to keep the five main Buddhist precepts: no killing, no stealing, no improper sexual conduct, no lying, and no use of intoxicants.

Because generosity, especially to the Buddhist monasteries, is an important virtue for Shans, gifts for the monks are a feature of many special occasions. Often a "money tree" will be paraded through the village, its branches decorated with banknotes and small household items for the monks to use. Dancers and musicians accompany the tree on its way to the monastery.

Shans sometimes hold a "Rocket Festival" in hopes of bringing on the rainy season to provide water for the rice and other crops. Large homemade fireworks are launched into the sky. Buddhist Lent occurs during the monsoon season, for three months. The monks stay at their monasteries, concentrating on their prayers and studies. Marriages and other festivities do not take place during Lent.

7 ● RITES OF PASSAGE

It was the old Shan custom for a mother to spend a month indoors, near a fire, after giving birth. When that month was over, the baby would be given a special bath in water that had coins and pieces of gold dropped into it.

Young boys usually become novice monks for one to three months. A colorful ceremony called *Poy Sang Long* is held as Buddhist Lent begins. The boys are costumed as little Shan princes. They are carried through the village on relatives' shoulders, or on ponies (sometimes even on elephants). Golden umbrellas shade them from the sun. At the monastery, the boys' heads are shaved, and they put on plain orange robes and begin learning the Buddhist scriptures.

In their mid-teens, many Shan boys get their first tattoos, usually from a *sayah* who uses a brass-tipped stick to inject magical ingredients in symbolic patterns. The chest, back, arms, legs, and tongue are common places for tattoos. The ink and designs are believed to give the wearer various powers against illness, evil-doers or weapons, or for cleverness. The tattooed person should keep Buddhist precepts of self-restraint to ensure the power of the tattoos. Men may continue to be tattooed, sometimes making their entire arms and legs blue-black from the ink. Shan women also get tattooed, but usually to a lesser extent than do men. Other ethnic groups often seek out the Shan *sayahs* as tattooists.

Death is considered the path to another existence, perhaps a better one. The dead are usually buried in a wooden coffin. Cremation ceremonies are held for monks and those who can afford to pay for the elaborate ritual. Musicians accompany the body to cremation site or burial ground.

8 ● RELATIONSHIPS

When visiting a Shan home, one removes the shoes before entering. Traditionally this even applies to small shops. It is also customary to remove one's shoes at Shan Buddhist temples and monasteries, and it is the usual practice to make an offering of money, flowers, or food for the resident monks. Shans treat the monks with respect, especially older monks or those known for their strict self-discipline.

Visitors to homes, or even offices or shops, are served tea. Shans are usually introduced using an honorific with their name, most often *Sai* for men and *Nang* for women, and it is polite to address them that way.

9 ● LIVING CONDITIONS

Currently there are many severe health problems among the Shans. There are few doctors or medical facilities, especially in rural areas. Malaria is prevalent, and children often die from it. Villagers suffer from tuberculosis and other respiratory diseases, and from goiter (caused by iodine deficiency). Medicine is too expensive for most people, and traditional "spirit doctors" cannot keep up with the present health crisis. HIV/AIDS has spread through the Shan state because of widespread injection of heroin refined from the locally grown opium, and because of the trade in young girls and boys to neighboring Thailand and China for prostitution. Generally ignorant about the disease, these young people who are forced into the "sex industry" have a very high rate of HIV infection.

Military rule in Myanmar has caused a decline in living standards for the Shans. Many have fled their original towns and villages because of forced labor, or have had their homes burned down by government troops seeking to secure the area. To get away from the conflict, they often settle in the hill country where it is hard to grow any crop other than opium.

In peaceful times, the marketplace is a center of Shan life. The markets are held quite early in the morning, and men, women, and children go there to buy food for the day, drink tea, and exchange information. Most of the vendors are women. Another center of Shan life is the Buddhist monastery, where many occasions are celebrated. Often the monastery is located on a hillside overlooking a village or town. Larger settlements have several monasteries, with tall whitewashed pagodas.

Shan houses are traditionally raised up on stilts, with the area underneath used for storage or a cool, shady place to sit. The roofs are thatched with leaf material. Inside, the Shans sit on the floor, eat at low tables, and at night sleep on mats. Cleanliness is

very important to Shans, so yards and village streets are swept often. In villages, Shans bathe in nearby streams or using buckets of rainwater.

The Shans like to travel, visiting friends and relatives or trading goods from town to town, but few have their own cars or motorbikes. Ox-carts are used for carrying farm products, and mules or ponies carry loads and riders up the hills. There are some airline flights and railway connections into the Shan state. A more common way to cover long distances is to share a ride on a truck, which may be carrying goods from China or Thailand.

10 ● FAMILY LIFE

The Shans have monogamous marriages, although in the old times of the aristocracy the *Sao-Phas* (princes) often had more than one wife. A bride price was traditionally paid to the bride's parents. Horoscopes are still important for determining if a couple is really meant for each other, and if so, when the wedding should take place. Shan weddings are not Buddhist ceremonies, although monks may attend. Usually, village elders or other respected persons will tie blessing string around the couple's wrists. A feast is then held for their families, neighbors, and friends. Married couples live on their own with their children, but may be joined by aging relatives or others needing help. Divorce is permissible in Shan society, especially in cases of domestic violence.

Shan families in Thailand have an average of two children, with parents hoping for one boy and one girl. In Myanmar, where birth control is rare, six children or more is

Recipe

Khai Soi ("fast-food" version)

Ingredients

Chicken flavored ramen noodles
3 Tablespoons canned unsweetened coco-
    nut milk
½ teaspoon turmeric
½ teaspoon paprika
Dash of tabasco sauce
½ cup finely chopped cooked chicken
Sliced green onion and chopped fresh
    cilantro as garnish
"Chow mein" noodles
Lime

Directions

1. Prepare chicken-flavored ramen noodles according to the directions on the
   package.
2. Mix in the canned unsweetened coconut milk, turmeric, paprika, tabasco
   sauce, and chicken.
3. Top with green onion, cilantro, and
   "chow mein" noodles. Serve with a
   wedge of lime. Just before eating,
   squeeze the lime wedge over the noodles.

a typical Shan family size. Shan families keep dogs, cats, and birds as pets. The dogs are used to guard houses and for hunting. Shan Buddhist monasteries often have many cats living there.

11 ● CLOTHING

Shan men wear baggy trousers, usually made of indigo-dyed homespun fabric. Called *koon*, the trousers have a huge waistband which is gathered and knotted in front. Women wear sarongs, called *phasin*, which are cotton or fancy embroidered silk sewn in a tube and wrapped tightly at the waist. There are traditional jackets and blouses to go with these, but younger people wear them with T-shirts and denim jackets for a comfortable mix of old and new.

Large conical bamboo or straw hats called *kup* provide shade for Shan men and women working in the fields or walking in hot sunlight. Shan men and women often wear large turbans wrapped from long lengths of cotton or bright terrycloth towels.

12 ● FOOD

Shans are fond of sticky rice, called *khao niw*. Eating with the right hand, they make a little ball of sticky rice and use it to soak up accompanying curry. *Khao niw* is also featured in the special treats the Shans make for seasonal festivals. In the cold season they cook *khao lam*, sweetened sticky rice, in bamboo tubes. A hot season specialty is *khao yak ku*, brown sugar-sweetened sticky rice with peanuts and grated coconut on top. As well as their fondness for sweets, Shans are known for their taste for sour foods, such as a spicy pickled cabbage similar to Korean *kim chee*.

Numerous varieties of fruit are grown in the Shan state, including temperate climate fruits like apples and strawberries not found elsewhere in Myanmar. Mango (*mak muang*) is a favorite fruit, both ripe and unripe, and is combined with meat such as pork for a Shan curry. Disks of fermented soybeans, called *thoo nao khep,* flavor many dishes. Corn and potatoes, originally from North America, are grown by Shan farmers.

Khao soi, Shan noodles with chicken-coconut curry, has become popular throughout Myanmar and Thailand.

13 ● EDUCATION

Being able to read and write in their native language has been a political cause for many Shans, who feel that the Burmese-dominated central government has deliberately suppressed Shan culture as a way to control Shan rebellion. Very little material is being published in Shan, as even Shan children's books and health pamphlets are considered suspect by the government. In many villages there are *sayahs*, men or women who can read old Shan texts on subjects such as astrology and herbal medicine, and use them to make predictions, cast spells, or treat illness. The sayah's power comes from book-learning as well as from the self-discipline needed to keep many Buddhist precepts.

Educational standards in the Shan state are low, with schools and teachers in short supply at every level. In many villages, the monastery is a source of education, at least for young boys. Children who do attend schools run by the Burmese government are likely to learn in Burmese rather than the Shan language.

14 ● CULTURAL HERITAGE

Shan literature has largely consisted of texts relating to Buddhist scripture, books of astrological and herbal lore, and histories of the aristocracy. "The Padaeng Chronicle" and "The Jengtung State Chronicle" are examples of such histories from the Keng Tung area and have been translated into English.

Typical Shan dances include one in which two young men in a costume portray a lion or yak-like creature, and another in which children dance dressed as mythical birds. Solo dance is a part of ceremonies involving ghosts and other special occasions. A popular social dance is the *ram wong*. Couples move around in a large circle, using simple steps and graceful hand motions. Dance music can be played by musicians walking or dancing in a procession, and it features long drums, gongs, cymbals, and bamboo flutes. There is also the ensemble music of the old Sao Pha courts, which was influenced by Burmese classical music and is played by seated musicians. A framed series of gongs, which can be hit all at once with a bamboo mallet, is a particularly Shan instrument for such ensemble music.

15 ● EMPLOYMENT

The Shans have traditionally been an agricultural society, producing bountiful crops of rice and vegetables including soybeans, garlic, and corn. Villagers exchange labor to plant and harvest each others' rice fields. Government quotas, confiscation, and forced relocation of farmers have brought on a severe decline in agricultural productivity, however. At the same time there has been an increase in cultivation of opium poppies for the heroin refineries.

In addition to farming, the Shans have been noteworthy traders. Men and women travel from village to village, peddling cloth, medicines, forest products, tools, and a great variety of other goods. Much of the trading stock is brought into Myanmar illegally from neighboring countries. Commodities including gemstones (rubies, sapphires, and jade), gold, cattle, and heroin, are smuggled out of the Shan state.

16 ● SPORTS

Soccer and volleyball are popular sports in the Shan state, as is *takraw*, in which a lightweight woven rattan ball is kept in play with the feet. Many Shans learn kung fu or a traditional Shan martial art in which swords are held with both hands. A more sedate game is *maknim*, in which the large seeds of the mucuna vine are set up in rows. Players take turns trying to knock them down by shooting another seed like a marble, kicking it off the top of the foot or rolling it off their clothing.

17 ● RECREATION

The Shans, like other people of Myanmar, enjoy marathon theater and dance performances that often last long into the night. Sometimes a traveling movie show comes to a Shan village, projecting a film (usually from Thailand) on an outdoor screen for everyone to watch. In recent years, the larger villages and towns have set up mini-movie theaters, small shops with a VCR and television showing foreign movies or locally produced videos. Radio is very popular in the Shan state, especially short-wave broadcasts such as the BBC or Voice of America programs, which are aired in Shan or Burmese.

18 ● CRAFTS AND HOBBIES

In some areas, Shan women weave colorful silk fabrics. Shans make embroidered cotton shoulderbags that are used all over Myanmar. Silverware, including decorated knives and swords, and basketry are other Shan crafts.

19 ● SOCIAL PROBLEMS

The Shans are endangered by the breakdown of their society under military rule. In 1996 alone, tens of thousands of Shan villagers were driven out of their homes by Burmese government troops, and the flow of refugees to Thailand from the Shan state has been steadily increasing for decades. Shan farmers are constantly under the threat of forced labor and caught in the crossfire of government troops, insurgent groups, and opium armies. In the towns and cities, Shan intellectuals and politicians have been imprisoned, killed, or exiled. The young people are in particular danger from the HIV/AIDS epidemic spread through the sex trade and drug use (heroin injection).

20 ● BIBLIOGRAPHY

Lintner, Bertil. *Burma in Revolt: Opium and Insurgency Since 1948.* Boulder, Colo.: Westview Press, 1994.

Mirante, Edith T. *Burmese Looking Glass: A Human Rights Adventure.* New York: Grove Press, 1993.

Sargent, Inge. *Twilight Over Burma: My Life as a Shan Princess.* Honolulu: University of Hawaii Press, 1995.

Smith, Martin. *Ethnic Groups in Burma.* London: Anti-Slavery International, 1994.

Tannenbaum, Nicola. *Who Can Compete Against the World: Power-Protection and Buddhism in Shan Worldview.* Ann Arbor, Mich.: Asian Studies Institute, 1995.

WEBSITES

Interknowledge Corp. Myanmar. [Online] Available http://www.interknowledge.com/myanmar/, 1998.

World Travel Guide. Myanmar. [Online] Available http://www.wtgonline/country/mm/gen.html, 1998.

Namibia

The people of Namibia are called Namibians. The largest ethnic group is the Ovambo, who live in northen Namibia and number about 665,000. The majority of whites, called Afrikaners, are of Dutch descent. The Coloureds (people of mixed descent) numbered 48,000, and there are about 32,000 San (Bushmen).

Namibians

PRONUNCIATION: nuh-MIB-ee-uhns
LOCATION: Namibia
POPULATION: 1.7 million
LANGUAGE: Afrikaans; English; indigenous languages (Oshivambo, Khoisan languages)
RELIGION: Christianity; animism

1 ● INTRODUCTION

Namibia sits in the extreme southwest corner of Africa, just north of the Republic of South Africa. Namibians lived under South African apartheid (separation of the races) for over forty years.

Namibia, known as South West Africa until 1966, fought a war for independence for twenty-two years. Over 50,000 Namibians are living in exile. Namibia's indigenous (native) population was first hunted, then herded into reserves, then forced to serve as soldiers for apartheid. Namibia has no year-round interior rivers and suffered a devastating drought in 1992. Its people suf-fer from extreme poverty. In spite of these terrible hardships, Namibia is one of the most starkly beautiful, peaceful, and progressive countries on the continent of Africa.

Namibia was the last of the African countries colonized by Europe to achieve independence. In 1966, the United Nations removed South Africa's authority over Namibia. It declared the South West African People's Organization, the liberation movement known as SWAPO, as the only legitimate representatives of the South West African peoples' interests.

2 ● LOCATION

Namibia is about half the size of Alaska. It is comprised of three distinct environments—the Namib Desert in the east; the more populous Central Plateau; and the Kalahari Desert in the west, famous for the Khoisan people (known as Bushmen) and majestic wildlife. All three regions are extremely dry. Most of Namibia's limited precipitation falls on the Central Plateau,

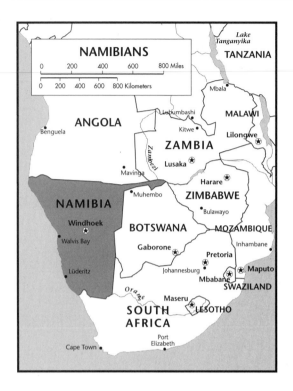

NAMIBIANS

"Basters." Most Namibians live in the north or on the plains surrounding the capital, where water is more plentiful.

3 ● LANGUAGE

Namibia's most common language is Afrikaans, imported from white South Africa. Considered the language of the oppressor, Afrikaans was replaced by English as the country's official language following independence. However, only 7 percent of the population speaks English. Oshivambo, spoken in the north, is the most widely used language. Some translations of "hello" follow:

LANGUAGE	GREETING
Afrikaans	Hallo
Oshivambo	Nawa
Damara	Matisa
Herero	Koree
Okavango	Mazwara

4 ● FOLKLORE

Not surprisingly, many Namibian folk heroes achieved their status through courageous battles with oppressors. One nineteenth-century Ovambo subchief, named Madume Ndemufayo, fought the Angolan Portuguese from the north and the Germans from the south, only to be captured and killed by the Germans. His exploits were passed on through oral tradition (storytelling), since native languages had never been written.

5 ● RELIGION

Namibians describe themselves as very spiritual. European missionaries found success here, and today 90 percent of Namibians are Christian, mostly Lutheran. Traditional religion was animistic, atttributing souls and

supporting cattle, goat and sheep herding, and marginal farming. A severe drought in 1992 sent 30,000 farmers to live as squatters (people occupying land without permission or rent) in the cities as their crops and animals died. In the late 1990s, the government was considering damming the Okavango River to provide a reliable water source.

The ancestors of the Khoisan people arrived in Namibia 2,000 years ago, followed by Bantu tribes from the north and east after AD 1500. The largest of these groups today is the Ovambo, who comprise half the population. Germans and South African Afrikaners, arriving in the nineteenth century, make up most of the 6 percent of the population that is white. As in South Africa, there is a large mixed-race population, known as "coloureds" or

Cory Langley

Although most Namibians are of African descent, a substantial minority is descended from the Dutch.

spiritual powers to natural objects and phenomena. While it is typical for Africans to incorporate traditional beliefs and practices into their religious life, less than 20 percent of Namibians claim to do so. Western churches hold great influence in Namibia.

6 ● MAJOR HOLIDAYS

Two important Namibian holidays fall on August 26. This day was first established in the nineteenth century as Red Day by the Herero in remembrance of their fallen chiefs. (The Herero is a group that depended on herding cattle in the region of Namibia around the mid-sixteenth century. They lost ground to other groups over rights

to grazing lands.) It is still marked by the wearing of dark red costumes. After independence, August 26 also became Heroes Day. This is an official holiday celebrating SWAPO's first armed battle with the South African military. Independence Day, March 31, bears the characteristics of independence days celebrated throughout the world: military parades, speeches by politicians, and plenty of food and festivities.

7 ● RITES OF PASSAGE

Much of Namibian ritual life involves cattle. Cattle have provided the economic cornerstone for most of Namibia's ethnic groups for centuries. *Lobola* (or bride-price) is a payment made by a man to the father of the woman he wants to marry before the marriage is approved. Lobola always includes cows.

Cows play a particularly important role in funeral rituals, too. When an Ovambo man dies, his body must remain in the house for at least one day before burial, during which time all his pets must be killed. Traditional Ovambo compounds, called *kraals,* have gates used by both cattle and humans.

At death, the Ovambo believe that the owner may not pass through this gate, or the cattle will die and the kraal will come to ruin. A new hole is cut for him to pass through. A bull is slaughtered, cooked without oil or flavoring of any kind, and a portion is eaten by everyone in the village. Then the kraal and all its contents must be moved at least 50 feet (15 meters). The cattle are not permitted to rest on the same earth that witnessed the death of their owner.

8 ● RELATIONSHIPS

Namibians feel strong dislike for the racial hatred of apartheid and the ethnic distrust common in many other African countries. They vow to greet each other as brothers and sisters. Many northern groups traditionally greeted one another with hugs. During the years before independence, the hug became a political symbol of secret camaraderie (loyalty and friendship) among those opposed to South African domination. Since independence, hugging has been making a comeback as a simple, friendly gesture.

Among some groups, women and youth bend at the knees as a sign of respect to older men. Basters (mixed-race Namibians) may kiss close friends and relatives on the lips. But the handshake is the most common form of personal introduction.

9 ● LIVING CONDITIONS

Living conditions vary widely among Namibians. The average annual salary for whites is $15,000, while the poorest blacks survive on $100 per year. However, some black Namibians count most of their wealth in cattle and are not deeply involved in the modern cash economy.

Housing has been a controversial issue during Namibia's short history. Under apartheid, blacks were only allowed to live in reservations called *bantustans,* or in single-sex dormitories if they worked in the cities or mines. Under such conditions, ten people typically shared one room. After independence, the government attempted to persuade black city dwellers and squatters to settle in and farm rural areas. Namibians rejected the plan as limiting their freedom of movement. Consequently, housing continues to be tight in urban areas.

Today, the average Namibian household has five to seven members. One-third of all dwellings have electricity, and slightly fewer have plumbing. Those without plumbing typically have lime-pit outhouses. Roughly 23 percent of Namibians own cars, mostly those in urban centers. In the rural areas, children often walk miles to school, and the donkey is often the best form of transportation.

Cory Langley

Herero women have adopted the German Victorian fashions of the nineteenth-century colonists. They wear long petticoated gowns with shawls, along with extravagant headdresses.

10 ● FAMILY LIFE

Family life, particularly the role of women, has changed drastically in Namibia in modern times. Polygyny (more than one wife), once the ideal in many ethnic groups, is now officially forbidden. Virginity before marriage had been the traditional ideal for women in many tribes, and women could even be banished for violating this custom. As of the late 1990s, one-third of all girls aged eighteen have at least one child, even though the average age for women at marriage is twenty-five. A related trend is the increase in households run by women, many of whom are single parents. Namibian women have legal access to birth control, as well as rights to demand child support for their children. Modern birth control is used by 25 percent of all women, far more than in most of Africa. Consequently, women average five children each, slightly lower than for the rest of the continent.

Despite women's gains in reproductive choice, their rights to family property are still not guaranteed. In most Namibian cultures, when a man dies, his parents and siblings often take his property from the widow and her children.

11 ● CLOTHING

Most Namibian city-dwellers dress in modern fashions, as in the West. Several examples of traditional dress stand out, however. Herero women have adopted the German Victorian fashions of the nineteenth-century colonists. They wear long petticoated gowns with shawls, along with extravagant headdresses. The Himba, the least-Westernized tribe in Namibia, typically wear leather thongs or skirts. They smear their bodies with ochre, a reddish pigment extracted from iron ore. Women wear elaborate braids and copper or leather bands around their necks, making their figures appear very elongated.

12 ● FOOD

Beef, mutton, milk products, millet, sorghum, peanuts, pumpkins, and melons are common Namibian subsistence (food) products. Mealie (corn) is a staple in the Namibian diet. While game hunting was traditionally practiced all over Namibia, it tended to take a back seat to livestock raising. Today, there are many private game parks to serve Western tourists interested in hunting. While fish and ostrich are both important exports, neither is a staple of the Namibian diet.

13 ● EDUCATION

Namibia's adult literacy rate (percentage of adults who can read and write) is one of the lowest in Africa south of the Sahel (southern Sahara Desert). As of 1993, 20 percent of Namibians had never been to school, and only 1 percent went on to university. There is a university in Windhoek, and some Namibians go to South Africa or Germany. In addition, several ministries have internal training colleges to better prepare civil servants (government administrators) for work.

14 ● CULTURAL HERITAGE

Whenever people struggle under a century of colonial rule, fight a long war for independence, live in exile, and concentrate on surviving in conditions of poverty, cultural heritage and valued traditions suffer. It has happened all over Africa. To help reverse this trend, the Namibian government has established a team of cultural preservationists—performers, artists, historians, and researchers. Their job is to record and then bring to life the cultural heritage of Namibia's tribes before it is forever forgotten. The preservationists combine tribal traditions to create traveling performances and exhibitions.

15 ● EMPLOYMENT

Namibians have a strong work ethic and are extremely self-reliant. Many elderly people

---

Recipe

Baked Mealie

Ingredients

2 cups corn (may be fresh, canned, or frozen)
2 eggs, lightly beaten in a bowl
¼ cup brown sugar, packed firmly into measuring cup
2 slices white bread, lightly toasted and cut into small cubes
¼ cup butter
½ cup unseasoned bread crumbs

Directions

1. Preheat oven to 325°F. Grease a 1½ quart casserole dish.
2. Combine corn, eggs, brown sugar, and bread cubes, and mix thoroughly. Pour into casserole dish.
3. Melt butter (20 to 30 seconds in microwave).
4. Stir bread crumbs into melted butter and spread over top of mixture in casserole dish.
5. Bake in oven for 45 minutes, or until top is browned.

---

expect to feed themselves from their own agricultural labor until they are physically unable to do so. Two-thirds of all Namibians are rural dwellers; most describe themselves as subsistence farmers (producing enough food for their family, with little or none left over) or herders. The government is currently trying to convince some tribes to discontinue the practice of keeping cattle as a "savings account," and to begin commercial ranching and beef export. Traditionalists consider cattle a legacy of their ancestors and object to selling off the herd for cash. Since independence, one of the government's primary goals is for Namibia to become less commercially dependent on South Africa.

16 ● SPORTS

As everywhere in Africa, soccer ("football" as it is known in Namibia) is the national sport with the most passionate followers. Children grow up playing it, sometimes using a ball made of twine. Track and field, called "athletics" by Namibians, is becoming more popular. Namibian Frankie Fredricks won a silver medal in the 100- and 200-meter dashes at the 1996 Olympic Games in Atlanta. Most Namibians get their physical exercise through daily chores. Many rural children must walk or run 3 miles (5 kilometers) a day to school. Most adults hoe and harvest regularly.

17 ● RECREATION

American popular culture is known all over the world. In Namibia in the late 1990s, Arnold Schwarzenegger movies were popular, and Michael Jackson and Michael Jordan were youth icons (idols). Most popular music, however, tends to come from South Africa, with its rich history of township jive. Performers such as Lucky Dube, Yvonne Chaka Chaka, and Mahlathini and the Mahotella Queens have captured the Namibian music market. The infectious rhythms of the Congo, farther to the north, are also gaining in popularity in Namibia.

18 ● CRAFTS AND HOBBIES

Traditional arts and crafts in Namibia focus on daily living. Woodcarving, despite the relative lack of trees, has a long history.

Cory Langley

Although Western-style dress is the norm in the cities, unique fashion styles exist in many parts of the country.

Beautiful utensils, knife handles and sheaths, and toy cars continue to be made from wood and sold. Baskets for holding everything from fish to grain to water are made out of the palm leaf, or, along the northern rivers, out of reeds.

19 ● SOCIAL PROBLEMS

Unemployment reached 35 percent in urban areas after the 1992 drought, and as of the late 1990s, unemployment remained high. After independence, the government did not nationalize industries (place them under government control). It also did not confiscate land or equipment from the white ruling class. As a result the economy has remained stable, but many black Namibians are impatient with the continued lack of economic justice.

20 ● BIBLIOGRAPHY

Cliffe, Lionel et al., *The Transition to Independence in Namibia.* Boulder, Colo.: Lynne Rienner, 1994.

Laurè, J. *Namibia.* Chicago: Children's Press, 1993.

Leys, Colin. *Namibia's Liberation Struggle: The Two-Edged Sword.* Athens: Ohio University Press, 1995.

Kaela, Laurent C. W. *The Question of Namibia.* New York: St. Martin's Press, 1996.

Sparks, Donald L. *Namibia: The Nation After Independence.* Boulder, Colo.: Westview Press, 1992.

WEBSITES

Government of Namibia. [Online] Available http://www.republicofnamibia.com, 1998.

Interknowledge Corp. [Online] Available http://www.geographia.com/namibia/, 1998.

Internet Africa Ltd. [Online] Available http://www.africanet.com/africanet/country/namibia/, 1998.

World Travel Guide. [Online] Available http://www.wtgonline.com/country/na/gen.html, 1998.

Nepal

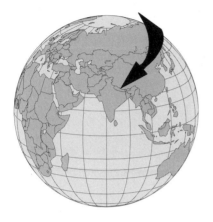

The people of Nepal are called Nepalis or Nepalese. Sherpas, the people who live in the Himalaya Mountains, have become well known as guides for mountain-climbing expeditions.

Nepalis

PRONUNCIATION: nuh-PAW-leez
ALTERNATE NAMES: Nepalese
LOCATION: Nepal
POPULATION: 21.5 million
LANGUAGE: Nepālī (Gorkhali) is official language; over thirty-six other languages and dialects
RELIGION: Hindu; Buddhist; Muslim; Christian; Jain

1 ● INTRODUCTION

Nepal is unique in the region of South Asia that includes India, Pakistan, Bangladesh, and Sri Lanka because it is the only country of any size to have maintained its independence. Nepal was never a British colony.

The Kathmandu Valley is the political and historical heartland of Nepal. There were cultures centered there as early as the eighth or seventh century BC. Indian inscriptions dated to the fourth century AD refer to a kingdom called "Nepala" in the Himalayan Mountains. The birth of modern Nepal can to be traced to the eighteenth century. The Gurkhas, a warlike people, are thought to have been princes fleeing Muslim persecution in western India. They established themselves in the mountains of what is now western Nepal in the mid-sixteenth century. In 1768, Prithvi Narayan Shah, the ninth king in the Gurkha dynasty, conquered the Kathmandu Valley, where the capital of modern Nepal, Kathmandu, is located.

Disputes over its southern border led Nepal (ruled by Gurkhas) into conflict with the British in India. Defeat during the Anglo-Gurkha war (1814–1816) saw Nepal's expansion halted and its borders fixed in their present locations. From 1816 to 1951, Nepal did not allow foreigners to enter—its borders were closed.

By the mid-twentieth century, the Nepali National Congress called for the establish-

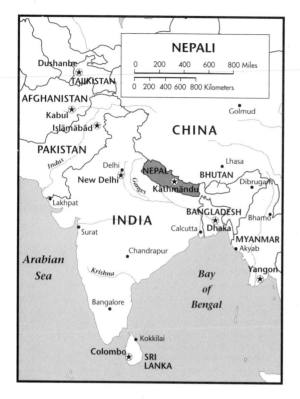

meters), roughly the size of Iowa. Nepal extends 500 miles (800 kilometers) in a generally east-west direction, but it is only approximately 80 to 140 miles (125 to 225 kilometers) wide in the north-south direction. The country is surrounded on the east, south, and west by India. China lies to the north.

Nepal is truly a mountain kingdom, with a quarter of its land over 9,800 feet (3,000 meters) in altitude. The only lowland of note lies in the extreme south, where the country extends into the plains near the Ganges River. The Terai is a narrow belt of land that was at one time a swampy, malaria-infested forest about 25 miles (40 kilometers) wide, but is now home to over a third of Nepal's population, much of its agriculture and industry, and several government wildlife reserves.

North of the Terai, the land rises to an elevation of 2,450 to 4,900 feet (750 to 1,500 meters), before descending to a series of east-west running valleys known as *duns*. From the duns, the terrain rises steadily toward the main ranges of the Himalayas. The Nepal Himalayas contain eight peaks over 26,200 feet (8,000 meters), including Mount Everest, the world's highest mountain at 29,028 feet (8,848 meters). Kanchenjunga, Dhaulagiri, and Annapurna are among the better-known peaks of this group.

The Kathmandu Valley lies north of the Mahabharat Lekh ranges at around 4,300 feet (1,300 meters) above sea level. It is the cultural and historical heart of Nepal, containing the modern capital of Kathmandu, and the cities of Patan and Bhaktapur.

ment of a democratic government. A new constitution was proclaimed in 1990. This created a true parliamentary democracy, legalized political parties, and made provisions for a popularly elected legislature. The first general election under the new system was held in May 1991. As of 1998, King Birendra Bir Bikram Shah Dev continued to rule as a constitutional monarch, but without much power.

2 ● LOCATION

Nepal is a landlocked state on the northern mountain rim of South Asia, the region that includes India, Pakistan, Bangladesh, Bhutan, and Sri Lanka. Its inhabitants number 21.5 million people, living in an area of 56,139 square miles (145,391 square kilo-

Market square in the Nepali midlands.

Nepal's climate and vegetation reflect the country's wide range of elevations. The Terai experiences an average temperature in June, the warmest month, of 95°F (35°C), while winter temperatures drop to 50°F (10°C). Rainfall is received during the summer monsoon, with amounts varying from 80 inches (200 centimeters) in the east to 40 inches (100 centimeters) in the west. As one moves northwards into the mountains, temperatures decrease and rainfall increases. Above 13,100 feet (4,000 meters), the climate is alpine, with short summers and long, severe winters. The higher elevations are under snow year-round.

The peoples of southern Nepal are like their Indian neighbors. Caste (social classification) remains the prime factor in relations. (For more information on castes, see the chapter on India in Volume 4.) There is considerable freedom of movement and intermarriage across the border between Nepal and India.

The term "Newar" is used to describe the inhabitants of the Kathmandu Valley regardless of their ethnic origin. Peoples of Mongoloid descent include the groups who traditionally have served as Gurkha soldiers. Technically, there is no single ethnic group called Gurkha, the name being derived from soldiers of the Kingdom of Gorkha whose ruler conquered the Kathmandu Valley in the eighteenth century.

The northern mountain belt is inhabited by the Sherpas who are closely related to the Tibetans.

3 ● LANGUAGE

Nepal's ethnic diversity is accompanied by linguistic diversity, with over thirty-six languages and dialects currently spoken by the Nepali people. Groups in the northern mountain belt speak languages belonging to the Tibeto-Burmese branch of the Sino-Tibetan language family. These include Tamang, Magar, Rai, and Limbu. Sherpa and Thakal are Bhutia dialects virtually indistinguishable from Tibetan. Newari, a Tibeto-Burman language written in the Devanagari (Hindi) script, is spoken in the Kathmandu Valley. Nepali (also known as Gorkhali) is spoken by 58 percent of the population and is the country's official language. An Indo-Aryan language related to Hindi, it is also written in the Devanagari script. Hindi, Bhojpuri, and Maithili are widely spoken in the Terai.

4 ● FOLKLORE

While each ethnic group has its own folk traditions, all Nepalis share in the mythology of Hinduism and Buddhism. The Himalayas, for example, are regarded as the home of the gods. Here, in the "snow-abode" *(hima-alaya),* is Gauri-Shankar, the peak where the god Shiva and his consort, Parvati, dwell. Annapurna, with her many peaks, is goddess of plenty. Ganesh Himal is named for Ganesh, the elephant-headed

Manjula Giri/EPD Photos
A woman from the middle hills region visits the market.

god of Hinduism. In Indian legend, every *rishi,* or yogi, who possesses divine power has a retreat in the mountain vastness of the Himalayas.

Another legend has it that, at the beginning of time, the Valley of Kathmandu was a beautiful turquoise lake. On this lake floated a lotus flower, from which shone a magnificent blue light. This was a manifestation of Swayambhu or Adi-Buddha, the first incarnation of Buddha. The lake was so beautiful, and the flame so sacred, that the devout came from far and wide to live along its shores, to meditate, and to worship. One such devotee was the sage Manjusri, who came from Central Asia to worship the flame. Wishing to approach the flame more closely, he sliced open the valley wall with his sword of wisdom. The waters of the lake drained away and the lotus settled on the valley floor. At this site, Manjusri built a shrine that was to become the sacred site of Swayambhunath.

5 ● RELIGION

Nepal is the only Hindu kingdom in the world. However, although Hinduism is the official state religion, Nepalis are highly tolerant of other religious beliefs. Freedom of religion is enshrined in law, but it is illegal to actively try to make religious converts. The religious makeup of the population is: Hindu (86.2 percent), Buddhist (7.8 percent), Muslim (3.8 percent), Christian (0.2 percent), Jain (0.1 percent), and others (1.9 percent).

Hinduism and Buddhism in Nepal have so influenced each other that it is sometimes difficult to distinguish between the two religions. Both Hindus and Buddhists, for example, worship at the Buddhist shrine of Swayambhunath. In addition, religion in Nepal has absorbed other elements of other beliefs that give it a unique character. Animal sacrifice accompanies almost every ritual and ceremonial event in Nepali life.

The temple of Pashupatinath in Kathmandu, dedicated to the Hindu god Shiva, is viewed as one of the most sacred in all of South Asia. It is one of the few Hindu temples from which non-Hindus are barred.

6 ● MAJOR HOLIDAYS

All the major Hindu and Buddhist celebrations are observed, as well as many that have their origins in ancient nature-worship beliefs. At the Seto Machhendranath festival held in Kathmandu in March, the image of the deity Seto Macchendra is placed in a towering chariot (rath) and pulled through the streets by hundreds of young boys. Gai Jatra is a festival when cows are decorated and led through the streets in procession. Many of the Buddhist festivals, such as the Mani Rimdu of the Sherpas, are accompanied by masked monks performing devil-dances.

One of the major celebrations of the Nepali festival year is Dasain, which is the Nepali name for Dasahara. It celebrates fertility and the victory of good over evil in the form of the goddess Durga's slaying of the buffalo-demon Mahisha. The festival lasts ten days, with numerous rituals and offerings to the gods. The ninth day of the festival is marked by the sacrifice of animals (chickens, ducks, goats, and buffalo) by every household, and by organizations such as the police force and military.

The secular holidays of Nepal include King Birendra's birthday (December 29) and National Democracy Day (February 19).

7 ● RITES OF PASSAGE

Hindu and Buddhist rituals and ceremonies are the most common. High-caste Hindu boy undergo the sacred thread ceremony (where a special cord is tied around the waist) as an initiation into adulthood. Among Buddhists, on the other hand, this initiation consists of boys adopting the saf-

Susan Rock

Nepalis are a rural people, with over 90 percent living in villages. Nepal's mountainous terrain makes for difficult transportation and communications.

fron clothes and lifestyle of the novice monk for a short period. Both Hindus and Buddhists cremate their dead, except for important lamas (Buddhist spiritual leaders), who are buried. Some groups at higher elevations (where wood is not available) dispose of their dead by exposing the corpses to be consumed by vultures and wild animals.

8 ● RELATIONSHIPS

The normal Nepali greeting is *Namaste*, said while joining one's own hands together, palms touching, in front of the body. A common greeting on the mountain trails is *Khana Khaiyo*, literally, "Have you eaten?"

This greeting indicates the difficulties in obtaining sufficient food.

9 ● LIVING CONDITIONS

Nepal is among the poorest and least developed countries in the world, a fact that is reflected in the nation's health and vital statistics. The average life expectancy at birth is fifty-three years. The leading causes of death are infectious and parasitic diseases, and respiratory problems. Infant mortality rates are high, amounting to 81 deaths per 1,000 live births. Fertility rates are also high, with 5.2 average births per childbearing woman in the population.

Nepalis are a rural people, with over 90 percent living in villages. These are usually clusters of houses sited on a hilltop or hillside, surrounded by agricultural land, and located near a source of water. Terracing of hillsides is quite common. Typical houses in the valleys are two-story, mud-brick structures with thatched or tin roofs. Stone and wood are the main construction materials in the mountain belt.

Nepal's mountainous terrain makes for difficult transportation and communications. Goods are often transported by pack animals or carried by porters over mountain trails. There are only 2,700 miles (4,400 kilometers) of paved roads. The rail system has only 63 miles (101 kilometers) of track and is of little economic significance. Royal Nepal Airlines, the country's air carrier, operates a schedule of domestic and international flights.

10 ● FAMILY LIFE

Social organization and family life differ among the various ethnic groups of Nepal. However, marriage between clans is practiced, with descent most commonly traced though the father's side. Hindus follow typical practices in terms of arranged marriages and the extended family structure. Monogamy is the norm, although some Tibetan-speaking peoples practice fraternal polyandry (two brothers may marry the same woman). Wife-capture is a practice among Tibetan-speaking groups. Customs concerning divorce and remarriage vary according to the community.

11 ● CLOTHING

Nepali clothing reflects the variety of peoples and cultures in the country. Each community has its own particular styles of dress, although certain broad patterns can be seen. Peoples of the Terai are virtually indistinguishable from their Indian neighbors. Groups in the northern mountain belt wear Tibetan-style clothes. The traditional Nepali dress is typically worn in the middle hills region. For men, this comprises trousers that taper from the waist to tight-fitting legs. Over this is worn a blouse-type shirt that reaches to mid-thigh and is tied at the waist with a belt, and a Western-style jacket. The Nepali cap, with its peak offset from the center, giving it a slightly lopsided look, completes the outfit. Ex-soldiers wear the badges of their former regiments with much pride. Women wear blouses and *saris* (cloth wrapped around the waist and over one shoulder), and they adorn themselves with gold ornaments and jewelry.

12 ● FOOD

Nepali food is generally similar to Indian cuisine. Rice, the staple cereal, is boiled and eaten with lentils *(dal)*, and spiced vegetables. Beef is not available, but poultry, goat, and buffalo meat are consumed. Meat is consumed mainly on special occasions and at festival times. Rice, too, is often unavailable to the average rural Nepali family. It is replaced by a dough made by mixing flour with boiling water, which is eaten with one's fingers just like rice. A flat bread *(chapati),* which is dry-roasted on a hot skillet, is a staple of the diet in the Terai.

Manjula Giri/EPD Photos

Over a third of Nepal's population and much of its agriculture and industry are found in the lowland region known as the Terai. Women of this region dress in the same style as their Indian neighbors to the south.

13 ● EDUCATION

Over one-third of the adult population has no formal schooling. Literacy (the ability to read and write) is only 38 percent for adult men and 23 percent for adult women.

14 ● CULTURAL HERITAGE

Traditions of music range from the sonorous chanting and huge horns, thigh-bone flutes, and conch shells of Tibetan sacred music to the songs and folk music of wandering professional troubadours. Dance forms include the classical *kumārī* of the Newars, and the masked devil-dances performed at Tibetan Buddhist festivals to scare off devils and demons.

15 ● EMPLOYMENT

Nepalis are overwhelmingly agricultural, with 93 percent of the labor force engaged in this sector of the economy. One unique tradition in Nepal, however, is military service in the Gurkha regiments of the British and Indian armies. The fighting abilities of the Gurkhas were recognized during the Anglo-Gurkha war of 1814–1816, after which they were recruited into the army of the East India Company. The Gurkhas have fought with distinction in campaigns around the world.

Another group that has carved out an occupational niche for itself is the Sherpas, who are well known as guides and porters for mountain-climbing expeditions.

16 ● SPORTS

Modern sports popular among Nepalis include soccer, cricket, basketball, table tennis and badminton. Despite the mountainous nature of the country, altitude and the rugged terrain make skiing impractical.

17 ● RECREATION

Most Nepalis are restricted to traditional forms of entertainment and recreation such as festivals, folk dances, and folk music. Radio Nepal broadcasts news and music, and for those who can afford television sets, Nepal Television commenced service in 1985. The cinema is popular in the cities, with most movies being supplied by India. Occasionally, Western films are shown.

There is an ancient tradition of theater in Kathmandu.

18 ● CRAFTS AND HOBBIES

Traditional Nepali crafts include woodcarvings, *khukhris* (curved knives), prayer wheels, musical instruments, and dance masks. The Nepalis still make their traditional crafts, but items are often made of lesser quality to sell to tourists.

19 ● SOCIAL PROBLEMS

Many of Nepal's social problems are related to poverty, overpopulation, and the nature of the country's environment. Only 17 percent of the country's land area is arable land, and Nepal has to import food to feed its population. Much of the population is engaged in subsistence agriculture, but the numbers of farmers unable to meet their basic food requirements is growing rapidly. More than 40 percent of the population is undernourished. Poor transportation and natural hazards such as flooding, landslides, and drought intensify the problems of agricultural production.

20 ● BIBLIOGRAPHY

Karan, Pradyumna P. *Nepal: A Cultural and Physical Geography.* Lexington, Ky.: University of Kentucky Press, 1960.

Rose, Leo E., and John T. Scholz. *Nepal: Profile of a Himalayan Kingdom.* Boulder, Colo.: Westview Press, 1980.

WEBSITES

Interknowledge Corporation. Nepal. [Online] Available http://www.interknowledge.com/nepal/, 1998.

World Travel Guide. Nepal. [Online] Available http://travelguide.attistel.co.uk/country/np/gen.html, 1998.

Sherpas

PRONUNCIATION: SHER-puhs
LOCATION: Nepal
POPULATION: 45,000
LANGUAGE: Sherpa (or Sherpali); Nepali
RELIGION: Nyingmapa sect of Buddhism

1 ● INTRODUCTION

The Sherpas are a tribe of Tibetan origin who occupy the high valleys around the base of Mount Everest in northeastern Nepal. In the Tibetan language, *Shar Pa* means "people who live in the east," and over time this descriptive term has come to identify the Sherpa community.

According to Sherpa tradition, the tribe migrated to Nepal from the Kham region of eastern Tibet over a thousand years ago. Historians, however, suggest that the Sherpas were nomadic herders who were driven out of their original homeland in eastern Tibet by warlike peoples sometime between the twelfth and fifteenth centuries AD. They migrated to the area around Tingri, but conflict with the local inhabitants caused them to move on in search of new pastures. They crossed the Himalayas and settled peacefully in their present homeland in northeastern Nepal.

2 ● LOCATION

The current Sherpa population is estimated to be around 45,000 people. They mainly live in the Khumbu and Solu Khumbu regions that lie to the south of Mount Everest. Sherpas also live to the east of this area in Kulung. In addition, Sherpas inhabit the valleys of the Dudh Kosi and Rolwaling

Rivers west of Solu-Khumbu, and they are also found in the Lantang-Helambu region north of Kathmandu. Kathmandu itself has a sizable Sherpa population, while small numbers of Sherpas can be found throughout Nepal, even in the Terai. Sherpa communities are also present in the Indian state of Sikkim and the hill towns of Darjiling and Kalimpong. The Sherpas are small in stature, relatively fair in complexion, with the distinctive facial features associated with peoples of Tibetan origin.

The Sherpas live on the flanks of the hill masses that jut south into Nepal from the crestline of the high Himalayas. Rivers such as the Dudh Kosi and Bhote Kosi have carved deep gorges into the mountains, leaving a complex terrain of steep ridges and narrow valleys. Wherever Sherpas are found, their settlements lie at the highest elevations of any human habitation. In Khumbu, their villages are found between 10,000 to 14,000 feet (approximately 3,000 and 4,300 meters). Winters at this altitude are severe, with snow covering the ground between November and February. No work can be done in the open. Most able-bodied Sherpas descend to lower elevations for the winter, leaving only the elderly in the villages. February sees the onset of spring, with warming temperatures and clear skies. People return to their villages for the New Year festival in late February, and the next three months are spent preparing fields and sowing crops. Summer temperatures vary according to altitude. At Nauje village (elevation 11,287 feet or 3,440 meters) in Khumbu, the July mean temperature is 54°F (12°C). May to August is the rainy season, with most of Nauje's annual precipitation of approximately 41 inches (105 centimeters)

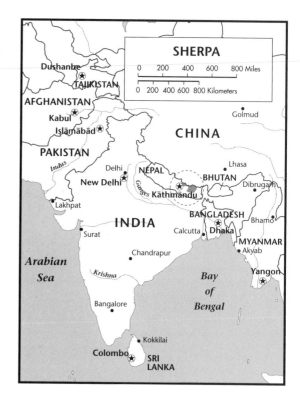

falling during this period. August to November heralds another period of fair weather, when the harvest is gathered in.

3 ● LANGUAGE

The language of the Sherpas, called Sherpa or Sherpali, is a dialect of Tibetan, although it has borrowed heavily from neighboring languages. It belongs to the Tibeto-Burman branch of the Sino-Tibetan language family. The Sherpas use the Tibetan script for writing. Sherpas use Nepali in their dealings with other peoples.

4 ● FOLKLORE

A unique element in Sherpa folklore is the Yeti, better known in the West as the "Abominable Snowman." According to one tale, Yetis were far more numerous in the past and would attack and terrorize local villagers. The elders of the village decided on a plan to eliminate the Yetis. The next day, the villagers gathered in a high alpine pasture and everyone brought a large kettle of *chāng* (maize beer). They also brought weapons such as sticks and knives and swords. Pretending to get drunk, they began to "fight" each other. Towards evening, the villagers returned to their settlement, leaving behind the weapons and large amounts of beer. The Yetis had been hidden in the mountains watching the day's events. As soon as the villagers left, they came down to the pasture, drank the rest of the beer, and started fighting among themselves. Soon, most of the Yetis were dead. A few of the less intoxicated escaped and swore revenge. However, there were so few left that the survivors retreated to caves high in the mountains where no one would find them. Occasionally, they reappear to attack humans.

Manjula Giri/EPD Photos

A Sherpa woman from the Himalaya. Sherpa villages cling to the sides of sheer mountain slopes or sit on top of steep escarpments. Sherpa settlements lie at the highest elevations of any human habitation in the world.

5 ● RELIGION

The Sherpas belong to the Nyingmapa sect of Buddhism. The oldest Buddhist sect in Tibet, it emphasizes mysticism and incorporates shamanistic practices and local deities borrowed from the pre-Buddhist Bon religion. Thus, in addition to Buddha and the great Buddhist divinities, the Sherpa also have believe in numerous gods and demons who are believed to inhabit every mountain, cave, and forest. These have to be worshiped or appeased through ancient practices that have been woven into the fabric of Buddhist ritual life. Indeed, it is almost impossible to distinguish between Bon practices and Buddhism.

Many of the great Himalayan mountains are worshiped as gods. The Sherpas call Mount Everest *Chomolungma* and worship it as the "Mother of the World." Mount Makalu is worshiped as the deity Shankar (Shiva). Each clan recognizes mountain gods identified with certain peaks that are their protective deities.

The day-to-day religious affairs of the Sherpas are dealt with by *lamas* (Buddhist spiritual leaders) and other religious practitioners living in the villages. It is the village lama, who can be married and is often a householder, who presides over ceremonies, and rituals. In addition, shamans (lhawa) and soothsayers (mindung) deal with the supernatural and the spirit world. They identify witches (pem), act as the mouthpiece of gods and spirits, and diagnose illnesses.

An important aspect of Sherpa religion is the monastery or gompa. There are some two dozen of these institutions scattered through the Solu-Khumbu region. They are communities of lamas or monks (sometimes of nuns) who take vows of celibacy and lead a life in isolation searching for truth and religious enlightenment. They are respected by and supported by the community at large. Their contact with the outside world is limited to the annual festivals to which the public is invited, and the reading of sacred texts at funerals.

6 ● MAJOR HOLIDAYS

The major festivals of the Sherpas are Losar, Dumje, and Mani Rimdu. Losar, which falls towards the end of February, marks the beginning of the New Year in the Tibetan calendar. It is celebrated with much feasting and drinking, dancing, and singing.

Dumje is a festival celebrated for the prosperity, good health, and general welfare of the Sherpa community. It falls in the month of July, when the agricultural work is complete, the trading expeditions to Tibet have returned, and the Sherpas are preparing to take their herds into the high pastures. Over a seven-day period, Sherpas visit their local monasteries and offer prayers to their gods. There is much eating and drinking, and members of the younger generation participate in singing and dancing.

The colorful Mani Rimdu celebrations are held four times a year, twice in Khumbu (at the Tami and Tengboche monasteries) and twice in Solu-Khumbu (at the Chiwong and Thaksindhu monasteries). Monks in colorful costumes and elaborate masks impersonate gods and demons and perform religious dances intended to scare the evil spirits.

Feasting and drinking accompany all Sherpa festivals and celebrations except for Nyungne. This is a penance for sins committed during the previous year. For three days, laypeople abstain from drinking and dancing and may even undergo a complete fast. They visit the gompa to recite sacred texts with the lamas, or repeat the mantra Om Mani Padme Hum. The principal mantra of the Buddhists, it is also found inscribed on prayer wheels. It has many interpretations, one of which is "Om, the Jewel of the Doctrine is in the Lotus of the World." Monks and nuns keep to the restrictions of Nyungne for two weeks.

7 ● RITES OF PASSAGE

The name-giving ceremony of a Sherpa child is an important event. The local lama (Buddhist spiritual leader) is informed of the birth and the time that it occurred. On the basis of this information, the lama determines the child's name and when the naming ceremony should take place. Children are often named after the day of the week on which they were born. Thus a baby born on Friday would be called "Pasang" (the Sherpa word for "Friday"). The lama, relatives, and neighbors are invited to celebrate the name-giving at a feast.

Children are usually brought up by their mothers, as the men are often away from home for much of the year. Young girls are introduced to household chores at an early age, while boys tend to have greater freedom for leisure and play. Boys undergo an initiation ceremony between seven and nine years of age, which is presided over by the lama and accompanied by feasting and drinking.

For the wedding ceremony (zendi), the boy's family dress in their best clothes and go in procession to the girl's house. There, they are entertained with food and drink and are expected to dance and sing in return. They visit houses of relatives, where the procedure is repeated. The feasting lasts for a day and a night, before the party returns home with the bride. The actual marriage is observed by putting a mark of butter on the forehead of the bride and groom. The bride is given a dowry by family and friends that usually consists of rugs, woolen carpets, yak-wool mats, and even cattle.

At the time of death, the body is washed and covered with a white shroud. The lama cuts off a lock of hair from the corpse so that the life breath (pran) of the departed may leave the body, and reads from the sacred texts. The lama decides if the deceased is to be buried, cremated, or given a water-burial. The lama also decides when to remove the corpse, which may not occur for several days. The body is seated on a frame and taken for cremation or burial. The funeral procession is accompanied by flags and novice lamas blowing conch shells and playing drums and cymbals. After death, the family performs rites for the benefit of the departed and undertakes a ritual purification of the home. Sherpas believe that the soul remains near the house for forty-nine days, and on the last of these days a grand feast is held to complete the last of the funeral rites.

8 ● RELATIONSHIPS

The Sherpas' most important rule of hospitality is that a visitor must not leave the house unfed or without a drink. Guests are entertained with Tibetan tea or beer. Visitors of high standing will be served a snack, or even a complete meal. Unlike some communities in South Asia, guests in Sherpa homes have complete access to both the kitchen and the area set aside for worship.

9 ● LIVING CONDITIONS

Sherpa villages cling to the sides of sheer mountain slopes or sit on top of steep escarpments. Sherpa settlements range from villages with a few houses to towns such as Khumjung or Namche Bazaar with more than a hundred houses. In the higher elevations, a house is usually built in the middle of its owner's fields. Where more flat land is available, however, houses are clustered together in a group at the center of the village's agricultural land. Larger villages may have a community temple, a community mill, and religious monuments called stupas and chorten. There are few proper roads, and villages are connected by tracks and trails. Goods are transported by pack animals or on the backs of the people.

Sherpa houses have two stories and are built of stone. The roofs are flat and usually made of wood, weighted down by heavy stones. The lower level is used to house livestock, fodder, food, and firewood, while the upper story holds the living quarters. The floor of this room is wooden, covered with carpets and rugs. There is no furniture; platforms and benches are used for sitting and sleeping. A small area of the house is set aside for an altar. Incense and butter lamps are kept burning before the shrine.

10 ● FAMILY LIFE

Sherpa society is divided into a number of clans called *ru*. A person is required to marry outside his or her clan. Although there is no ranking of individual clans, they fall into two groups, the *khadeu* and *khamendeu*. The former are of higher status and anyone marrying into the lower group loses this standing.

Sherpas choose their own marriage partners. The marriage process is a lengthy one that may stretch over several years. Following a betrothal, the boy has the right to live with his fiancée in her parents' house. This arrangement may continue for several years, during which the relationship may be broken off. Once the respective families feel that the marriage will be successful, a ceremony is carried out that formally confirms the marriage negotiations. Several months or even years may pass again before the wedding date is fixed.

Sherpa families are small by South Asian standards. The nuclear family is the norm in Sherpa society, with households consisting of parents and their unmarried children. A newly married son is supposed to receive a house on completion of the marriage. Interestingly, a man does not return home until he has a child; he lives with his in-laws until such time as his wife gives birth. Most mar-

Susan D. Rock

Sherpa families are small by South Asian standards. The nuclear family is the norm in Sherpa society, with households consisting of parents and their unmarried children.

riages are monogamous, although fraternal polyandry (having more than one husband) is permitted and is even considered to be prestigious. According to this practice, two brothers marry the same woman. Divorce is quite frequent among the Sherpas.

11 ● CLOTHING

Sherpa dress is similar to that worn by Tibetans. Both men and women wear a long inner shirt over a pant-like garment, both made out of wool. Over this, they wear a thick, coarse, wraparound robe *(bakhu)* that reaches to below the knees and fastens at the side. A sash is belted around the waist.

Both males and females wear high, woolen boots with hide soles. The uppers are colored maroon, red, and green (or blue), and the boots are tied on with colored garters. An unusual feature of women's dress is the multicolored striped aprons worn to cover the front and back of the bodies below the waist. Both married and unmarried women wear the rear apron, while the front apron is worn only by married women. Various ornaments and a distinctive cap called a *shyamahu* complete the dress of the Sherpa woman.

Traditional Sherpa dress is rapidly disappearing among Sherpa men. Many younger men who have worked for mountaineering expeditions wear Western-made high-altitude clothing.

12 ● FOOD

The Sherpa diet is dominated by starchy foods, supplemented by vegetables, spices, and occasionally meat. In addition, Sherpas drink Tibetan tea (tea served with salt and butter) at all meals and throughout the day. A typical breakfast consists of Tibetan tea and several bowls of gruel made by adding *tsampa,* a roasted flour, to water, tea, or milk. Lunch is eaten in the late morning and may include boiled potatoes which are dipped in ground spices. Sometimes a stiff dough made from a mixture of grains *(sen)* is eaten with a thin sauce made from spices and vegetables, or meat if it is available. A typical dinner is a stew *(shakpa)* consisting of balls of dough, potatoes, and vegetables. Dairy products, especially butter and curds, are important in the Sherpa diet. Sherpas eat meat, but as practicing Buddhists they will not kill animals themselves.

A favorite beverage of the Sherpas is *chang,* a beer made from maize, millet, or other grains. This is consumed not only at meals, but also at most social and festive occasions. It has considerable symbolic and ritual significance in Sherpa society.

13 ● EDUCATION

Although primary schools are slowly being introduced into Sherpa areas, few Sherpas have any formal schooling. As might be expected, literacy rates (the percentage of people who can read and write) are low, as are parental expectations for their children.

14 ● CULTURAL HERITAGE

The Tibetan tradition of religious dance-dramas known as 'cham can be seen in the Mani Rimdu festivals of the Sherpas. Elaborately choreographed, with monks dressed up in costumes and masks, the Mani Rimdu dances enact the triumph of Buddhism over the demons of the Bon religion. The temple orchestras that accompany these dramas are unique in the makeup of their instruments, which include drums, cymbals, handbells, conch shells, 10-foot (3-meter) telescopic horns, large oboes, and flutes made from human thighbones. The distinctive chant used by monks in their religious observances is also in the tradition of Tibetan sacred music.

15 ● EMPLOYMENT

Traditional Sherpa economic activities were centered on agriculture and trade. At lower elevations, such as in Solu-Khumbu, where conditions allow cultivation, Sherpas raise maize, barley, buckwheat, and vegetables. Potatoes were introduced to the Sherpas only eighty years ago but have now become the mainstay of their diet. In Khumbu, with its higher altitudes, farming gives way to pastoralism. Khumbu Sherpas raise cattle and the yak, a cattle-like animal that does well at higher elevations. Yaks provide wool and milk by-products such as butter, which are sold or bartered for grain. Hybrids of domestic cattle and the yak are are used as pack and plow animals.

Trade between Nepal and Tibet is of considerable historical importance in the region. Sherpas, because of their location and ability to handle high altitudes, have traditionally played a major role in the trade that moves through Nangpa La and other passes across the mountains. Salt, sheep's wool, meat, and yak are still brought from Tibet into Nepal, in exchange for food grains, rice, butter, and manufactured goods.

The Sherpas' reputation as excellent porters and guides on mountain-climbing and trekking expeditions has brought them a new source of income and, for some Sherpas, a comfortable living.

16 ● SPORTS

Sherpas enjoy playing cards and gambling with dice. Wrestling and horseplay is popular among both boys and girls.

17 ● RECREATION

Sherpa entertainment and recreation is largely limited to their traditional pastimes of singing, dancing, and drinking beer.

18 ● CRAFTS AND HOBBIES

Sherpas rely on the artisan castes to provide the material necessities of life. Some Sher-

pas have developed skills in religious painting and in liturgical (religious) chanting. The Sherpas have a tradition of indigenous folk songs and dancing.

19 ● SOCIAL PROBLEMS

Sherpa society has a high incidence of alcoholism and related medical problems. Similarly, although the situation is beginning to change, the lack of education among the Sherpas reflects to a large extent their isolation and the low level of development in Nepal as a whole. Tourism has provided many Sherpas with wealth, but serious environmental damage has occurred with its development. Inflation, increasing dependence on a tourist-based economy, problems with drug-running, and the migration of wealthy Sherpas to Kathmandu are all indications of a changing Sherpa society.

20 ● BIBLIOGRAPHY

Brower, Barbara. *Sherpa of Khumbu: People, Livestock, and Landscape.* Delhi, India: Oxford University Press, 1991.

Fürer-Haimendorf, Christoph von. *The Sherpas of Nepal: Buddhist Highlanders.* Berkeley and Los Angeles: University of California Press, 1964.

Ortner, Sherry B. *Sherpas Through Their Rituals.* Cambridge: Cambridge University Press, 1978.

Sherpa, Donna M. *Living in the Middle: Sherpas of the Mid-Range Himalayas.* Prospect Heights, Ill.: Waveland Press, 1994.

WEBSITES

Interknowledge Corporation. Nepal. [Online] Available http://www.interknowledge.com/nepal/, 1998.

World Travel Guide. Nepal. [Online] Available http://travelguide.attistel.co.uk/country/np/gen.html, 1998.

The Netherlands

The people of the Netherlands are called Netherlanders or Dutch. Ethnically, they are a unified people, but ethnic makeup changed slightly in the 1980s and 1990s when about 300,000 immigrants and returning Dutch arrived from from Indonesia, and more than 140,000 arrived from Suriname.

Netherlanders

PRONUNCIATION: NEH-thur-lann-duhrs
ALTERNATE NAMES: Dutch
LOCATION: The Netherlands
POPULATION: 15 million
LANGUAGE: Dutch
RELIGION: Roman Catholicism; Protestantism (including the Dutch Reformed Church); small populations of Muslims, Hindus, and Jews

1 ● INTRODUCTION

The Netherlands is a small, flat country located on the shores of the North Sea in western Europe. The whole country is often referred to as Holland, although this term is actually the name for certain provinces in the northwestern part of the country. Over many centuries, Netherlanders (also called "Dutch") literally built their nation by building dikes, dunes, and windmills to hold back the sea. Its coastal location has historically made it an important trading center. Through the efforts of the Dutch East India and Dutch West India trading companies in the seventeenth century, the Netherlands acquired colonial territories (people and land that they ruled) on every continent. In the seventeenth and eighteenth centuries, the Netherlands was one of the world's most powerful nations.

Meanwhile, scientists report that the nation's lowlands are sinking at the rate of 1.5 feet (45 centimeters) per century, and the North Sea is rising at a steady rate. Netherlanders cannot rest in their ongoing struggle against the sea.

2 ● LOCATION

The name "Netherlands" means "lowlands." Much of the western part of the country is *polders* (low-lying lands) that have been reclaimed from the sea by dikes and dunes.

NETHERLANDERS

0   100   200   300 Miles

0 100 200 300 Kilometers

NORWAY
Oslo

North
Sea

SWEDEN
Göteborg

DENMARK
København
(Copenhagen)

Newcastle
upon Tyne

UNITED
KINGDOM

Rostock
Hamburg

NETHERLANDS
Amsterdam

Berlin
Hannover

London

GERMANY

Brussels

Leipzig

BELGIUM

Rhein
Bonn

Le Havre

Frankfurt

Seine

LUXEMBOURG

Prague

Paris

Strasbourg

Stuttgart

Munich

FRANCE

AUSTRIA

Zürich

Thames

In addition, windmills, called "polder mills," pump excess underground water to keep these areas dry and farmable.

Most of the 15 million Netherlanders belong to the same ethnic group, descended from western and northern European tribes. Some diversity has been added by immigrants from the former Dutch colonies of Indonesia and Suriname, and foreign workers from Turkey, Morocco, and southern Europe. Throughout history, Netherlanders have been known for tolerance of different ethnic and religious groups. They welcomed Jews and Huguenots (French Protestants) in the sixteenth and seventeenth centuries. They played a role in helping Jews flee Nazi persecution in World War II (1939–45). The most famous of these Jewish refugees was Anne Frank. The famous *Diary of a Young*

Girl, kept by Anne during the war years, bears witness to the courage of ordinary Netherlanders who risked their lives attempting to save this German Jewish family.

3 ● LANGUAGE

Dutch, a Germanic language, is the official language in all twelve provinces of the Netherlands. It is the language in everyday use everywhere but in Friesland, where ancient Frisian is spoken. Dutch dialects can vary enough to make it difficult for speakers from different regions to understand each other.

COMMON WORDS

English	Dutch	Pronunciation
man	man	mahn
woman	vrouw	vrow
mother	moeder	MUD-ur
father	vader	VAD-ur
yes	ja	yah
no	nee	nay
right	rechts	rex
left	links	lehnks
breakfast	ontbijt	OHNT-bee-yet
lunch	middageten	MID-dog-ett-uhn
dinner	avondeten	A-vond-eff-uhn
milk	melk	mehlk
beer	fier	beer

4 ● FOLKLORE

Netherlands mythology is strongly linked to the sea and characters associated with it, such as mermaids and pirates. There is also a tradition of tales about devils who tempt people with riches in order to gain their souls. One of the popular subjects of these tales is the Devil, *Joost*. Over time, many popular tales, riddles, and rituals were suppressed (discouraged or banned) by wealthy townsfolk, but some survived as part of the country's Christian traditions. The Dutch

Father Christmas (named, like the American Santa Claus, for Saint Nicholas) is called Sinterklaas. He has a dark-faced assistant called Black Peter who is said to carry disobedient children to Spain in a sack.

5 ● RELIGION

An estimated 37 percent of Netherlanders are Roman Catholic. Thirty percent belong to six major Protestant groups, of which the largest is the Dutch Reformed Church. There are smaller populations of Muslims, Hindus, and Jews. Since the mid-nineteenth century, Netherlanders have practiced a kind of religious "apartheid," separating Protestant and Catholic schools, newspapers, political parties, radio stations, and other institutions. This system has weakened somewhat since the 1960s, but it still controls many facets of life in rural areas.

6 ● MAJOR HOLIDAYS

Legal holidays include New Year's Day (January 1), the Queen's birthday (April 30), Memorial Day (May 4), Liberation of the Netherlands (May 5), and Christmas (December 25–26). In addition, many Netherlanders observe the other standard holidays of the Christian calendar. Netherlanders are great celebrators of birthdays. On their birthdays, Netherlanders stay in bed late and family members come into the bedroom singing "Lang Zal Hij Leven" ("Long May He Live") for men and "Lang Zal Zij Leven" ("Long May She Live") for females. Gifts are presented, and the festivities continue at school or work, and, in the evening, with a party for family and friends. The Queen's birthday is considered an especially important occasion. It is marked by flag displays, parades, and girls wearing orange ribbons in their hair in honor of the royal family, the House of Orange. The Memorial Day holiday in the spring has two contrasting parts. At 8:00 PM on May 4, people throughout the country stop whatever they are doing to remember those who have died in war and to pray for peace. The next day, May 5, is a time of festivals and celebrations.

7 ● RITES OF PASSAGE

The Netherlands is a modern, industrialized, Christian country. Hence, many of the rites of passage that young people undergo are religious rituals, such as baptism, first communion, confirmation, and marriage. Religious minorities observe their own rituals. In addition, many families mark a student's progress through the education system with graduation parties.

8 ● RELATIONSHIPS

On the whole, Netherlanders are reserved people who do not speak readily to strangers. Public interaction, usually marked by close eye contact, is direct but formal. (Close friends, however, greet each other with a kiss on the cheek.) Restraint and moderation can be seen in many aspects of Netherlander life, from cars (medium-sized and -priced) to clothing (casual and plain). The primary Netherlander focus is on the family and on being *gezellig thuis* or "cozy at home." Popular Dutch sayings include:

Je krijgt de wind van voren
You'll face the wind. (Comparable to the American phrase "face the music.")

Ik roei met de riemen ik heb.
I'll row with the oars I have. (Similar to "I'll make the best of the situation.")

Gods molens malen langzaam.
God's mills grind slowly.

9 ● LIVING CONDITIONS

Traditionally, the Dutch have tried to make their homes *gezellig,* which means "homey" or "cozy." They favor knick-knacks such as colorful tiles and blue-and-white Delft porcelain. Most homes have colorful flower gardens in front. The Dutch national flower, the tulip, is grown in almost every garden. Due to the nation's high population density (many people living close together), Dutch cities suffer from overcrowding and housing shortages. Many people have taken to living in houseboats, usually converted barges. In the mid-1980s there were over 2,000 such boats anchored on the canals in the center of Amsterdam, about half of them illegally.

10 ● FAMILY LIFE

The Dutch place great value on family life. A traditional Dutch saying is *Eigen haard is goud waard* (Your own hearth [home] is worth gold). The nuclear family—called the *gezin*—has traditionally been at the center of Dutch life, especially since the nineteenth century. Since 1945, there has been an increase in the incidence of unmarried people living together, and these arrangements are widely accepted as common law marriages. The divorce rate has risen as well. Netherlanders tend to have small families and to give a great deal of care and attention to their children. Home birth has always been popular in the Netherlands.

11 ● CLOTHING

In everyday life, the Dutch wear typical, modern Western-style clothing for both formal and casual occasions. People who work outdoors often still wear the *klompen* (wooden shoes) popularly associated with the Dutch. Traditional folk costumes vary from region to region. Most feature baggy black pants and wide-brimmed hats for men. Women wear full black dresses with embroidered bodices and lace bonnets. The popular image of Netherlanders often includes a woman wearing wooden shoes and the white cap of the Volendam region with its high peak and wing-like folds at the sides. Traditional costumes may still be seen in Volendam and Marken, where they are a tourist attraction.

12 ● FOOD

Netherlander food is wholesome and simply prepared, often with butter but not thick sauces or strong spices. Seafood is widely eaten, especially herring. Dairy products are a dietary staple, and the Dutch are known worldwide for their cheeses, such as gouda and edam. Many desserts come with whipped cream, and popular beverages include tea, coffee, beer, and *Jenever*, a gin made from juniper berries.

The Netherlander breakfast and lunch are generally cold meals of sliced bread, meat, and cheese. Dinner is a large meal typically including soup and a main dish consisting of meat and vegetables. Popular snacks include french fries—*patat frites*—often served with mayonnaise or ketchup, and waffles smothered in whipped cream or caramel sauce.

Netherlanders are great cookie bakers (and eaters). Spice cookies, *Speculaas*, are embossed with windmills or Sinterklaas on horseback. Children also enjoy using the

---

Recipe

Speculaas
(Netherlander Christmas cookies)

Makes about 28 thin cookies.

Ingredients

$2/3$ cup butter or margarine
1 cup flour
1 egg
$1/2$ cup brown sugar
$1/8$ teaspoon cloves
$1/8$ teaspoon cinnamon
$1/8$ teaspoon allspice
Pinch of cardamom

Note: Use all four, or any combination of at least two, spices.

Directions

1. Using a fork or a pastry blender, combine butter and flour well until there are no large lumps of butter.

2. Add the egg and brown sugar and mix well.

3. Add the spices.

4. Spread the dough on a 14x17-inch cookie sheet. (It will be thin.) Chill for at least 2 hours or up to 24 hours, covered with plastic wrap.

5. Use a knife to cut a grid pattern on the dough, making 28 rectangular shapes 2x4 inches.

6. Stamp each cookie with a mold dipped in flour. Bake at 350°F for about 10 minutes.

Adapted from Rombauer, Irma S. and Marion Rombauer Becker. *The Joy of Cooking.* Indianapolis, Ind.: Bobbs/Merrill, 1972.

---

dough to make letterbankets, number or letter shapes, with the cookie dough.

13 ● EDUCATION

Netherlanders are a well-educated people with virtually no illiteracy. Schooling is compulsory (required) between the ages of six and sixteen. At the age of twelve, students take an exam that qualifies them to enter either general, pre-university, or vocational school. (It is generally possible to change schools at a later time.) At the age of sixteen, school certificate exams are taken in a variety of subjects. Students in the pre-university (often called "gymnasium") track can advance automatically to a university at the age of eighteen. Others must take an exam. Higher education is offered at eight universities and five technical institutes.

14 ● CULTURAL HERITAGE

The seventeenth century was the golden age of Dutch painting. Especially famous are the work of such masters as Rembrandt van Rijn, Jan Vermeer, and Jacob van Ruisdael. These works depict everyday scenes of middle-class life. The great nineteenth-century painter Vincent van Gogh was born and lived most of his life in the Netherlands. (He moved to Arles, France, two years before his death in 1890.) The twentieth-century *De Stijl* movement, which advocated simplicity, is represented in the works of Piet Mondrian and Theo van Doesburg. The Netherlands was home to two great phi-

Susan D. Rock

Cheese auction at Alkmaar, Netherlands, Dairy products are a dietary staple, and the Dutch are known worldwide for their cheeses, the most popular being Gouda, which is round and flat, and Edam, which is shaped like a ball.

losophers, Desiderius Erasmus in the fifteenth century, and Baruch Spinoza in the seventeenth. The nineteenth-century novel Max Havelaar, by Edouard Douwes Dekker, caused a public outcry over Dutch treatment of the people in its colonies. The novel led to eventual government reforms.

15 ● EMPLOYMENT

The Netherlander economy expanded from 1945 until 1973, when economic growth slowed due to rising world oil prices. Over the next decade unemployment skyrocketed. Eight percent of the work force were unemployed in 1991. The main industry of the twentieth century has been the production of petrochemicals. Agriculture, which accounts for only 4 percent of workers, is still an important part of the national economy. Many Netherlanders specialize in dairy farming and flower-growing. It is common in the Netherlands to go into the family business and eventually take it over from the older generation. About 40 percent of the labor force is female. Foreign workers, who first entered the country in large numbers in the 1960s, perform low-paying, unskilled work.

16 ● SPORTS

At least 4 million people belong to sports clubs. The largest is the Royal Netherlands

Football (soccer) Association, which claims about a million members. The Netherlands won the European soccer championship in 1988. Other popular sports are tennis (with some 500,000 enthusiasts), swimming, and hockey. In Friesland, the Frisians enjoy some unique pastimes around the canals.

17 ● RECREATION

Netherlanders enjoy many forms of outdoor recreation. Fishing is popular, as are boating, sailing, and camping. Throughout the country, bicycles are used for recreational outings and races, as well as transportation. Winter sports include skating, curling, ice boating, and many kinds of races and endurance tests. Netherlanders also enjoy wind-assisted skating, performed wearing a kite-like triangular sail on one's back. As many as 17,000 people compete in the 125-mile (200-kilometer) Elfstedentocht skating race over frozen canals connecting eleven towns in Friesland. (However, in many years temperatures do not drop low enough for this event to be held.) Another traditional sport popular in Friesland is *fierljeppen*, a form of pole-vaulting.

18 ● CRAFTS AND HOBBIES

Traditional Dutch crafts include pottery, tile work, glassware, and silver. The famous blue-and-white Delft pottery has been produced in the city of that name since 1653. Plates, vases, pitchers, and many other decorative pieces are still made. Workers enter the trade at age sixteen or seventeen and receive eight years of training. The designs were originally copied from fine Chinese porcelain that entered Holland during the seventeenth century.

19 ● SOCIAL PROBLEMS

The generous Netherlands program of social benefits has been abused by people claiming sickness or disability. In the early 1990s, one-fourth of Amsterdam's population was living on welfare. There are often strict educational requirements for employment. As a result, the Dutch economy suffers both from high unemployment and a labor shortage. Absenteeism at work is also a problem. Overcrowding in cities has resulted in the illegal occupation of buildings by squatters (people who neither own nor pay rent for the place where they live). Amsterdam is one of Europe's main entry points for illegal drugs. As of the late 1990s, the government was addressing the resulting drug problem with strong antidrug laws.

20 ● BIBLIOGRAPHY

Catling, Christopher. *Amsterdam. Insight Guides.* Singapore: APA Press, 1991.

Fradin, Dennis. *The Netherlands. Enchantment of the World Series.* Chicago: Children's Press, 1983.

Kristensen, Preben, and Fiona Cameron. *We Live in the Netherlands.* New York: Bookwright Press, 1986.

Moss, Joyce, and George Wilson. *Peoples of the World: Western Europeans.* Detroit: Gale Research, 1993.

Netherlands in Pictures. Minneapolis, Minn.: Lerner Publications Co., 1991.

van Stegeren, Theo. *The Land and People of the Netherlands.* New York: HarperCollins, 1991.

WEBSITES

Embassy of the Netherlands, Washington, D.C. [Online] Available http://www.netherlands-embassy.org/, 1998.

Netherlands Board of Tourism. [Online] Available http://www.goholland.com/, 1998.

World Travel Guide. [Online] Available http://travelguide.attistel.co.uk/country/nl/gen.html, 1998.

Frisians

PRONUNCIATION: FREE-zhuhns
LOCATION: The Netherlands
POPULATION: 600,000
LANGUAGE: Dutch; Frisian; English; French; German
RELIGION: Protestant; Mennonite

1 ● INTRODUCTION

The Frisians live in Friesland, one of the Netherlands' northern provinces. They value their independence as a unique ethnic group. Friesland is the only province of the Netherlands to retain its own language. Like the other low-lying parts of the Netherlands, Friesland struggles to protect its land from flooding. It owes its existence to dikes (artificially constructed mounds of earth) extending the length of the coastline, and to windmills—the most famous of Dutch symbols—that drain the land.

Under the Treaty of Utrecht, in 1579, Friesland joined with the six other northern provinces, including Holland, to form the "Seven United Provinces," the forerunner of the modern Netherlands. Friesland maintained a high degree of regional autonomy (independence) within the union. Friesland became part of the Kingdom of the Netherlands established at the Congress of Vienna in 1814.

2 ● LOCATION

Friesland is one of the northernmost provinces of the Netherlands. It is bounded on the west, southwest, and north by water, and on the east and south by other provinces. It has an area of 1,297 square miles (3,357 square kilometers), most of it below sea level. This land was reclaimed from the sea about 2,000 years ago. There is a continuing struggle against storms and flooding. In addition to the waters of its long coastline, Friesland has some thirty inland lakes. Friesland's population is approximately 600,000 people. Most Frisians live their entire lives in Friesland, but some have migrated to other parts of the Netherlands as well as to Germany, Denmark, and North America.

3 ● LANGUAGE

Dutch is the official language in Friesland, as in the rest of the Netherlands. About half of Friesland's 600,000 residents speak both Dutch and Frisian. Frisian is a Germanic language similar to both Dutch and English. Most Frisian speakers use the language at home, and speak Dutch in the workplace and other public settings. It is also common to combine the two languages into a hybrid (mixture) called "town Frisian." Many Netherlanders—including Frisians—speak (or at least understand) English, French, and German, all taught in the secondary schools. The fishing village of Hindelopen is unusual in that it has its own dialect. With a population of 900, it is believed to be the smallest town in the world to publish its own dictionary.

4 ● FOLKLORE

Friesland has a large body of folklore that has survived from pre-Christian times. Popular tales and superstitions feature a variety of devils, ghosts, witches, elves, wizards, and trolls. There are also female spirits who either help or harm travelers. According to a popular folk belief, funeral processions should follow a winding path to confuse the spirit of the deceased so it will not be able to return and haunt the living. For the same reason, the coffin is traditionally carted around the cemetery three times before being buried.

"The Seven Wishes" is a traditional Frisian folktale. The story is set in a time when the land was populated by Little People, including an old fisherman named Jan and his wife, Tryn. One day Jan caught a magic silver fish that promised him seven wishes, on condition that he choose wisely. The humble fisherman's only desire was for a new boat because his old one was about to fall apart. However, his wife got carried away by greed, demanding a new house, furnishings, servants, and other luxuries. Finally, she demanded absolute power, and the fish took away everything it had given them. The old woman learned her lesson. The couple realized that what truly mattered to each of them was the other, and they contentedly returned to their modest existence.

5 ● RELIGION

Protestantism is the majority religion in Friesland. About 85 percent of Frisians belong to one of two Calvinist churches—the Dutch Reformed Church, or the Reformed Church. Five percent of Frisians are Mennonites. Some Frisians still hold certain pre-Christian beliefs (called *byleauwe*). These date back to the period before the introduction of Christianity to Friesland by the Franks (a Germanic tribe) in the eighth and ninth centuries AD.

6 ● MAJOR HOLIDAYS

Frisians observe the Dutch legal holidays: New Year's Day (January 1), the Queen's birthday (April 30), Memorial Day (May 4), National Liberation Day (May 5), and Christmas (December 25–26). They also observe other standard holidays of the Christian calendar, including Good Friday, Holy Saturday, Easter Monday, Ascension, and Whitmonday. Easter is considered an especially important holiday. It is observed with a special dinner and an Easter egg hunt similar to those in the United States. The Queen's birthday is another important occasion, marked by flag displays and parades. On this day girls wear orange ribbons in their hair in honor of the royal family, the House of Orange. Frisians, like other Dutch people, observe Christmas by attending church services. In the Netherlands, the gift-giving that people in other countries associate with Christmas takes place on December 6. This day is devoted to St. Nicholas (*Sinterklaes,* the Dutch equivalent of Santa Claus). According to tradition, St. Nicholas and his helper, called Black Peter, sail to the Netherlands from Spain to give children candy and other gifts.

7 ● RITES OF PASSAGE

Frisians live in a modern, industrialized, Christian country. Hence, many of the rites of passage that young people undergo are religious rituals. These include baptism, first communion, confirmation, and marriage. In addition, many families mark a student's progress through the education system with graduation parties.

8 ● RELATIONSHIPS

The shared perpetual struggle against the sea has given Frisians a strong sense of community. This is expressed in the concept of *buorreplicht* (neighbor's duty). Helping one's neighbors in times of trouble was so necessary to survival that it was actually a formal law under emperor Charlemagne (742–814) in the Middle Ages (AD 768–814). The sense of communal responsibility has survived as a tradition. Relations with one's neighbors have even more importance than kinship (family ties) in holding Frisian communities together. Like their neighbors in the northern province of Groningen, Frisians tend to be seen as unsophisticated by Netherlanders living in the southern part of the country.

9 ● LIVING CONDITIONS

The traditional old-fashioned Frisian farm house consists of modest-sized living quarters. These are connected to a barn by a narrow section containing a kitchen, milk cellar, and butter-churning area. The living quarters are generally divided into an all-purpose family room and a formal parlor where visitors are received. Tile roofs have largely replaced the older thatched roofs.

10 ● FAMILY LIFE

The nuclear family—called the *gezin*—plays a central role in Dutch life. However, there has been an increase in the number of unmarried couples living together since 1950. This trend, known as "homing," is as common in Friesland as in other regions. The divorce rate for Frisians is also similar to that elsewhere in the Netherlands, as is the growing number of single-parent families. Instead of the elaborate church weddings of the past, many Frisians today have a civil (nonreligious) wedding. The average age at marriage has risen. More young people are choosing to complete their higher education before starting a family.

11 ● CLOTHING

Like other Dutch people, the Frisians wear modern Western-style clothing for both casual and formal occasions. One difference, however, is their preference for wooden shoes. They wear the modern variety, made of lightweight poplar (a kind of wood) and generally painted black with leather trim.

12 ● FOOD

Frisians prefer wholesome, simply prepared food, often cooked in butter. Dietary staples include seafood and dairy products, including the world-famous Dutch cheeses like gouda and edam. Desserts are often served with whipped cream, and popular beverages include tea, coffee, and beer. The Frisians eat a typical Dutch breakfast of sliced bread, meat, and cheese. Lunch generally consists of bread with jam and butter, cold meat, and buttermilk. A large dinner, served at about 6:00 PM, typically includes soup and a main dish containing meat and vegetables. French fries *(patat frites)*—typically served with mayonnaise or ketchup—are popular snacks, as are waffles smothered in whipped cream or caramel sauce.

13 ● EDUCATION

As in the rest of the Netherlands, students in Friesland must attend school from the ages of six to sixteen. The Frisian language is taught in the public schools, but not in the Christian private schools. At the age of twelve, all Dutch students take an exam that qualifies them for either a general, a pre-university, or a vocational school. At the age of sixteen, they take school certificate exams in a variety of subjects. There are no universities in Friesland, but higher education is offered at eight Dutch universities and five technical institutes.

14 ● CULTURAL HERITAGE

Friesland has enjoyed relative autonomy (self-rule) for much of its history. This has given its people a strong sense of ethnic and cultural identity, reinforced by the preservation of their language, folklore, and folk art.

The town of Franeker houses the world's oldest planetarium, built in the 1770s by Eise Eisenga in his own home. Eisenga's model accurately demonstrates the movement of the planets (except for Uranus, which had not been discovered yet). It has needed only minor adjustments since it was built over 200 years ago.

15 ● EMPLOYMENT

The economy of Friesland is based primarily on agriculture. Many Frisians living in inland areas work on small family farms, raising crops or dairy cattle. The dairy products, construction, and tourist industries are also important employers.

16 ● SPORTS

Popular sports in Friesland include cycling, sailing, canoeing, and ice skating. Friesland is also home to the famous Elfstedentocht skating race, held once every five or six years, when it is cold enough for all the region's canals to freeze over. As many as 20,000 people skate a 125-mile (200-kilometer) course over the frozen canals connecting Friesland's eleven towns. Another traditional sport popular in Friesland is *fierljeppen*, pole-vaulting across the canals in the warmer months.

17 ● RECREATION

Frisians enjoy spending much of their leisure time outdoors. Favorite activities include camping, hiking, and a variety of sports. One pastime unique to Friesland is *wadlopen* ("mudwalking") across the salt flats and mud of the shallow Waddenzee at low tide. This unusual activity provides vigorous exercise as well as an opportunity for birdwatching. Wadlopen is often undertaken in organized group outings. Socializing at the weekly livestock market in Tjouwert serves as informal recreation for many Frisians.

18 ● CRAFTS AND HOBBIES

Frisian craftspeople are renowned for their tile work, pottery, and embroidery. Friesland is also noted for the unique folk art that goes into the creation of *ûlebuorden* (owl boards). These are elaborately decorated barn gables that include carved swans. They have holes through which owls can fly in and out of the barn. Once a functional creation, ûlebuorden are now considered decorative artifacts.

19 ● SOCIAL PROBLEMS

Frisians experience many of the social problems found in all modern, industrialized countries, such as increasing drug use among young people and rising incidence of crime.

20 ● BIBLIOGRAPHY

Catling, Christopher, ed. *The Netherlands. Insight Guides.* Boston: Houghton Mifflin, 1991.

Gall, Timothy, and Susan Gall, ed. *Worldmark Encyclopedia of the Nations.* Detroit: Gale Research, 1995.

Gratton, Nancy E. "Frisians." *Encyclopedia of World Cultures.* Boston: G. K. Hall, 1992.

Mahmood, Cynthia Keppley. *Frisian and Free: Study of an Ethnic Minority of the Netherlands.* Prospect Heights, Ill.: Waveland Press, 1989.

Spicer, Dorothy Gladys. *The Owl's Nest: Folktales from Friesland.* New York: Coward-McCann, 1968.

Van Stegeren, Theo. *The Land and People of the Netherlands.* New York: HarperCollins, 1991.

WEBSITES

Embassy of the Netherlands, Washington, D.C. [Online] Available http://www.netherlands-embassy.org/, 1998.

Netherlands Board of Tourism. [Online] Available http://www.goholland.com/, 1998.

World Travel Guide. [Online] Available http://www.wtgonline.com/country/nl/gen.html, 1998.

New Zealand

The people of New Zealand are called New Zealanders. About 80 percent of the population is classified as European; the majority are of British descent. Almost 15 percent of the population report Maori (native) ancestry. The Maori are a Polynesian group with a distinctive culture and a well-ordered social system. The non-Maori Polynesian population is about 4 percent. Chinese and Indians total almost 1 percent of the population.

New Zealanders

PRONUNCIATION: new ZEE-lun-duhrs
ALTERNATE NAMES: Kiwi (nickname)
LOCATION: New Zealand
POPULATION: 3.4 million
LANGUAGE: English; Maori
RELIGION: Christianity (Church of England, Presbyterian, Roman Catholic, and Methodist); New Zealand Christian sects (Ratana and Ringatu); Hinduism; Judaism

1 ● INTRODUCTION

New Zealand is an island nation in the southwestern Pacific Ocean. It is separated from Australia by the Tasman Sea. New Zealand was a British colony until 1907 and did not achieve full independence from Great Britain until 1947.

New Zealand's original inhabitants, the Maori, migrated from Polynesian islands in three separate waves between AD 950 and 1350. The first European to discover New Zealand was Abel Tasman, a navigator for the Dutch East India Company, in 1642. In the 1790s, the islands began to attract whalers from Europe who established the first settlements on the coast. In 1814, the first missionary station was set up in the Bay of Islands.

Europeans and Australians began arriving in New Zealand in large numbers in the 1830s. In 1840, the Maori chieftains entered into a compact with them, the Treaty of Waitangi. Under this agreement the Maori granted sovereignty (authority) over their land to Britain's Queen Victoria while retaining territorial rights, and New Zealand became a British colony. More settlers arrived after gold was discovered in 1861. After the Maori Wars (1860–70), resulting largely from disputes over land rights and sovereignty, New Zealand rapidly increased

high-level contacts with the New Zealand government, a ban that was removed (annulled) in 1990.

In December 1989, New Zealand established a Cabinet-level committee to create a government policy for extensive Maori land claims.

2 ● LOCATION

New Zealand is situated in the southwest Pacific Ocean. It is about the size of the state of Colorado. New Zealand consists of two main islands—North Island and South Island—and several dozen minor ones. Most of its large cities, including the capital city of Wellington, are located on North Island. North Island is also known for its two active volcanoes. South Island is the larger of the two islands and the location of the scenic Southern Alps.

Over 85 percent of New Zealand's population is of European (mostly British) descent. The Maori, New Zealand's first inhabitants, are the country's most significant minority group. They represent close to 10 percent of the population. People of non-Maori Polynesian descent, as well as those with Chinese, Indian, and southeast Asian ancestry, account for the remainder of New Zealand's population.

3 ● LANGUAGE

English is the universal language of New Zealand. However, Maori, a Polynesian language, is still spoken by the Maoris and taught in Maori schools. New Zealand English resembles British English in a number of ways. In addition, New Zealanders have many unique words and expressions of their own. Both males and females are

in wealth and population. With the introduction of refrigerated shipping in 1882, New Zealand became one of the world's great exporters of dairy, produce, and meat. In 1907, New Zealand was made a Dominion (territory) of Great Britain. In 1947, the New Zealand government formally claimed complete independence while remaining a member of the British Commonwealth.

Since 1984 New Zealand has actively pursued an antinuclear policy. It refused to admit a U.S. warship to one of its ports because of the possibility that there were nuclear arms on board. In 1986 the United States responded by canceling its military obligations to New Zealand under a 1951 agreement. The United States also banned addressed informally as "mate." The word "she" is used for "it" in a very general sense, as in "she'll be right," which means "everything will be all right."

COMMON ENGLISH WORDS AND PHRASES

New Zealand	American English
bach or crib	cottage or vacation house
fizzy	soda pop
mob	herd of sheep or cattle
rousterer	professional sheep shearer
panel beater	auto body shop
hogget	year-old lamb
gumboots	rubber rain boots
hotel	public bar
mozzies	mosquitoes
peckish	slightly hungry
prang	car or bicycle accident
sandshoes	sneakers

MAORI WORDS AND PHRASES

Maori	English
Aotearoa	land of the long white cloud (Maori name for New Zealand)
aroha	love and understanding for others
Maoritanga	the Maori tradition and way of life
marae	a Maori meeting house or the area surrounding it
pakeha	a white, or non-Maori, New Zealander

4 ● FOLKLORE

Guy Fawkes Day, an institution with English roots, is celebrated by burning an effigy of Guy Fawkes. In 1605 Fawkes was discovered lurking in the cellar of the Parliament building in London with barrels of gunpowder, waiting to blow up Parliament as it opened in the morning. In parts of New Zealand, children recite Guy Fawkes rhymes in a type of competition. Adults throw pennies to the children who recite the loudest or the best. Sometimes, certain adults heat pennies on a shovel held over a fire before throwing them. The anxious children pick up the hot pennies, regardless of the burns they receive. Some children carry painful reminders of Guy Fawkes Day for weeks.

The Maori have a rich folklore tradition that is reflected in their native art, song, and dance. Some of their legends involving journeys contain highly detailed and accurate descriptions of New Zealand's terrain and of the surrounding waters.

5 ● RELIGION

The majority of New Zealanders are Christian. Most of the population belongs to one of four main churches: the Church of England, the Presbyterian Church, the Roman Catholic Church, and the Methodist Church. There are many other Protestant groups, two Christian sects native to New Zealand (Ratana and Ringatu), and small communities of Hindus and Jews. About one-fourth of New Zealanders do not belong to any religious denomination.

6 ● MAJOR HOLIDAYS

Nationwide legal holidays in New Zealand include Christmas and Boxing Day (December 25 and 26), Easter, New Year's Day (January 1), and Labor Day (the fourth Monday in October). The official birthday of Britain's current queen, Elizabeth, is celebrated on the first Monday in June. A holiday unique to New Zealand is Anzac Day (April 25). On that day, New Zealanders and Australians who died in both world wars are honored at dawn services throughout the country. Another date with national significance is Waitangi Day (February 6), commemorating the signing of the Treat of Waitangi between the Maori and Great Britain in 1840.

7 ● RITES OF PASSAGE

Rituals marking major life events such as birth, marriage, and death are generally observed within the Christian religious tradition.

8 ● RELATIONSHIPS

New Zealanders like to refer to themselves as "kiwis." The name is derived from the kiwi, a rare flightless bird unique to their country. (The kiwi fruit, originally known as the Chinese gooseberry, was renamed to reflect its connection with New Zealand. However, the popularity of the name kiwi comes from the bird, not the fruit.) People from New Zealand also refer to themselves as "En Zedders," a name based on the abbreviation "NZ" ("Z" is pronounced "zed" in New Zealand, as it is in Britain). The Maori word *pakeha* is used for New Zealanders of European descent.

A common greeting among New Zealanders is "good day," pronounced so that it sounds like "geday." New Zealanders often address each other informally as "mate," reflecting the British ancestry of many of the country's inhabitants. The Maoris have a traditional greeting, called *hongi*, in which they touch faces so that their noses are pressed together. It is believed that their spirits mingle through this gesture.

9 ● LIVING CONDITIONS

Most people in New Zealand live in single houses with large yards and flower or vegetable gardens. The average home has three bedrooms, a living room, dining room, kitchen, laundry, bathroom, and garage. Most are built of wood and have sheet-iron or tiled roofs. Besides the garden, a common sight outside a New Zealand house is a clothes-drying rack covered with laundry spinning in the wind. Most families own their own homes. However, high-rise apartment buildings can be found in the major cities. More than half of the total housing stock has been constructed since 1957.

10 ● FAMILY LIFE

Most families in New Zealand have two or three children and enjoy a high standard of living. Many own a home with three or four bedrooms and an attached garage.

Maori families are larger than those of the *pakeha,* or white, population. Maori households may include relatives besides the nuclear family, such as grandparents, uncles, and aunts.

11 ● CLOTHING

New Zealanders wear modern Western-style clothing. They prefer to dress casually. Men in white-collar jobs sometimes even wear shorts, knee socks, white shirts, and ties to work.

Maoris generally dress like other New Zealanders, but still wear their traditional costumes for special occasions. The most distinctive feature of these costumes is the striped, fringed skirt woven from flax that is worn by both men and women. Women wear

Susan D. Rock

Houses on a New Zealand hillside.

them over brightly colored dresses. Over their dresses the women may also wear long white capes decorated with black fringes.

12 ● FOOD

New Zealanders eat three main meals a day. Breakfast consists of eggs, sausage, and bacon. Lunch is typically a meat pie, hamburger, or sandwich. Dinner is a full meal generally featuring some type of meat dish, often lamb. The most popular traditional dinner entree is roast lamb with mint sauce, typically served with roasted potatoes, roast kumara (New Zealand's sweet potato), and roast pumpkin. In addition, it is common to have a midmorning snack called "morning tea" and a bedtime snack called "supper." British-style afternoon tea is still popular, complete with scones, cakes, and other pastries, especially when entertaining guests.

The most famous Maori culinary tradition is the *hangi*. The hangi is a feast that may only be prepared in the regions of the country where there are hot springs. A pit is dug in the ground and filled with rocks, and meat and vegetables are placed into it. The food is left to steam for several hours. The hangi is offered by resort hotels in the northern part of the North Island, where the traditional meal is enjoyed by tourists.

13 ● EDUCATION

New Zealanders are a well-educated people. The adult literacy rate (ability to read and write) is 99 percent. Education is free and required for children between the ages of six and fifteen. Most state schools are coeducational, but some private schools are not. For children in isolated areas, a public correspondence school enables them to send their homework assignments by mail.

In some regions there are special state schools for Maori children, but most Maori children attend public schools.

Young people may leave school at age fifteen to work. However, most stay in school through the eleventh grade (called the "fifth form"), earning a school certificate. Students planning to attend college continue their secondary education until the age of seventeen or eighteen, when they take university qualifying exams. New Zealand has six universities.

14 ● CULTURAL HERITAGE

New Zealand enjoys the rich cultural heritage provided by both its Maori and European traditions. In recent years, Maori weaving and woodcarving have enjoyed a revival. Many galleries and museums display Maori art. The Maori also preserve their traditional songs and dances.

Since World War II (1939–45), a lively art scene has grown up in New Zealand. Leading artists include Frances Hodgkins, Colin McCahon, and Sir Toss Woollaston. Well-known authors include acclaimed short story writer Katherine Mansfield, as well as Frank Sargeson, Janet Frame, and Sylvia Ashton-Warner. Native New

Zealander Kiri Te Kanawa is an internationally acclaimed opera singer. New Zealand's motion picture industry, assisted and promoted by the New Zealand Film Commission, has produced a number of internationally known movies. Notable films of the 1990s include *The Piano*, *Once Were Warriors*, and *Heavenly Creatures*.

15 ● EMPLOYMENT

In 1992, New Zealand had a civilian work force of 1.5 million people. Roughly 28 percent were employed in community or personal services, 20 percent in wholesale or retail trade, 16 percent in manufacturing, and 10 percent in agriculture. Unemployment grew in the early 1990s due to slow economic growth. In 1992, there were 160 registered trade unions. Since 1977 employers have been required to pay men and women the same minimum wage.

16 ● SPORTS

New Zealanders enjoy many kinds of sports. Rugby, a game similar to football in the United States, is the national game. The national team, called the All Blacks (a name that refers to their uniform), plays teams from Australia, France, Britain, and other countries, and is known throughout the world. Cricket is also very popular, as are a variety of water sports including sailing, surfing, kayaking, canoeing, and rafting. Bruce Kendall, a New Zealander, won an Olympic gold medal in yacht racing in 1988. In 1995, New Zealand won the coveted America's Cup yachting trophy. In the winter, skiing is a favorite pastime in New Zealand, where the ski season runs from June to late October.

17 ● RECREATION

Almost every household in New Zealand has a television set. New Zealanders enjoy watching both local programming and popular shows from Britain and the United States. Camping is a universal summertime activity among New Zealanders. Beach houses (called "bachs" or "cribs") are also popular vacation spots. Most family trips are taken during summer vacations from school, which run from late December to early February.

18 ● CRAFTS AND HOBBIES

The Maoris are known for their weaving and their intricate woodcarving, a skill that is passed from one generation to the next. Other New Zealand crafts include stained glass, glass blowing, and pottery.

19 ● SOCIAL PROBLEMS

Free market reform policies instituted by New Zealand's government since the mid-1980s have lowered inflation and increased economic growth. However, they have also resulted in high unemployment and led to cutbacks in educational spending and social services. New Zealand, a country proud of its traditionally egalitarian ways, has seen a growing division between rich and poor. There have also been rising tensions between the Maori and pakeha (white) populations, and an increase in violent crime.

20 ● BIBLIOGRAPHY

Fox, Mary Virginia. *New Zealand*. Chicago: Children's Press, 1991.

Hawke, G. R. *The Making of New Zealand*. Cambridge: Cambridge University Press, 1985.

Keyworth, Valerie. *New Zealand: Land of the Long White Cloud*. Minneapolis, Minn.: Dillon Press, 1990.

King, Jane. *New Zealand Handbook*. Chico, Calif.: Moon Publications, 1990.

Lealand, Geoffrey. *A Foreign Egg in Our Nest?: American Popular Culture in New Zealand*. Wellington, New Zealand: Victoria University Press, 1988.

McLauchlan, Gordon, ed. *The Illustrated Encyclopedia of New Zealand*. Auckland, New Zealand: D. Bateman, 1992.

The Oxford Illustrated History of New Zealand. New York: Oxford University Press, 1990.

WEBSITES

Embassy of New Zealand, Washington, D.C. [Online] Available http://www.emb.com/nzemb/, 1998.

World Travel Guide. New Zealand. [Online] Available http://www.wtgonline.com/country/nz/gen.html, 1998.

Maori

PRONUNCIATION: MOW-ree
LOCATION: New Zealand
POPULATION: Approximately 525,000
LANGUAGE: Maori; English
RELIGION: Christianity; traditional Maori, based on ancestor worship

1 ● INTRODUCTION

The ancestors of the present-day Maori created an outpost of Polynesian culture on the North and South islands of New Zealand. They remained relatively isolated from external contact until 1769. In that year, English navigator and explorer Captain James Cook (1728–79) initiated a permanent European presence in New Zealand. As a result, Maori culture would be dramatically changed in less than a century.

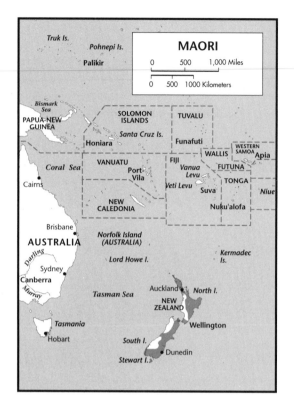

MAORI

0   500   1,000 Miles

0   500   1000 Kilometers

In 1840, some 500 Maori chiefs signed the so-called Treaty of Waitangi with the British government. The treaty promised the Maoris that they would keep their lands and property and have equal treatment under the law as British subjects. However, the British later seized Maori lands and made the people move to reservations. As a result of war and disease, the Maori population fell drastically by 1896. Since World War II (1939–45), the government's policies have been more favorable to the Maoris. In recent years, the government of New Zealand has acknowledged its responsibility to the Maoris after a series of protests and court rulings. In October 1996, the government agreed to a settlement with the Maoris that included land and cash worth $117 million,

with the Maoris regaining some traditional fishing rights. The Maori have been striving to revive aspects of their traditional culture, reclaim artifacts of their cultural history from foreign museums, and regain their ancestral homelands.

As of 1997, the Maori of New Zealand numbered close to 525,000 people, or about 15 percent of New Zealand's total population. The term "Maori" refers to a number of different tribal and subtribal groups that view themselves and each other as very distinct.

2 ● LOCATION

The islands of New Zealand are the present-day homeland of the Maori. New Zealand consists of two islands: the North Island and the South Island. The North Island is hilly with areas of flat, rolling terrain. The South Island is larger and more mountainous. Prior to the arrival of humans, both islands were densely forested.

Archaeologists refer to two branches of Maori: the archaic, and the traditional. The archaic Maori were probably the original inhabitants of New Zealand. They relied on the moa, a large, flightless bird that they hunted into extinction. Their culture dates back to around AD 1000. The traditional Maori are believed to have migrated to the North Island around the fourteenth century. The original homeland of the traditional Maori was in the Society Islands of Polynesia. Maori migrants left there to escape warfare and the demands of excessive *tribute* (taxes).

3 ● LANGUAGE

Maori belongs to the Tahitic branch of the Eastern Polynesian language group. (Eastern Polynesian is, in turn, a branch of the larger Austronesian language family.) Prior to European colonization of New Zealand, there were two distinct Maori dialects: North Island Maori; and South Island Maori, which is now extinct. The Maori of today speak English. Preschools that offer instruction in Maori language have sprung up all over the country at a rapid rate as a result of Maori activism.

4 ● FOLKLORE

Traditional Maori folklore describes an original couple, *Rangi* (sky) and *Papa* (earth). These two were locked in sexual union until the god Tane was able to push them apart and provide for the creation of human life. Maori folklore focuses on oppositions between pairs, such as earth and sky, life and death, and male and female.

5 ● RELIGION

Like other New Zealanders, many Maori today are Christian (primarily Anglican, Presbyterian, and Roman Catholic). Before contact with outside cultures, Maori religion was based on the important concepts of *mana* and *tapu.* Mana is an impersonal force that can be both inherited and acquired by individuals in the course of their lives. Tapu refers to sacredness that was assigned by status at birth. There was a direct relation between the two: chiefs with the most mana were also the most tapu. The English word "taboo" derives from this general Polynesian word and concept of a mysterious superhuman force. Ancestor worship was important in traditional religion.

6 ● MAJOR HOLIDAYS

Christian Maori celebrate the major Christian holidays as do other New Zealanders. Holidays as Westerners view them did not exist in Maori society before contact with other cultures. Rituals were performed according to the religious calendar and the harvest and collection of foodstuffs.

A controversial New Zealand national holiday for the Maori is Waitangi Day (February 6). This holiday commemorates the 1840 signing of the treaty that was supposed to guarantee their rights and privileges. In 1994, Maori radicals disrupted the Waitangi Day national celebration, forcing the government to cancel the festivities.

7 ● RITES OF PASSAGE

Modern Maori rites of passage are similar to those of other New Zealanders. Specific Maori traditions are still practiced at certain events. At weddings, for example, a relative of the groom traditionally challenges the father of the bride to a fight. The bride's father then approaches the challenger and is instead warmly greeted.

The Maori once practiced what anthropologists call "secondary burial." When a person died, the body would be laid out on ceremonial mats for viewing by relatives and other members of the village. After a few days, the body was wrapped in mats and placed in a cave or a tree, or buried in the ground. After one year had passed, the body was removed from the primary burial and the bones were cleaned and painted with red ochre (a pigment). These remains were taken from village to village for a second period of mourning. Following that, the bones were buried in a sacred place.

8 ● RELATIONSHIPS

Maoris today, like other New Zealanders, typically address each other informally and emphasize friendliness in relationships. Maori customs—practices before the Maoris came into contact with other cultures—were taken less seriously by the 1990s.

One such Maori custom, called *hakari* (feasting), was an important aspect of Maori culture. The Maori feasts brought together a number of different families and other social groups. A man of status would provide food and gifts for those who attended. In the end, he and his family would be left with very little in the way of material possessions or reserves of food. However, his status would have been increased enormously.

Premarital sexual relationships were considered normal for Maori adolescents. Both males and females were expected to have a series of private relationships before they married. When Maori females became sexually active, they were to publicly acknowledge this so that they could become tattooed. Tattooing marked their ritual and public passage into adulthood. It was also considered extremely attractive and erotic.

The Maoris have a traditional greeting, called *hongi,* in which they touch faces so that their noses are pressed together. It is believed that their spirits mingle through this gesture.

9 ● LIVING CONDITIONS

Today, 80 percent of the Maori live in the urban areas of New Zealand. However, until the 1920s, they lived almost entirely in rural areas. Maori housing today therefore typically reflects that of other urban New Zealanders.

Traditionally, Maoris in coastal areas relied on travel by canoes. These included single-hulled canoes as well as large double-hulled canoes. *Waka taua* were large Maori war canoes that were powered by both sail and paddles. As with other New Zealanders, travel today is by modern road, rail, water, and air transport.

10 ● FAMILY LIFE

Since most Maoris live in urban industrialized areas, family life is similar to that of other urban New Zealanders. Intermarriage between Maoris and *Pakehas* (the Maori term for whites) is common. Most Maoris have Pakeha cousins or other Pakeha relatives. Maori households may include relatives besides the nuclear family, such as grandparents, uncles, and aunts.

The system of referring to members of the immediate and extended family in Maori culture differs from that found in American culture. In the Maori system, a person's brothers, as well as the male cousins on both the mother's and father's side, would all be called "brother." Similarly, a person's sister, as well as all female cousins, would be called "sister."

11 ● CLOTHING

Maoris typically wear modern Western-style clothing. However, they still wear their traditional clothing for special occasions. Traditional Maori clothing was some of the most elaborate in Polynesia. Intricately decorated cloaks were an important item of dress for individuals of high status within Maori society.

Tattooing among the Maori was highly developed and extremely symbolic. Maori facial tattoos were created by two methods. One was by piercing and pigmenting the skin with a tattooing comb. The other was by creating permanent grooves in the face with a chisel-like instrument. Male facial tattooing, called *ta moko,* was done in stages in a male's life through adulthood. Females were also tattooed in Maori society. Female facial tattooing was known as *ta ngutu.* Designs were placed on the chin and lips. There is a growing revival of this art among younger Maori women nowadays.

12 ● FOOD

Maoris typically eat the same kinds of foods as other New Zealanders. Breakfast consists of eggs, sasage, and bacon. Lunch may be a meat pie or sandwich. Dinner is a full meal with a meat dish as the main course. The traditional Polynesian foodstuffs of taro (a starchy root), yams, and breadfruit were not well adapted for cultivation on the temperate islands of New Zealand.

The most famous Maori culinary tradition is the *hangi.* The hangi is a feast that may only be prepared in the regions of the country where there are hot springs. A pit is dug in the ground and filled with rocks. Meat and vegetables are placed on top of the rocks in the pit. The food is left to steam for several hours.

Susan D. Rock
These Maori men are dressed in tradional clothing as part of a cultural demonstration for a group of tourists. Maoris typically wear modern Western-style clothing.

13 ● EDUCATION

Public education has now become the norm for most urban Maori. A number of preschools based on Maori cultural education have also been established throughout New Zealand. Education is state-supported and required in New Zealand between the ages of six and fifteen. Students planning to attend one of the country's six universities continue their secondary education until the age of seventeen or eighteen. At that time, they take university qualifying exams.

14 ● CULTURAL HERITAGE

The *haka* dance of the Maori is one of the best-known cultural traditions of Polynesia. These dances are accompanied by song and body percussion created by clapping hands, stomping feet, and slapping thighs. There is a leader and a chorus that responds to the leader's lead vocal line. The dance itself involves energetic postures representing warlike and aggressive poses.

Maori chanting follows very strict rules for performance, rhythmic structure, and continuity. To break a chant in midstream is to invite disaster or even death for a community. These chants often tell of genealogies (family lines) or the exploits of ancestors.

15 ● EMPLOYMENT

Maoris today work at the same types of jobs and professions found in any urbanized industrial economy. About two-thirds are engaged in the service sector (jobs that directly serve the public).

Traditional Maori culture developed a high degree of specialized labor. Artisans such as tattoo artists, canoe builders, house builders, and carvers were all classified as *tohunga* in Maori. This title implies a quality of sacredness and translates best into English as "priest." These artisans paid homage to the gods of their various occupations. They were initiated into their crafts through a series of rituals. All artisans were

descended from chiefly lines in traditional Maori society.

16 ● SPORTS

New Zealand, like its neighbor Australia, has rugby and cricket as its national sports. Maori boys and men participate in and follow rugby competitions in New Zealand. Traditional competitions among men in Maori society stressed aggressiveness; they provided practice for real-life conflicts.

17 ● RECREATION

The modern Maori have become consumers of video, television, and film. As well, they have also become producers of their own stories in these media. Traditional storytelling and dance performance have been preserved by the Maori in this manner, serving both as cultural archives and as entertainment.

18 ● CRAFTS AND HOBBIES

The New Zealand Maori are accomplished artists in a number of media. Collectors and the general public are most familiar with Maori carving and sculpture. They also have a tradition of figurative painting dating back to the late nineteenth century. Maori subtribes each have their own unique artistic styles.

Traditionally, large meeting houses of the Maori were decorated with elaborately carved facades containing figures of their ancestors. The entire structure was conceived as a representation of an ancestor.

19 ● SOCIAL PROBLEMS

The vast majority of all contemporary Maori are urban dwellers. The Maori continue to suffer the social problems that accompany urban life in conditions of poverty. In some urban areas, Maori unemployment rates exceed 50 percent. The film *Once Were Warriors* (1994) provides a Maori perspective on the social problems of alcoholism, domestic violence, and under-employment or unemployment.

20 ● BIBLIOGRAPHY

Bishop, Russell. *Maori Art and Culture.* London: British Museum Press, 1996.

Gell, A. *Wrapping in Images: Tattooing in Polynesia.* Oxford: Clarendon Press, 1993.

Hazlehurst, Kayleen M. *Political Expression and Ethnicity: Statecraft and Mobilisation in the Maori World.* Westport, Conn.: Praeger, 1993.

Tregear, Edward. *The Aryan Maori.* Papakura, New Zealand: R. McMillan, 1984.

WEBSITES

Embassy of New Zealand, Washington, D.C. [Online] Available http://www.emb.com/nzemb/, 1998.

Kupenga Maori. The Maori Net. [Online] Available http://www.maori.org.nz, 1998.

World Travel Guide. New Zealand. [Online] Available http://www.wtgonline.com/country/nz/gen.html, 1998.

Polynesians

PRONUNCIATION: PAHL-uh-nee-zhuns

LOCATION: Polynesia, a vast string of islands in the Pacific Ocean, including Hawaii, New Zealand, Easter Island, Tonga, and French Polynesia

POPULATION: Unknown

LANGUAGE: Native languages of the islands; Maori; Tahitian; French; English

RELIGION: Christianity with elements of native religion

1 ● INTRODUCTION

The Polynesians are the original inhabitants of a vast string of islands in the Pacific Ocean, from New Zealand in the south to Hawaii in the north. The western boundary is Easter Island. *Polynesia* means "many islands" in Greek. The cultures of the region share many traits with each other. Their differences are often subtle and not readily perceived by outsiders.

2 ● LOCATION

In the Pacific region, there is an important distinction between "high" islands and "low" islands. Tahiti, a typical high island, is relatively large with steep slopes, rich plant life, and many waterfalls and rushing streams. Coastal plains are absent or extremely limited on high islands. Atolls (ring-shaped islands made of coral) are the most common low islands in Polynesia. These are typically "desert islands" that are low-lying, narrow, and sandy with few, if any, surface streams. Low islands have less biodiversity (variety of plant and animal species) than do high islands.

At the time of the first known European contact with the Polynesian world in the 1500s, there were probably around half a million people scattered throughout the region. European powers competed for ownership of most of Polynesia's inhabited islands. The indigenous (native) populations suffered greatly at the hands of the Europeans. They lost their traditional lands and resources, and suffered discrimination against their cultures and languages.

3 ● LANGUAGE

The Polynesian languages are part of the larger Austronesian language family that includes most of the languages of the Pacific Basin. Polynesian languages form a subgroup of this extensive language family.

Many Polynesian languages face an uncertain future. Attempts have been made to revitalize the Hawaiian language through educational programs at the university and the elementary school levels. Tahitian has been used as a *lingua franca* (common language) throughout the Tuamotuan Islands, the Marquesas, the Gambiers, and the Austral Islands since before European contact. It is threatening the survival of the native languages of those islands. In New Zealand, all speakers of Maori—the indigenous Polynesian language of the island chain—are bilingual in English.

4 ● FOLKLORE

Polynesian societies have an exceptionally rich body of folklore and mythology. Myths relate the origins of human beings as well as the origins of cultural practices and institutions. There is a considerable body of mythology regarding the origins of tattoo-

ing in Polynesian cultures. Some origin myths describe the process of migration from one island to another via ocean-going canoes. Cultural heroes are important figures in the folklore of Polynesian societies.

5 ● RELIGION

Polynesian religion changed dramatically with the coming of European missionaries in the early part of the nineteenth century. From what is known of precontact (before European contact) practices, there was considerable variation in religious ideas and practices throughout Polynesia. In Hawaii, for instance, chiefs were genealogically related to gods and, as a result, were believed to possess sacred power called *mana*. The Hawaiian system recognized four major gods and one major goddess.

The concept of *tapu*, English "taboo," was important in all Polynesian societies. This refers to anything forbidden due to sacredness. There were rules that served to protect through forbidding certain actions. In the Marquesas Islands, a woman's menstrual cloth itself was not tapu; however, it was tapu to touch it.

Today, most Polynesians are followers of Christianity, both Catholicism and Protestantism. Some traditional beliefs and mythologies have been incorporated into Christian ideology.

6 ● MAJOR HOLIDAYS

Holidays in most contemporary Polynesian societies are events related to the state or the church. In the French possessions like the Marquesas, Bastille Day (July 14) is an important holiday. (Bastille Day is a French national holiday. It commemorates the fall of the Bastille, a French fortress formerly used as a prison that was captured by revolutionaries on July 14, 1789.) Many islanders now celebrate a number of Catholic holidays due to influence of missionaries in the colonial era.

7 ● RITES OF PASSAGE

The Marquesas Islanders had a birth feast on the day a child was born. On that occasion, the maternal uncles and the paternal aunts of the newborn would cut their hair. An ornament-maker would fashion hair ornaments for the child to wear later in life. The newborn was brought presents by family and friends, and a type of shrine was built by the infant's father.

Passage into puberty was often accompanied by tattooing rituals in many Polynesian societies. In some societies only men were tattooed. In others, both men and women were tattooed. The practice of tattooing in Polynesia carries with it cultural and symbolic meanings. There have been recent revivals of the art of tattooing in societies such as the Maori of New Zealand.

Another puberty ritual performed in some Polynesian societies was "fattening." Male and female youths were secluded, kept inactive and out of direct sunlight, and fed large amounts of food for a period of time to make them more sexually desirable. This ritual is no longer performed.

In the Marquesas, death was accompanied by ritualized wailing on the part of women, and the performance of formalized chanting on the part of men. Women would also perform a specific dance called *heva*. During this dance they would take off all their clothes and move in an extremely exaggerated manner. Finally, the female relatives of the deceased would do physical harm to themselves by cutting their hands and faces with sharks' teeth and other sharp objects. Christian missionaries saw these behaviors as pagan and quickly found ways to put a stop to them.

8 ● RELATIONSHIPS

Greetings in Polynesian societies vary from island to island. Status determines the nature and extent of the social interaction of individuals in these societies. In rural Tahiti, for example, the standard greeting is, "Where are you going?" The two expected responses are: "Inland" (away from the coast) or "Seaward" (toward the coast). The interaction can continue with the question, "What's new at the inland/seaward end?" This is usually an opener for a conversation.

Premarital sexual relations are typically very casual in most Polynesian societies. However, once a permanent relationship is established, casual sexual relations outside of the relationship are not permitted. The choice of a marriage partner is less fixed than in many cultures of the world. In the times before Christian influence, the preference in some Polynesian societies was for cross-cousin marriage—a woman would marry her mother's brother's son or her father's sister's son. Missionaries forbade this type of marriage pattern. The present patterns allow for freedom of choice in marriage partners, similar to that found in American society.

9 ● LIVING CONDITIONS

Traditional Polynesian societies did not feature large villages. Instead, families clustered together in neighborhoods that focused on a set of shared buildings for social, ceremonial, and religious life. Many Polynesians had separate sleeping quarters for bachelors. In some parts of Polynesia, households were built on elevated stone platforms. Religious shrines were important parts of the household structure.

Households of the nobility had carved items of furniture including headrests and stools. Sleeping mattresses were also available for members of noble households. In many parts of Polynesia, lighting from torches or coconut oil lamps was common inside houses at night. Polynesia seemed like a virtual paradise to Europeans who ventured there. Nowadays, Polynesian houses and communities are the products of native design and Western materials.

10 ● FAMILY LIFE

In societies such as Tahiti with distinct social classes, marriage was traditionally prohibited among individuals from different classes. Children born of sexual relations between members of different classes were killed at birth. These practices were discontinued as a result of missionary activity in Tahiti.

In many Polynesian societies, polygamy (multiple spouses) was practiced. In the traditional society of the Marquesas Islanders, a woman could have more than one husband at a time. (This practice, called polyandry, is fairly rare in cultures of the world.) It was very uncommon to find a man who had more than one wife in the Marquesas. Monogamy—having only one spouse at a time—is now the universal practice in Polynesia.

The role and status of women in relation to men varies between island societies in Polynesia. In the Marquesas, women have always enjoyed a status nearly equivalent with men. One traditional indicator of this equality was that women were allowed tattooing almost as extensive as that of men. In many other Polynesian societies, this was not the case, as women held positions of lower status than men.

11 ● CLOTHING

Typical Polynesian clothing in precontact times was similar for men and women. A section of bark cloth was worn as a loincloth by men or as a waistcloth by women. Decorated bark cloth known as *tapa* was the main item of traditional clothing in Tahiti. (It is no longer manufactured there.) A number of ornaments were worn for ceremonial events. Elaborate feather headdresses were signs of nobility. Both men and women wore ear ornaments.

Traditional patterns of dress have disappeared except for performances or special ceremonial or cultural events. Current fashion in Polynesia spans the range that it does in any Westernized developing country.

12 ● FOOD

Most traditional Polynesian societies rely on fishing and horticulture (growing flowers, fruits, and vegetables). European accounts of the region indicate that the Marquesas Islands were unique in their reliance on breadfruit, a large starchy fruit native to the Pacific islands. Taro root is another important foodstuff in Polynesia. Early Hawaiians relied on taro as a staple starch in their diet.

In some parts of Polynesia—Hawaii, Tahiti, and the Marquesas in particular—men and women used to eat separately. In general, this pattern is no longer followed except in the most traditional communities and in certain ceremonial contexts.

13 ● EDUCATION

Western-style education has become the standard in Polynesia. Many Polynesians attend colleges and universities both inside and outside the region.

14 ● CULTURAL HERITAGE

Polynesia has a rich tradition of vocal and instrumental music. Some types of musical expression have been lost and some new ones have been created as a result of missionary activity in the region. Christian hymns have had considerable influence in the style of vocal music in Polynesia. The Tahitian vocal music known as *himene* (from the English word "hymn") blends European counterpoint (two or more lines of music sung at the same time) with Tahitian drone-style singing.

One of the most well-known Polynesian musical instruments is the Hawaiian ukulele. It is the Hawaiian version of the Portuguese mandolin, which came to the islands with Portuguese immigrants in the 1870s. The primary use of Hawaiian flutes and drums was to accompany the graceful and erotic dance known as the *hula*.

15 ● EMPLOYMENT

Throughout the Polynesian world there is a traditional division of labor along the lines of gender. Men are responsible for fishing, construction, and protection of the family units. Women are responsible for collecting and processing horticultural products and for manufacturing basketry items and bark cloth. Both sexes participate in gardening activities. Throughout Polynesia, modern types of employment are to be found in the cities and towns.

16 ● SPORTS

Arm wrestling was a traditional Polynesian form of male entertainment as a competition of strength. Other forms of competition between males were common throughout the islands as ways to prepare for battle. Because native warfare is no longer practiced in Polynesia, these forms of competition have either disappeared or have been modified. Surfing was also popular in many parts of Polynesia, although it was only in Hawaii that surfers stood on their surfboards. The worldwide sport of surfing originated through European observation of this traditional Polynesian pastime.

17 ● RECREATION

Most parts of Polynesia have running water and electricity. Television has made its way into most Polynesian communities. In some parts of the region, Polynesian peoples are taking control of the images of themselves presented in the popular media, producing popular films as well as documentaries.

18 ● CRAFTS AND HOBBIES

Decoration of everyday objects of utilitarian nature is common in most Polynesian societies. Woodcarving has been particularly well developed among the Maori of New Zealand. In most Polynesian societies, the designs and patterns that appeared on bark cloth or woodcarvings also appeared on the human body in the form of tattoos. In some societies, tattooing was the primary art form. Many traditional art forms, including tattooing, are being revived in many Polynesian societies.

19 ● SOCIAL PROBLEMS

The right to self-determination (the right to make their own decisions) is important for many Polynesian peoples. Increased nuclear testing in French Polynesia is a central concern for the region and the world. Groups like the Maori continue to deal with the social problems of alcoholism and domestic violence. The recent film *Once Were Warriors* is a moving, insightful portrayal of the modern life of the Maori.

20 ● BIBLIOGRAPHY

Gell, A. *Wrapping in Images: Tattooing in Polynesia*. New York: Oxford University Press, 1993.

Goldman, I. *Ancient Polynesian Society*. Chicago: University of Chicago Press, 1970.

Hooper, Anthony, and Judith Huntsman. *Transformations of Polynesian Culture*. Auckland, New Zealand: The Polynesian Society, 1985.

Melville, Herman. *Typee*. New York: Wiley and Putnam, 1876.

WEBSITES

Embassy of New Zealand, Washington, D.C. [Online] Available http://www.emb.com/nzemb/, 1998.

World Travel Guide. New Zealand. [Online] Available http://www.wtgonline.com/country/nz/gen.html, 1998.

Nicaragua

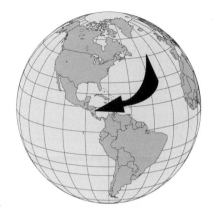

The people of Nicaragua are called Nicaraguans. The population is estimated to be about 70 percent mestizo (mixture of white and Amerindian or native), 14 percent white, and 13 percent black. Amerindians (native people), including the Sumu and Miskito, account for the remaining 4 percent.

Nicaraguans

PRONUNCIATION: nih-cah-RAH-gwuhns
ALTERNATE NAMES: Nicas
LOCATION: Nicaragua
POPULATION: 4.4 million
LANGUAGE: Spanish; English; indigenous dialects
RELIGION: Roman Catholicism; Protestantism (Moravian church)

1 ● INTRODUCTION

Nicaraguans inhabit Nicaragua, a country in central America. Nicaragua was originally occupied by Indians, who were conquered by the Spanish explorers and colonists in the 1520s. As a result, as of the late 1990s, over two-thirds of Nicaraguans were Mestizo—of mixed Indian and Spanish descent. In 1821, Nicaragua was one of the five Central American provinces that declared independence from Spain, but many people of Spanish descent had made their home in the country and decided to stay. Until the early 1900s, Nicas (as Nicaraguans call themselves) enjoyed peace and relative prosperity. Many coffee and banana plantations were established during this time.

Since 1909, the governments of the United States, the former Soviet Union, Cuba, and others have involved themselves in Nicaraguan affairs, primarily to protect their respective country's business interests. Since the 1970s, a group known as the Sandinistas have been believed to have connections with the former Soviet Union (and its successor, Russia) and Cuba. The United States prohibited trade with Nicaragua and supported anti-Sandinista groups called Contras. Some 30,000 people died in over ten years of fighting. In 1989, a cease-fire (truce) was followed by elections. The Sandinistas were defeated and surrendered political power to the UNO opposition coalition (groups working together) led by Violeta Barrios de Chamorro.

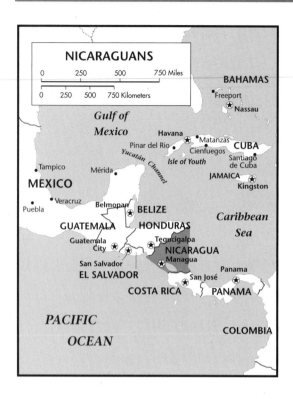

NICARAGUANS

| 0 | 250 | 500 | 750 Miles |
| 0 | 250 | 500 | 750 Kilometers |

3 ● LANGUAGE

Spanish is the official language and the one spoken by most Nicaraguans. However, English is the most common language in the Caribbean half of the country, as well as in the capital city of Managua. It is the native tongue of the Creoles, blacks who came from Jamaica and other islands colonized by the British. The Miskito, Nicaragua's main indigenous group, live in this Caribbean region. Their ancestry is mixed Indian, African, and European. They speak Miskito, an Amerindian language.

Nicaraguans have two family names: the mother's family name, which acts as a surname (last name), followed by the father's family name. For example, Mario Garcia Sanchez would be addressed as Señor Garcia. Garcia is Mario's mother's family name, and Sanchez is his father's.

2 ● LOCATION

Nicaragua is the largest country in Central America, about the size of the state of New York. It is bounded on the north by Honduras, on the south by Costa Rica, on the east by the Caribbean Sea, and on the west by the Pacific Ocean. The country includes the central highlands (including a belt of mountains that has twenty-five volcanoes), as well as lowlands on both coasts.

More than half of Nicaragua's population live in the Pacific lowlands. Over two-thirds of Nicaraguans are Mestizo—of mixed indigenous Indian and ethnic Spanish descent. About 17 percent are of European descent, about 9 percent are black, and 5 percent are native Indian.

4 ● FOLKLORE

Indian folklore attributes the creation of the world to magic. Spanish folk practices survived in Nicaragua in combination with Indian folklore. A lively interest in witchcraft developed from these roots. For example, people with love potions to sell can always find customers. The *cuadro*, a picture of a saint found in most households, is often credited with magical powers derived from native cult idols. Feasts for local patron saints are often held at the times of planting and harvesting. They reflect folk beliefs that divine intervention will result in bountiful crops

Nicaragua's original Indian inhabitants worshiped the Corn Goddess (*Cinteotl*) as an aspect of the Mother Goddess (*Chicome-*

coatl). An annual feast called *Xóchitl* was held in honor of Cinteotl.

Nicaraguan folk literature abounds in tall tales and fantastic heroes. In fables, Uncle Coyote is constantly outwitted by the jokester and trickster Uncle Rabbit.

5 ● RELIGION

Approximately 90 percent of Nicaraguans are Roman Catholic. City dwellers and those from the middle and upper classes are most likely to attend Mass (church service) and receive the sacraments (baptism and communion, for example). The lower classes tend to be less religious. There is a shortage of priests, and the Catholic Church's ability to reach people in rural areas is limited. During the civil war, the bishops were hostile to the ruling Sandinistas. However, some priests and nuns have been activists in support of the Sandinistas, combining religious faith with the support for the struggle for freedom. Their beliefs are sometimes referred to as "liberation theology."

The 10 percent of the population that are Protestant chiefly live in the Caribbean part of the nation. The Moravian Church, a Protestant Christian denomination, is the most common in this region.

6 ● MAJOR HOLIDAYS

La Purísima is the most important holiday in Nicaragua. This is a week-long celebration of the Feast of the Immaculate Conception held around December 8. Elaborate altars to the Virgin Mary are built and decorated in homes and workplaces. People, especially children, go from altar to altar singing songs and reciting prayers.

Cory Langley

A child receiving first communion, usually at the age of nine, is given many gifts. A girl's fifteenth birthday is a time of special celebration, denoting that she has come of age. Among the middle and upper classes, dating does not begin until later.

The *posadas* are held on nine consecutive nights, ending on Christmas Eve (December 24). They are celebrated with nightly caroling processions commemorating the Holy Family's wanderings in search of shelter in Bethlehem. Holy Week (Easter) processions are common as well. The capital city, Managua, holds a *fiesta* (celebration) in honor of St. Dominic, the city's patron saint, in early August. Masaya has a feast to St. Jerome on September 30, complete with Indian dancers in costume. It also has a religious pilgrimage (journey) on March 16 to bless the waters of Lake Masaya.

Secular (nonreligious) holidays include Independence Day, September 15, commemorating the 1821 Central American declaration of independence from Spain;

Cory Langley

The civil war of the 1980s left Nicaragua struggling to keep its economy going. In the mid-1990s, 75 percent of Nicaraguans were living below the poverty line. Squatter settlements (people living without owning or paying rent for their dwelling) are found on the outskirts of the cities. The dwelling above was constructed with any materials the builder could find.

and Liberation Day, July 19, marking the 1979 overthrow of the government.

7 ● RITES OF PASSAGE

The baptism ceremony for the newly born is important. Godparents, chosen at that time, are expected to concern themselves with the welfare of the child and to provide aid in times of hardship. A child receiving first communion, usually at the age of nine, is given many gifts. A girl's fifteenth birthday is a time of special celebration, denoting that she has come of age. Among the middle and upper classes, dating does not begin until later. Among adults, birthdays have lit-

tle importance, but a person's saint's day may be marked.

8 ● RELATIONSHIPS

The style of greeting practiced by Spanish-speaking peoples is generally more demonstrative than in the United States. This is especially true of Nicaraguans. Friends almost always shake hands when greeting and parting, and often embrace. Women often kiss on one or both cheeks as well as embracing. People often stand closer to one another in conversation than is usual in the United States. A common casual greeting, especially among teenagers, is *Hola!* (Hi).

Visitors may drop in on friends without notice. People of social standing are greeted with respectful titles such as *Señor, Señora,* and *Señorita* (Mr., Mrs., and Miss, respectively). Older people are often addressed by the respectful titles of *don* or *doña.*

The concept of honor is important in Nicaragua. Personal criticism is considered to be in poor taste. Urban residents often adopt modern values, while people in rural areas tend to be more traditional. The concept of *machismo,* in which men are seen as more important than women, is still common in rural areas.

9 ● LIVING CONDITIONS

The civil war of the 1980s left Nicaragua struggling to keep its economy going. In the mid-1990s, 75 percent of Nicaraguans were living below the poverty line. Health care declined after the Sandinistas lost power in 1989. Most people suffer from malnutrition and do not have access to adequate health care. Most are also poorly sheltered. In rural areas, the most basic dwelling is a dirt-floor straw or palm-frond hut supported by poles and sticks. Its counterpart in towns and cities is a low adobe structure with a tile roof. Squatter settlements (people living without owning or paying rent for their dwelling) are found on the outskirts of the cities. The more substantial homes of the middle and upper classes are of Spanish or Mediterranean style.

10 ● FAMILY LIFE

Nicaraguans rely on their families for support, since community and church ties tend to be weak. Individuals are judged on the basis of their families, and careers are advanced through family ties. The nuclear family of father, mother, and children is often joined by a grandparent, aunt or uncle, or orphaned children. Newly married couples may take up residence with one or the other set of parents. Godparents, although unrelated by blood or marriage, are also important to the family structure.

Except for the middle and upper classes, marriage is not often formalized. (The man and woman live together as a couple without going through a wedding ceremony.) The average woman has five or six children. Abortion is illegal except to save the woman's life. However, illegal abortions are not uncommon. Women have major representation in the government, labor unions, and social organizations, but not in business. Many women are heads of households and, in addition to their domestic duties, have joined the labor force.

11 ● CLOTHING

Typically women wear simple cotton dresses, while many men wear work shirts, jeans, sneakers or sandals, and straw hats. Even businessmen will often wear sport shirts, or leave off their jackets in hot weather in favor of the *guayabera*—a long cotton shirt.

Traditional dress for women varies. It may consist of a long, loose cotton skirt and short-sleeved cotton blouse, both brightly colored and embroidered. A shawl, jewelry, and flowers in the hair complete the outfit. (Women go barefoot.) For men, the native costume is blue cotton trousers, a long-sleeved collarless white cotton shirt, a sheathed machete (large knife) strapped to the waist, a straw hat, and sandals.

12 ● FOOD

Beans and corn tortillas are the basics of the Nicaraguan diet. The local form of the tamale is the *nacatamal*, wrapped in a banana-like leaf rather than a corn husk. In addition to cornmeal, the nacatamal may contain rice, tomatoes, potatoes, chili, cassava root, and a small piece of meat. The Christmas Eve meal consists of nacatamales with a special filling, along with *sopa borracha* (drunken soup)—slices of caramel or rice-flour cake covered with a rum-flavored syrup.

Meals usually last longer than they do in the United States, accompanied by pleasant conversation. The main meal is eaten at midday, often followed by a *siesta*, or afternoon rest during the hottest time of the day, when work is difficult.

13 ● EDUCATION

School is required and free between the ages of six and thirteen. In the mid-1990s, over three-fourths of primary-school-age children were in school. However, a much smaller percentage of older children were attending secondary school. Nicaragua has six universities.

14 ● CULTURAL HERITAGE

The marimba, a kind of xylophone, is popular in Nicaragua. In Masaya, the traditional capital of Nicaragua, the marimba is sometimes accompanied by the oboe, "ass's jaw," and a single-string bow with gourd resonator. In the east the music is typically Afro-Caribbean, played with banjos, accordions, guitars, and drums.

Recipe

Glorious Plantains

Ingredients

2 ripe plantains (very soft)
1 Tablespoon cooking oil
¼ cup (2 ounces) sugar
1 Tablespoon cornstarch
½ teaspoon cinnamon
2 cups (16 ounces) milk
4 Tablespoons grated cheese
½ teaspoon vanilla extract
1 Tablespoon butter

Directions

1. Slice the plantains into rounds and brown them in the cooking oil in a frying pan.
2. Combine the sugar, cornstarch, and cinnamon in a bowl.
3. Add the milk and mix well.
4. Add the grated cheese and vanilla.
5. Use half the butter (½ tablespoon) to grease a glass pie pan.
6. Pour half the milk mixture into the greased pan, then place the fried plantains on top.
7. Cover with rest of the milk mixture and dot with the remaining butter.
8. Bake at 350°F for 30 minutes, or until the milk is set.

Note: Do not use small yellow bananas, use only plantains, which must always be cooked prior to eating. They are called *platanos verdes* when green and *platanos maduros* when ripe.

Courtesy of Embassy of Nicaragua.

Traditional dance is more popular in Nicaragua than anywhere else in Central

Rita Velazquez

In the mid-1990s unemployment and underemployment (having more qualifications than the job requires) were estimated at 60 percent of the work force.

America. Dances often include masked characters, some pink and large-nosed, meant to mock the Spanish.

Foremost of Nicaragua's writers was the poet Rubén Darío (1867–1916).

15 ● EMPLOYMENT

Nicaragua's economy is in a terrible state. In the mid-1990s unemployment and under-employment (having more qualifications than the job requires) were estimated at 60 percent of the work force. Social class is based on whether or not one works with one's hands. Those who work with their hands represent 80 percent of the people

and are classified as lower class. Nearly 50 percent of the work force lives by farming. Most farmers use hand tools and oxen-drawn plows on small subsistence plots— land whose crops fill their own basic needs with no excess for profit. Most industrial workers are employed in food-processing plants.

16 ● SPORTS

In most of Central America, soccer (*futbol*) reigns supreme. However, in Nicaragua (and Panama) baseball is the most popular sport. Nicaraguans were playing in organized leagues in the 1890s. By the early 1960s even the isolated Miskito Indians were playing regularly. Nicaragua's most famous player is major-league star pitcher Dennis Martínez, who retired in the late 1990s. Also popular are boxing, basketball, volleyball, and water sports. Children's games abound; one authority has put their number at over one hundred.

17 ● RECREATION

Fiestas (festivals) are an important part of public life. They include such events as cockfighting, bull-riding, and bull-baiting. Dancing in clubs is popular. Lobo Jack's in Managua is the largest disco in Central America. Most films shown in Nicaragua's theaters are in English, with Spanish subtitles. Even though the family is the most important unit of society, youth clubs for socializing are becoming more popular.

18 ● CRAFTS AND HOBBIES

Locally made earthenware (clay pottery) is decorated much as it was before the Spanish conquest. Other handicraft items include hammocks, baskets, mats, embroidery, leatherwork, coral jewelry, and carved and painted gourds and dolls.

19 ● SOCIAL PROBLEMS

In spite of the fact that the civil war had ended, at least 270 people died in political violence between 1990 and 1994. Police, army, and Sandinistas killed former Contras, and northern Contra bands committed similar acts, often because of land disputes. Previously undeveloped tracts of rain forest are being cut down at an alarming pace to grow crops and gather fuel wood. Health care is suffering from shortages of food, medicine, and basic medical supplies. Mal-

nutrition and tropical diseases, such as yellow fever and malaria, are serious problems.

20 ● BIBLIOGRAPHY

Glassman, Paul. *Nicaragua Guide.* Champlain, N.Y.: Travel Line, 1996.

Haverstock, Nathan A. *Nicaragua in Pictures.* Minneapolis, Minn.: Lerner Publications Co., 1987.

Merrill, Tim, ed. *Nicaragua: A Country Study.* 3rd ed. Washington, D.C.: U.S. Government Printing Office, 1994.

WEBSITES

Green Arrow Advertising. Nicaragua. [Online] Available http://www.greenarrow.com.nicaragu/nicaragu.htm, 1998.

World Travel Guide. Nicaragua. [Online] Available http://travelguide.attistel.co.uk/country/ni/gen.html, 1998.

Sumu and Miskito

PRONUNCIATION: SOO-moo and MISS-key-toe
LOCATION: Nicaragua; Honduras (Eastern coasts)
POPULATION: 215,000
LANGUAGE: Sumu; Spanish
RELIGION: Protestantism (Moravian Church); Catholicism

1 ● INTRODUCTION

The Sumu and Miskito are indigenous (native) groups living on the eastern coasts of two Central American countries, Nicaragua and Honduras. The area is commonly known as the Atlantic or Miskito (also spelled Mosquito) Coast. The Sumu and Miskito are traditional enemies. The Miskito is the largest, and the Sumu the second-largest, native group in the region.

The Miskito are a mixed-race people resulting from intermarriage between escaped African slaves and other Amerindians. In the seventeenth century, English traders and settlers in the area wanted help in their colonial rivalry with the Spanish. They introduced the Miskito to guns and ammunition to get their assistance. The Miskito used these weapons to expand their territory, as well as to dominate the Sumu, demanding tribute (money) from them, and often capturing them for use as slaves.

The persecuted Sumu ultimately retreated inland. The Sumu population declined sharply as a result of Spanish, British, and Miskito aggression and the spread of European diseases. The Miskito became the most important non-European population on the coast. From the mid-seventeenth century to the late nineteenth century, the Miskito prospered.

In the late nineteenth century, banana growers began bringing in black English-speaking laborers from Caribbean islands controlled by the British. These laborers (and their descendants) became known as Creoles, and replaced the Miskito as the area's dominant nonwhite group. Both the Miskito and the Sumu were relegated to a lower social status.

In 1979, the Nicaraguan government tried to tighten its control over the native peoples of the Atlantic coast. The Miskito resisted and tried to form an antigovernment alliance among the native groups of the region. They gave the alliance the name *Misura*, combining the groups' names: *Mis-kito, Sumu,* and *Rama* (a small native group). However, most of the Sumu did not want to become involved in the hostilities, and tried to stay out of the conflict. When Violeta Barrios de Chamorro was elected president in 1990, she established a new ministry to serve as a liaison with the peoples of the Atlantic coast. The Sumu have drawn international attention because the violence since 1979 has decreased their numbers to the point that they have nearly disappeared.

2 ● LOCATION

The Sumu live in isolated inland villages along the main rivers of what is known as the Atlantic or Miskito Coast, located in Nicaragua and Honduras. (Many of the areas they occupy can be reached only by water.) While the Miskito Coast is extremely diverse geographically, most Sumu live in the tropical rain forest.

There are three main subgroups among the Sumu. Each speaks its own variant of a common language. During the prolonged warfare of the 1980s, the Sumu suffered persecution at the hands of both the government and the Miskitos. A great number of their settlements were destroyed. Many Sumu fled to refugee camps in Honduras, but most have been repatriated (returned to their homeland) in the years since 1985. Those who have returned are attempting to rebuild their shattered communities. Altogether, there are thought to be about 150,000 Mikito in Nicaragua and 50,000 in Honduras; and about 14,000 Sumu in Nicaragua and 1,000 in Honduras.

3 ● LANGUAGE

Both the Sumu and Miskito languages are derived from the Chibchan Indian language family of South America. Outside influences have caused both groups to borrow words from the other's language, as well as from English and Spanish. Most Sumu and Miskito are multilingual, speaking Spanish in school and their native language at home. In addition, many learn to speak the other native language (either Sumu or Miskito). Few Sumu or Miskito know how to write in their own language.

4 ● FOLKLORE

The Sumu traditionally believed in a Sun god, called Mapapak, who lived in the heavens. Other forces of nature, including the Moon and the wind, were also worshiped. A variety of spirits (*walasa, nawah,* and *dimalah*) were thought to have either harmful or helpful influences on human beings. They were even thought capable of causing death. Much Sumu folklore has been preserved by its shamans (holy people), called *sukia,* who also serve as priests, exorcists, herbalists (healers), and spiritual advisors.

5 ● RELIGION

The Sumu and Miskito in Nicaragua mostly belong to the Moravian Church, a Protestant sect. Practice of traditional religion declined with the arrival of Moravian missionaries in the nineteenth century. The Sumu traditional religion involved Sun and Moon worship and a belief in both good and evil spirits, practices that some Sumu continue to this day. Miskito traditional religion included belief in spirits (*lasas*) and omens in addition to worship of the moon.

6 ● MAJOR HOLIDAYS

The major holidays of the Christian calendar are celebrated, including Christmas (December 25) and Easter (late March or early April). They are combined with the traditional practices of singing, dancing, and drinking.

7 ● RITES OF PASSAGE

Festivities mark major events in the life-cycle, such as weddings and funerals. Both the Sumu and Miskito mark major life events—births, marriages, deaths—with Christian ceremonies.

8 ● RELATIONSHIPS

The Sumu family traditionally functioned as an independent, self-sufficient economic unit. Men cut down trees and hunted, while women performed agricultural work and household chores. Today, both men and women participate in the cash economies (employment for wages) of the countries in which they live.

Among the Miskito, it is common for villagers to magnify personal quarrels into major feuds between communities.

9 ● LIVING CONDITIONS

Both Sumu and Miskito dwellings are typically wooden, split-bamboo, or post-and-pole structures. Roofs are thatched or corrugated tin, and floors are made of board, split bamboo, or palm branches. They mostly consist of one room—although some have interior divisions—and generally have windows and doors. Instead of having a foundation, houses are usually raised several feet or meters off the ground on posts.

Traditional herbal remedies are used in conjunction with Western-style medicine. Herbal remedies using roots, leaves, bark, and seeds are still used for a variety of purposes, including the treatment of poisonous snake bites. However, modern medicine is beginning to replace traditional folk remedies for many illnesses.

10 ● FAMILY LIFE

Most Sumu and Miskito live in extended families with two or three generations under one roof. Sumu men formerly had more than one wife, but today monogamy (having only one spouse) is the rule. Courtship customs include the giving of gifts by the man to the young woman's parents. These may include food and firewood. Once married, the couple generally lives with either the wife's or the husband's parents until their own house is built. At one time, marriage with outsiders was strictly forbidden. Today it is common for the Sumu and Miskito to marry blacks, mestizos (mixed-race peoples), or members of other native groups— even their traditional enemies. In addition to their domestic responsibilities, women take part in farm work, including planting, weeding, and harvesting.

11 ● CLOTHING

Formerly, Sumu and Miskito women made loincloths and skirts from pounded tree bark or locally woven cotton. Other clothing was made from cotton that was spun, dyed, and woven by hand. Today, however, like other inhabitants of Nicaragua and Honduras, Sumu and Miskito wear mass-produced Western-style clothing, mostly lightweight cotton.

12 ● FOOD

Dietary staples for the Sumu and Miskito include root crops, such as sweet manioc (cassava) and yams; plantains and green bananas, which are boiled or baked; rice and beans; and fish. Corn is pounded to make tortillas. A fermented beverage called *mishla* or *wasak* is made from ripe plantains and bananas mashed together with corn, palm fruits, and other ingredients, and mixed with water. Fish and wild game are eaten when available. The Sumu also keep chickens, ducks, turkeys, pigs, and cows.

The Miskito eat two main meals each day. The morning meal is eaten shortly before dawn. The late-afternoon meal is eaten after people return from work.

13 ● EDUCATION

Honduras and Nicaragua, where most Sumu and Miskito live, both have free, required primary education. However, the educational systems of both countries are inadequate, with low enrollment and graduation rates. Consequently, adult illiteracy (inability to read and write) is high. Estimates of the adult illiteracy rate are as high as 80 percent in rural areas, where most Sumu and Miskito live. Schools are understaffed and undersupplied, with as many as eighty students per classroom. In the 1980s, the Nicaraguan government instituted the first bilingual education programs for native people, taught in the Miskito language.

14 ● CULTURAL HERITAGE

Many of the traditional Sumu flute melodies imitate bird calls. Accompaniment is provided by rattles and drums.

15 ● EMPLOYMENT

The Sumu have traditionally lived by subsistence agriculture (farming that provides for the farmer's basic needs with little surplus for marketing). The Miskito, in addition to subsistence agriculture, have engaged in hunting and fishing as well. Both groups have raised root crops, corn, plantains, bananas, and other produce. Villagers traditionally helped each other with major tasks, such as house-building. They had a system of labor exchange called *biribiri.* Today, however, the exchange of labor has been replaced by payments of produce, supplies, or cash.

16 ● SPORTS

Baseball, soccer, basketball, and volleyball are popular in Nicaragua and Honduras. Cockfighting is a favorite spectator sport among the Sumu and other groups living along the Miskito Coast.

17 ● RECREATION

Holidays and other special occasions are marked with singing and dancing. The Sumu also celebrate by drinking alcoholic beverages including *mishla,* a fermented beverage made from fruit and water.

A favorite pastime of the Miskito is *kihrbaia* (strolling), especially on Sundays.

18 ● CRAFTS AND HOBBIES

Traditional Sumu crafts included spinning, weaving, and dyeing cotton for clothes and household items such as sheets. These crafts have been replaced by the production of decorative items that can be sold. These include carved tree gourds, bark tapestries, and *majao* bags. Bark is also used for making blankets and mosquito netting. Twine for weaving bags and hammocks is made from pounded bark.

The Miskito weave bskets and make gourds into functional items They also produce bark cloth that is made into bed coverings.

19 ● SOCIAL PROBLEMS

The Sumu, Miskito, and other native groups in eastern Nicaragua and Honduras generally have limited opportunities in terms of income, education, and employment. Many hold low-paying, dangerous mining jobs.

Drug traffickers from Colombia, hoping to use Nicaragua as a place to ship drugs, have been actively resisted by the Miskito.

20 ● BIBLIOGRAPHY

Americas Watch Committee. *The Sumus in Nicaragua and Honduras: An Endangered People.* New York and Washington, D.C.: Americas Watch, 1987.

Helms, Mary W. *Asang: Adaptations to Culture Contact in a Miskito Community.* Gainesville: University Presses of Florida, 1971.

Olson, James S. *The Indians of Central and South America: An Ethnohistorical Dictionary.* New York: Greenwood Press, 1991.

WEBSITES

Green Arrow Advertising. Nicaragua. [Online] Available http://www.greenarrow.com/nicaragu/nicaragu.htm, 1998.

World Travel Guide. Nicaragua. [Online] Available http://www.wtgonline.com/country/ni/gen.html, 1998.

Niger

The people of Niger are called Nigeriens. The Hausa are the largest ethnic group living in Niger, forming 53 percent of the total population. To learn more about the Hausa read the chapter on Nigeria in this volume. The Djerma-Songhai, the second-largest group, make up 22 percent of the population. Nomadic livestock-raising peoples include the Fulani, or Peul (10 percent), the Tuareg (10 percent), and the Kanuri (4 percent). For more information on the Fulani, see the chapter on Guinea in Volume 4.

Nigeriens

PRONUNCIATION: nee-jir-YENS

LOCATION: Niger

POPULATION: 8.8 million (1994)

LANGUAGE: Hausa; Zarma; Songhay; Fulfulde; Tamasheq; Manga or Boudouma; Arabic, Tubu, or Gourmantche; French

RELIGION: Islam; small numbers of Catholics and Protestants; spirit possession; indigenous religious practices

1 ● INTRODUCTION

Niger is a landlocked, drought-ridden country in the heart of West Africa. Its population is made up of distinct ethnic groups . Niger is located in one of Earth's harshest ecological regions. Historically, groups that have wielded power in the area of present-day Niger include the Songhay, Hausa, and Tuareg. Some Fulani live in the southwest.

After conquering the region, the French created the colony of Niger in 1922.

Niger was granted independence from France in 1960. However, the end of colonial rule has not brought economic success to this West African nation. The severe drought of the 1970s focused the world's attention on the plight of this people and other rural peoples of the Sahel region. In January 1996, Nigeriens saw their country return to military rule.

2 ● LOCATION

Niger has a flat and monotonous landscape. Two-thirds of its territory is located in the central Sahara Desert. In 1994, the population of Niger was estimated to be 8.8 million.

Over the last fifty years, dwindling resources in the rural areas have forced many people to migrate to the cities to look for work. Niamey, the capital, has grown as people have arrived from all parts of the country.

3 ● LANGUAGE

Altogether, over twenty-one languages are spoken in Niger. Hausa, which is spoken by over half the population, has become the *lingua franca* (common language) of the country. Other major languages include Zarma, Songhay, Fulfulde, and Tamasheq. Many Nigeriens speak more than one language. Nigeriens who have attended Western-style schools also speak French. Recently, the government has recognized ten languages as national languages.

4 ● FOLKLORE

The people of Niger believe they are surrounded by spirits that regularly act in the lives of humans. These spirits are thought to grant health, protection, or good luck to people who obey their requests. Other spirits may cause family conflicts, money problems, or lengthy illnesses. Hausa-speaking peoples explain the origin of these harmful spirits with the following myth.

Adamu, the first man, and Hawa, the first woman, had given birth to fifty sets of twins. One day, their creator told them that he wanted to see the children. They were afraid that he would keep them for himself. So the cunning Hawa told her husband that they would hide the more beautiful twin of each pair in a cave. They would then show the supreme being only the remaining twins. The powerful god saw that they had deceived him. He decided to punish Adamu and Hawa by making the hidden twins invisible forever. It is believed that the spirits who plague people are the descendants of the beautiful twins who are condemned to remain invisible.

5 ● RELIGION

Today, about 95 percent of the Nigerien population is Muslim (followers of Islam). However, many followers of the prophet Muhammad still believe in pleasing the spirits of the traditional religions. Thus, Nigeriens enlist the help of the spirits to pass an examination, to ensure safe return from a trip, or to receive protection from jealous relatives. Children are given Muslim names. Most Nigerien men observe the Islamic practice of praying five times a day.

Recently, reformist religious groups, such as *Izala*, have made many converts among Nigerien young people. Izala advocates simple living and Islamic education for all. It condemns traditional customs such as the use of amulets (magic charms).

Catholics and Protestants make up less than 1 percent of Niger's population.

6 ● MAJOR HOLIDAYS

Salaried workers do not work on January 1. However, most of the people, being Muslim, do note celebrate the secular (non-religious) new year, but celebrate the Muslim holiday accoring to the lunar calendar. Labor Day (May 1) and Proclamation of the Republic (December 1) are also national holidays. On April 15, Nigeriens celebrate the coup (takeover of the government) that ousted Diori, the first president of independent Niger. Nigerien independence is celebrated on August 3. The anniversary of the Republic is December 18.

As Muslims, most Nigeriens celebrate Muslim holidays such as the end of Ramadan (the month of fasting). For the birthday of Muhammad and the Muslim New Year, men go to the mosque to pray. Nigeriens also celebrate the holiday known as *Tabaski*, which commemorates the story of the sacrifice of Abraham and the saving of the life of Isaac. On this day, families slaughter a ram and then cook it on an open fire and feast with friends and relatives.

7 ● RITES OF PASSAGE

Marriage, especially to a first spouse, is considered a major change of status for both men and women. In the Hausa language, for instance, there is no word for a woman who has reached adulthood but has never been married. Marriage is mainly considered the union of two family groups, rather than two individuals.

A Nigerien woman is considered to be an adult when she bears her first child. The Tuareg celebrate this event by blessing the mother's tent. There is also a lively display of wrestling by the wealthiest and most prestigious women. On the sixth day after a baby's birth, female relatives perform the *kishakish* ritual. The newborn is brought out of the tent for the first time and given a name. A ram is usually killed and the baby's head is shaved.

Under Islam, burial of the dead is a simple matter. The body is buried immediately after death. Relatives, friends, and neighbors come to offer their condolences to the grieving family. In most cases, there is no crying. Restraint and dignity (meaning no showing of emotion) are expected of everyone.

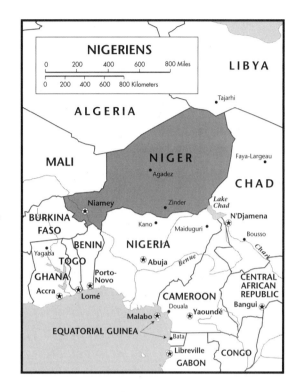

8 ● RELATIONSHIPS.

Nigeriens are hospitable people who always have food available for guests and visitors. Because of the influence of Islam in daily life, there is a strong segregation (separation or division) between the sexes. Once she has married, it is considered improper for a Muslim wife to look her husband directly in the eye or to confront him.

Greetings in the Hausa language are complex. They involve asking about the other person's health, the health of that person's children, and whether that person has had a good day, night, morning, and so forth. But to the question *Ina kwana?* (How was the night?) it is appropriate to answer *Lahiya lau* (Fine) even if one is at death's door.

Cory Langley

A Nigerien woman baking. In Niger, where drought is a constant threat to human survival, the staple food is millet.

Among the rural people, there are traditional youth associations, the *Samarya*, that provide opportunities for recreation and for group work that benefits the community.

9 ● LIVING CONDITIONS

Niger remains a very poor country, struggling to become stronger and more self-sufficient. Most rural communities have no electricity. In many villages, women still draw water daily from the same shared well.

Most people in rural areas cannot go to to a hospital or clinic. Almost one-third of Niger's children do not reach the age of five.

10 ● FAMILY LIFE

Traditionally, members of extended families put their money together and used it for the needs of the family group. Today, though, the economic unity of the extended family has broken down. Young men are now responsible for raising money on their own when they are ready to marry.

Women spend most of the day taking care of the children and preparing meals. According to Islam, men can have up to four wives at the same time. There is no limit to how many wives they can marry in their lifetime, as long as they keep divorcing their previous wives. Women who are divorced usually go back to their parents' home and live there until they remarry.

Among the Hausa, a woman cannot show affection for her eldest children in public. She cannot even speak their names. Nor can she call her husband by his name, joke with him, or contradict him. Grandparents, on the other hand, enjoy an affectionate, teasing relationship with their grandchildren.

11 ● CLOTHING

Most Zarma, Songhay, and Hausa women wear colorful custom-made cotton blouses and wraparound dresses of the same fabric. Tuareg and Fulani women wear dark clothes dyed with indigo. In cities and towns, professional women may wear Western clothes. Many women wear a small head scarf or even a large veil that covers their shoulders. Female members of the Izala religious Muslim sect are covered from head to ankle by a large, tent-like veil, the *hijabi*.

Many Nigerien men wear a flowing, sleeveless brocade gown over a matching shirt and drawstring pants. When they do not wear a turban, men often wear an embroidered rimless hat. Among the Tuareg, it is not the women, but the men, who cover their faces with a veil.

12 ● FOOD

The staple food in Niger is the grain millet. Millet is the main ingredient in the traditional midday meal of *fura*. It is a porridge consisting of millet flour, water, spices, and sometimes milk or sugar. Millet is eaten in the evening meal as a thick paste. This paste is covered with a spicy sauce made with meat, tomato paste, or other ingredients such as onions, squash, or eggplant. Along

the Niger River, the Songhay prepare a thick paste of corn, to which they add meat or smoked fish. In addition to millet and sorghum, Nigeriens eat beans or rice. They also enjoy snacks of skewered meat, grilled tripe (the lining of an animal's stomach), fried bean meal, or ground peanut cakes. During the cricket season, women fry the insects for snacks.

Observant Muslims do not eat pork or drink alcohol.

13 ● EDUCATION

Schooling in Niger is free and compulsory (required) between the ages of seven and fifteen. Students can attend either a Western-style school, with instruction in French, or an Islamic school, where they are taught in Arabic. Only a small number of Nigeriens are literate (can read and write) either in French or in Arabic. Even fewer finish high school or go to college.

Many parents believe that if children attend government schools, they will forget their traditions.

14 ● CULTURAL HERITAGE

The history and traditions of Nigerien people are often recalled at social gatherings and celebrations by the *griots*, who are singers, messengers, and historians. Their praise-singing is accompanied by a variety of percussion instruments. These include the *ganga*, a medium-size drum, and the *kalangu*, an hourglass-shaped drum held under the armpit. Among the Tuareg, three women are needed to play the *tinde*, a type of drum, which is often accompanied by a flute (*tassinsack*).

Cory Langley

Many Nigerien women and girls wear colorful cotton blouses and wraparound skirts of the same fabric.

The Nigerien theater, in its present form, was introduced by the French colonists. Plays are performed in schools, in village cultural centers, and on national radio and television. The plays are mostly comedies. They are improvised (made up on the spot) around a chosen theme. They are often performed in Hausa, the language most widely understood in Niger.

A well-known Nigerien writer is Boubou Hama, a former president of the National Assembly. His autobiography, *Kotia Nima*, received the major literary prize of Sub-Saharan Africa in 1970.

15 ● EMPLOYMENT

Most Nigeriens are farmers. They grow millet, sorghum, and beans as primary crops. In addition, almost all of them are involved in secondary work such as trade, smithing (working with metals), or tailoring. One-sixth of the workforce is engaged in live-stock production. The pay for civil servants (government workers) is low, and some do not even receive a monthly salary.

16 ● SPORTS

Wrestling tournaments draw large crowds, and every city now has a wrestling arena. Soccer is a popular source of entertainment for young boys and men. Horse races also attract many spectators.

Among Fulani herders, young men engage in *soro*, a competitive game in which a man violently hits his partner on the chest with a large stick. The receiver of the blow pretends not to be hurt; he simply smiles at the audience to demonstrate his self-control in the face of great pain.

17 ● RECREATION

The people of Niger enjoy music, whether they listen to Islamic chanting on the radio or attend a concert honoring local authorities. Storytelling is an important form of entertainment for children and adults alike. Spirit possession ceremonies are public performances that can draw large crowds. At these events, men and women stomp their feet to the sounds of the drums (calabashes) and a one-stringed violin.

Wedding celebrations in cities and towns provide an evening of dancing to the sound of African pop music.

Although it is still a luxury, television is becoming more and more popular among Nigeriens. Parents and children enjoy American TV series like *Dynasty* or *Columbo.* Some Nigeriens with televisions in their homes charge their neighbors entrance fees to view programs or videos. In some rural communities, villagers can watch television using equipment powered by solar batteries.

In the cities, young people attend open-air movie theaters. There they can view melodramas from India or karate films.

In rural areas, market days are opportunities to meet friends or relatives and catch up on the latest news.

18 ● CRAFTS AND HOBBIES

Nigeriens are skilled craftspeople. Zarma craftwomen, for example, are known for their large earthenware water jars decorated with white geometric motifs. Songhay pottery is decorated with ocher (yellowish), black, or white triangular motifs. Hausa earthenware jars have a wide opening at the top.

Tuareg and Hausa craftsmen are famous for their fancy leather work—beautiful boots, colorful sandals, and goatskin bags.

Multicolored, hand-woven cotton blankets are among a woman's most treasured possessions.

The Tuareg manufacture a wide range of jewelry. They produce rings, necklaces, and wrist and ankle bracelets made of braided strands of silver or copper.

19 ● SOCIAL PROBLEMS

Widespread migration from rural areas to cities and towns has brought a variety of social ills. Violent crime, juvenile delinquency, and alcoholism have increased significantly. Drug use among workers is reported to be increasing. Growing numbers of unemployed young men become involved in smuggling and other crimes. Infanticide (the killing of babies), the rape of young girls, and teenage prostitution are happening more often.

20 ● BIBLIOGRAPHY

Charlick, Robert B. *Niger: Personal Rule and Survival in the Sahel.* Boulder, Colo.: Westview Press, 1991.

Coles, Catherine, and Beverly Mack, ed. *Hausa Women in the Twentieth Century.* Madison: University of Wisconsin Press, 1991.

Miles, William F. S. *Hausaland Divided: Colonialism and Independence in Nigeria and Niger.* Ithaca, N.Y.: Cornell University Press, 1994.

WEBSITES

World Travel Guide, Niger, 1998. [Online] Available http://www.wtgonline.com/country/ne/gen.html, 1998.

Tuareg

PRONUNCIATION: TWAH-reg

LOCATION: Saharan and Sahelian Africa (mostly Niger, Mali, Algeria, Libya, and Burkina Faso)

POPULATION: About 1 million

LANGUAGE: Tamacheq

RELIGION: Islam, combined with traditional beliefs and practices

1 ● INTRODUCTION

The Tuareg are an Islamic African people. They are classified as *seminomadic*, meaning that they travel with their herds on a seasonal basis but also have a home area where they grow some food crops.

The Tuareg are best known for the men's practice of veiling their faces with a blue cloth dyed with indigo. Early travelers' accounts often referred to them as the "Blue Men" of the Sahara Desert, the region where many Tuareg live. It is believed that the Tuareg are descendants of the North African Berbers, and that they originated in the Fezzan region of Libya. They later expanded into regions bordering the Sahara, bringing local farming peoples into their own society.

By the fourteenth century, trade routes to the wealthy salt, gold, ivory, and slave markets in North Africa, Europe, and the Middle East had sprung up across Tuareg territory. The Tuareg grew rich as livestock breeders and traders in the Saharan and *Sahelian* regions. (The *Sahel* is the region south of the Sahara Desert that is marked by times of drought but is not a real desert.

In the late nineteenth century, European exploration and military expeditions led to French rule of the Tuareg homeland. By the early twentieth century, the French had brought the Tuareg under their colonial control. They ended Tuareg trade activities, including the collection of tariffs and the protection services for camel caravans crossing the Sahara.

2 ● LOCATION

Most of the Tuareg live in the Saharan and Sahelian regions—southern Algeria, western Libya, eastern Mali, northern Niger, and northeastern Burkina Faso. The landscape includes flat desert plains, rugged savanna (grassland), and volcanic mountains. Due to drought and famine, many Tuareg have migrated to rural areas and cities farther south. Political tensions with the governments of Mali and Niger have also caused migration.

The total Tuareg population has been estimated at about 1 million.

3 ● LANGUAGE

The major language of the Tuareg is Tamacheq, which is in the Berber language group. A written script called Tifinagh is used in poetry and also appears in Saharan rock art. Many of the Tuareg also speak Songhay, Hausa, and French, and read Arabic.

4 ● FOLKLORE

There are many proverbs, riddles, myths, and folk tales among the Tuareg. Animal tales depicting human moral questions are popular with children. They feature the jackal, hyena, and rabbit—animal characters widespread in African folklore.

Many Tuareg groups have myths about female ancestors who were founders of traditions. One is Tagurmat, who fought a battle on Mount Bagzan in the Air region. Her twin daughters are said to have founded the herbal healing profession.

Another popular figure in myth and folk tales is Aligouran, a character in a series of adventures involving an uncle and his nephew.

Many stories are about spirits, called *jinn,* who are believed to play tricks on humans beings who are traveling alone in the desert.

5 ● RELIGION

Most Tuareg are Muslims. But their traditional belief system and rituals overlap with Islam. For example, there is a widespread belief in spirits. Most spirits are considered evil and are believed to cause illnesses. Some Tuareg perform fortune-telling with cowrie shells, lizards, mirrors, and the Koran (the sacred text of Islam).

Unlike women in many other Islamic societies, most Tuareg women do not wear veils in public. They may also independently inherit property and begin the process leading to a divorce.

Islamic holy men, called *marabouts,* are believed to possess a special power of blessing, called *al baraka.* They educate children in verses from the Koran and they officiate at ceremonies marking rites of passage and Muslim holidays.

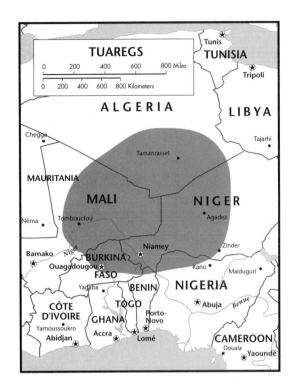

6 ● MAJOR HOLIDAYS

The Tuareg celebrate Muslim holy days, as well as secular (nonreligious) state holidays. *Tabaski* commemorates the story of Abraham's willingess to sacrifice his son. Each household slaughters a goat or ram, feasts on its meat, and prays at the prayer ground. The Tuareg celebrate *Ganni* (also called *Mouloud*), the Prophet Muhammad's birthday, with special sacred and secular songs and camel races. The end of the month-long Ramadan fast is celebrated by animal sacrifice, feasting, prayer, and evening dancing festivals. Secular holidays that the Tuareg celebrate include Niger Independence Day (August 3) and Niger Republic Day (December 18). On these days, there are camel races and feasting in

Cory Langley

Compounds in the less nomadic rural communities may include several tents and a few cone-shaped grass buildings. Some of the wealthier Tuareg, who have settled in oasis areas, have adobe houses.

the countryside, and parades and speeches in the towns.

7 ● RITES OF PASSAGE

Name day is held one week following a baby's birth. On the evening before the name day, the older female relatives carry the baby around the mother's tent. They give him or her a secret name in the Tamacheq language. The next day, the baby's hair is shaved in order to cut off the baby's ties to the spirit world. At the mosque, the marabout (Islamic holy man) and the father give the baby an Arabic name from the Koran. As the marabout pronounces the

baby's official Koranic name, he cuts the throat of a ram. Then there are feasts, camel races, and evening dancing festivals.

Tuareg men begin to wear a veil over the face at approximately eighteen years of age. This signifies that they are adults and are ready to marry. The first veiling is performed in a special ritual by a marabout. He recites verses from the Koran as he wraps the veil around the young man's head.

Weddings are very elaborate, lasting for seven days. There are camel races and evening festivals featuring songs and dances. The groom's family arrives in the bride's village on gaily decorated camels and donkeys. Older female relatives of the bride build her a special tent.

Burial takes place as soon as possible after a person has died. It is quickly concluded with a graveside prayer led by a marabout. Burial is followed by *iwichken,* or condolences. Relatives and friends gather at the home of the dead person, and the marabout offers a prayer and blessing. The guests eat a memorial feast.

8 ● RELATIONSHIPS

Like many other African societies, the Tuareg have very elaborate greetings. In the Air regional dialect, *Oy ik?* signifies "How are you?" This is followed by *Mani eghiwan,* meaning "How is your family?", and additional greetings such as *Mani echeghel?* (How is your work?). The usual polite response to these questions is *Alkher ghas,* or "In health only." Exchanging gifts is an important sign of friendship between women.

The Tuareg in rural areas still recognize social categories from the time before colonization. These are based on family descent and inherited occupation. For example, *imajeghen* (nobles) refers to Tuareg of noble birth, while *inaden* refers to the smiths and artisans. In principle, people are supposed to marry within their own social category. However, this practice has been breaking down for some time, especially in the towns.

9 ● LIVING CONDITIONS

Compounds in the less nomadic rural communities may include several tents and a few cone-shaped grass buildings. Some of the wealthier Tuareg who have settled in oasis areas have adobe houses.

Since the early 1960s, when independent states were established in their regions, the Tuareg have lost economic power. They tend to be underrepresented in city and town jobs, including government positions. In rural areas, their once-strong local economy has been weakened by drought and by the decreasing value of livestock and salt.

10 ● FAMILY LIFE

In rural communities, a nuclear family (parents and their children) live in each tent or compound (living area). Each compound is named for the married woman who owns the tent. She may make her husband leave the tent if she divorces him.

Fathers are the disciplinarians of the family. But other men, especially maternal uncles (uncles on the mother's side), often play and joke with small children. Grandmothers also have a close, affectionate relationship with the children. Cousins have a relaxed relationship marked by teasing and joking. Relationships with in-laws are reserved, distant, and respectful.

Traditionally, the Tuareg have married within their own social category, preferably to a close cousin. In the towns, both of these traditions are breaking down. In rural areas, they remain strong. However, many individuals marry close relatives only to please their mothers. Later they divorce and marry nonrelatives. Some wealthy Tuareg men practice polygamy (having more than one wife at the same time).

Two-thirds of a family's property goes to the sons as an inheritance; one-third, to the

Cory Langley

Most of the Tuareg live in southern Algeria, western Libya, eastern Mali, northern Niger, and northeastern Burkina Faso. Due to drought and famine, many Tuareg have migrated to rural areas and cities farther south.

daughters. A political office usually passes from father to son.

Women who lack daughters of their own often adopt nieces to help with the housework.

11 ● CLOTHING

The veil that Tuareg men wear on their faces has several meanings. It is, first of all, a symbol of male identity. It is also thought to protect the wearer from evil spirits. In addition, it is considered an attractive adornment and can be worn in various styles. The face veil is worn differently in different social situations. It is worn highest (covering the nose and mouth) to express

respect in the presence of chiefs, older persons, and in-laws.

Once they marry, Tuareg women wear a head scarf that covers their hair. In rural areas, Tuareg men wear long Islamic robes. Women wear wraparound skirts and embroidered blouses. In the towns, clothing is more varied. It includes West African tie-dyed cottons, and also fashionable European styles for some wealthier people.

12 ● FOOD

Almost 95 percent of the daily diet in rural areas consists of grains. Protein is added by dairy products (milk and cheese). Fruits such as dates and melon are eaten in season.

Dried and pounded vegetables are added to sauces. Meat is eaten primarily on holidays and at rites of passage.

A very sweet, thick beverage called *eghajira* is also consumed on special occasions. It consists of pounded millet, dates, and goat cheese mixed with water, and it is eaten with a ladle.

In the towns, the diet is slightly more varied. However, it still consists mostly of nonmeat protein. Along the Niger River, some fish are caught and added to the diet.

13 ● EDUCATION

Until recently, many Tuareg resisted sending their children to secular (nonreligious) schools because they did not like or trust the government. Nowadays, however, more Tuareg recognize the importance of formal education. Most rural residents finish at least primary school. Some continue on to junior and senior high schools in the towns. Very few Tuareg attend universities.

Koranic (Islamic) schools are important and respected among the Tuareg.

14 ● CULTURAL HERITAGE

Music and poetry are of great importance during courtship, rites of passage, and festivals. Distinctive styles of music and dance are associated with various social classes. Sacred music is performed on Muslim holidays. Secular music is performed on instruments including the *anzad* (a bowed, one-stringed lute) and the *tende* drum.

15 ● EMPLOYMENT

Most camel herding and all caravan trade are still done by men. Men plant and irrigate gardens, and women harvest the crops.

Because of natural disasters and political tensions, it is difficult to make a living only from nomadic herding. Most rural Tuareg today combine different occupations, including herding, oasis gardening, caravan trading, and migrant labor. Others produce arts and crafts for the tourist trade or work as security guards in the towns. In the towns, a few Tuareg have become businessmen or teachers.

16 ● SPORTS

In the countryside, most everyday occupations involve hard physical labor. The Western concept of "exercise" as a separate category does not exist.

In the towns, there are organized athletics at schools, including soccer and racing. There is also traditional wrestling.

17 ● RECREATION

In the towns, television, films, parades, and culture centers offer entertainment. Films from India and China are popular.

In the countryside, most residents provide their own entertainment. Children make their own dolls and other toys. Adults dance, sing, and play musical instruments at festivals. In addition, people of all ages play board games with stones and date pits.

Some newspapers and magazines are available.

18 ● CRAFTS AND HOBBIES

Tuareg crafts consist mainly of metalworking (silver jewelry), leather working (boxes and saddles for camels), and woodworking (delicately decorated spoons and ladles).

19 ● SOCIAL PROBLEMS

Development programs from the 1940s into the 1970s failed to help the Tuareg because the programs worked against their traditional herding patterns. Between 1991 and 1995, Tuareg who had received military training and arms in Libya carried out a separatist rebellion. They demanded the right to rule their own region. Since that time, there has been continued off-and-on fighting in some regions of Mali and Niger. Some of the Tuareg have been forced into refugee camps.

20 ● BIBLIOGRAPHY

Clarke, Thurston. *The Last Caravan.* New York: Putnam, 1977

Nicolaisen, Johannes, and Ida Nicolaisen. *The Pastoral Tuareg: Ecology, Culture and Society.* New York: Thames and Hudson, 1997.

Rochegude, Anne. *Tarlift, Tuareg Boy: My Village in the Sahara.* Translated and adapted by Bridget Daly. Morristown, N.J.: Silver Burdett, 1985.

WEBSITES

World Travel Guide. Niger. [Online] Available http:// www.wtgonline.com/country/ne/gen.html, 1998.

Nigeria

The people of Nigeria are called Nigerians. The main ethnic groups, distinguished by different languages, are the Hausa, the Igbo (Ibo), the Yoruba, and the Fulani. The Hausa have been officially estimated to constitute 21 percent of the population; Yoruba, 20 percent; Igbo, about 16.1 percent; and Fulani, 12 percent. For information on the Fulani, see the chapter on Guinea in Volume 4.

Nigerians

PRONUNCIATION: nigh-JEER-ee-uhns
LOCATION: Nigeria
POPULATION: 111.7 million
LANGUAGE: English; English Creole; Bantu; and Chadic languages
RELIGION: Traditional African religion; Islam; Christianity

1 ● INTRODUCTION

The territory that is now Nigeria has witnessed the rise and decline of many different kingdoms and empires since AD 600.

In the 1880s, the British took control of the palm oil plantations at the mouth of the Niger River and created the colony of Nigeria by combining the territories of a number of local kingdoms and chiefdoms. They established a capital at Lagos in 1914. In 1960, Nigeria won its independence from the British. Since then, the government of Nigeria has been challenged to unite a diverse group of peoples. The three major groups are the Hausa and Fulani in the north, the Yoruba in the west, and the Igbo in the east.

2 ● LOCATION

Nigeria shares borders with Benin, Niger, Chad, and Cameroon. From the Gulf of Guinea on the Atlantic Ocean in the south, plateaus and plains cover much of the country. To the east, the Gotel and Mandara Mountains form a border with Cameroon. With the equator just to the south, the climate is tropical in the central regions and arid in the north.

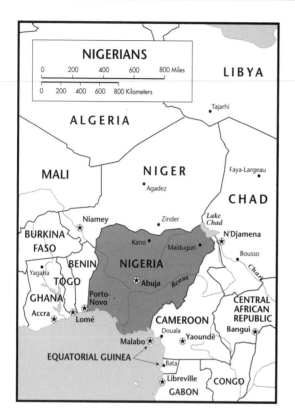

With nearly 112 million people, Nigeria is the most populous country in Africa and the sixth most populous in the world. It is also one of the world's most ethnically diverse countries, with more than 250 distinct groups.

3 ● LANGUAGE

English is the official language, but English Creole is the language most people speak. Each of the ethnic groups has its own language also. These include Bantu and Chadic languages.

4 ● FOLKLORE

Proverbs, chants, folk stories, and riddles are popular.

5 ● RELIGION

Almost 50 percent of all Nigerians are Muslim (followers of Islam), and about 40 percent are Christian. Many also continue some traditional African religious practices. As a part of their traditional religions, most ethnic groups have names for a supreme being who they believe created the universe. The Yoruba call him Olorun (Lord of Heaven) and the Hausas call him Ubangiji (God). Lesser gods and deities act as contacts between humans and the supreme being.

6 ● MAJOR HOLIDAYS

The main secular (nonreligious) holiday is National Day (October 1). Muslim holidays include *Tabaski* (commemorating Abraham's sacrifice) and Eid al-Adha (the end of Ramadan). Christians celebrate Easter and Good Friday (in March or April).

Nigerians also celebrate many cultural festivals throughout the year. One example is the Argungu Fish and Cultural Festival on the banks of the Sokoto River. During this celebration, hundreds of fishermen jump into the river at once. This scares the fish into the air, and into their nets.

7 ● RITES OF PASSAGE

Nigerians typically celebrate rites of passage with music, dance, and ceremony. At his or her naming ceremony a child becomes a member of the community. At initiation, an adolescent assumes the responsibilities of adulthood. A woman becomes part of her husband's family after marriage. At death, a community member joins the spirit world.

A 1993 documentary film (*Monday's Girls*) illustrates one ethnic group's initiation rite for girls. The young women (initiates) participate in a five-week coming-of-age ceremony (*Iria*), which transforms them into marriageable women. They are secluded in a house and "fattened up" for the ceremony. The initiates are pampered and must do no work. Elderly women shear the initiates' hair. They are taught how to be mothers and take care of their husbands. The old women paint the initiates' bodies. The initiates then appear in public to be inspected by the elders.

8 ● RELATIONSHIPS

The equivalent of "good morning" is *Isalachi* in the Igbo language, and *Yayadei* in Hausa. As elsewhere in Africa, two men may hold hands and stand near each other when talking. Their sense of personal space is closer than that of Americans.

As in most parts of Africa south of the Sahara Desert, passing an object with the left hand or with only one hand is considered impolite. Children learn to offer and accept objects with both hands. Some Nigerians consider waving to be an insult, particularly if it is done close to the face.

9 ● LIVING CONDITIONS

About 70 percent of Nigerians live in villages without indoor plumbing and electricity. Women and children have to walk up to half a mile to draw drinking water from a water source.

Nigerians build simple rectangular or cylindrical houses of reed, mud brick, or cinder block. Several families of migrant workers often live together in a few rooms,

Corel Corporation

Woman winnowing grain in Gumel, Nigeria. About 43 percent of Nigerians work in agriculture.

sharing common cooking areas and latrines. Lower- and middle-income workers can afford small- to medium-sized houses. Some have indoor plumbing. The more prosperous Nigerians have Western-style furniture, as well as refrigerators and televisions.

10 ● FAMILY LIFE

Most Nigerian families live together in compounds (living areas). Nuclear families (parents and their children) share the same hut. The father is generally the head of the household. Family members respect their elders.

Under Islamic law, a Muslim man can have up to four wives if he can support them. The groom will pay a bride price to the family of his bride. In the cities young people date, much as they do in the West, but this type of dating is rare in the villages. Because weddings are expensive, many couples live together until they can afford to give a proper wedding feast.

There are some Nigerian women who are internationally respected leaders in academia and business. However, Nigerians still regard single (unmarried) women as an oddity.

11 ● CLOTHING

Western-style clothes are increasingly replacing traditional garments. This is especially true in the cities. In rural areas, many women and men wear long loose robes in either white or bright colors. Women often wear scarves or turbans.

European fabrics have replaced handwoven cloth. European makeup and costume jewelry, too, are replacing traditional cosmetics and ornaments.

12 ● FOOD

Nigerians rise early, and therefore may eat a number of times a day. Early breakfast begins at 5:00 AM and late dinner is eaten at 9:00 PM. Breakfast may consist of rice and mango or fried plantains. At around 11:00 AM people might eat *efo* (stew) or *moyin-moyin*, bean pudding made with steamed black-eyed peas.

Nigerians generally like their food hot and spicy. Cooks use plenty of red hot peppers in the dishes themselves or on the side. Typically, stews or sauces are made from greens or fish and, if one can afford it, meat or chicken. These are eaten with rice or yams. Cassava and corn are popular too. Nigerians in the coastal regions drink palm wine and locally brewed beer. Muslims are great tea drinkers. In the cities, coffee houses and pubs are very popular.

13 ● EDUCATION

The Nigerian formal educational system is patterned after the British school system. At the age of six or seven, children begin primary school. Muslim children learn Arabic and religious teachings in Koranic schools (schools where teaching is based on the Koran, the Muslim scriptures). Young people in rural areas receive basic instruction in farming and other skills through apprenticeships. Nigeria also has preschools, special education, adult education, and classes for the gifted and talented.

Nigeria has one of Africa's most developed systems of higher education. There are at least twenty-five institutes of higher learning, including six universities. Many Nigerians still view advanced education as unnecessary for girls. As of the late 1990s, more than 60 percent of males could read and write, compared with only 40 percent of females.

14 ● CULTURAL HERITAGE

Nigerians have a long history of music, traditional dancing, visual art, and oral literature. Modern drama, opera, cinema, films, and written literature build on this heritage.

Traditional dancing at festivals combines music, drama, poetry, storytelling, and elaborate masks, costumes, and body painting. Music and dance accompany child-naming, marriage, burial, housewarming, and harvesting. Dramatic dances are performed at initiations.

Modern Nigerian authors are gaining international recognition. Nigeria's most famous author is Chinua Achebe. His novels *Things Fall Apart* and *A Man of the People* provide harsh critiques of colonialism and contemporary Nigerian society. Both works are often taught in American college classrooms.

15 ● EMPLOYMENT

Most of the labor force works in service jobs, while about 42 percent work in agriculture. Occupations in the cities vary greatly. Unskilled workers carry water, sell cooked food on the street, wash clothes, and peddle household items. Many people work in trade and retail, and small, informal businesses.

16 ● SPORTS

Traditionally Nigerians have taken part in wrestling, archery, foot and horse races, and gymnastics. Soccer now tops the list of modern competitive sports. Nigeria has produced three world boxing champions. Other sports include table tennis, basketball, polo (especially in the north), cricket, and swimming.

17 ● RECREATION

Visiting friends and relatives is a popular form of recreation. Many middle-class Nigerians have televisions and stereos. City dwellers enjoy watching films on video and in movie theaters. For music and dancing, the older generation still appreciates live bands. Younger people prefer Afro-Beat and Juju music. These two contemporary styles

Jason Lauré

In rural areas, many women and men wear long loose robes of either white or bright colors. Women often wear scarves or turbans. Western-style garments are increasingly replacing traditional apparel, especially in the cities.

originated in the Nigerian capital city, Lagos.

18 ● CRAFTS AND HOBBIES

Nigerian folk art ranges from ivory carvings to body painting to wall decoration. In the northern plains, craftspeople use long grasses to weave colorful and durable baskets, fans, tables, and floor mats. Wood carvers make figures for shrines, portraits, and masks. Artists cast sculptures in bronze and brass, produce glass and metal work, and make quality leatherwork and calabash (gourd) carvings. Nigerian pottery is valued all around the world.

19 ● SOCIAL PROBLEMS

Problems facing Nigeria include a corrupt government and business community. Embezzlement of oil revenues, bribery, and ethnic favoritism are all common practices. Nigeria has been a center for drug trafficking to Europe and the United States. Crime afflicts its cities. Regional ethnic rivalries exist between the people who are Muslim in the north and those who are Christians in the south.

20 ● BIBLIOGRAPHY

Adeeb, Hassan. *Nigeria: One Nation, Many Cultures.* New York: Benchmark Books, 1996.

Metz, Helen Chapin, ed. *Nigeria: A Country Study.* Washington, D.C.: U.S. Government Printing Office, 1992.

Owhonda, John. *Nigeria: A Nation of Many Peoples.* Discovering Our Heritage. Parsippany, N.J.: Dillon Press, 1998.

WEBSITES

World Travel Guide. Nigeria. [Online] Available http://www.wtgonline.com/country/ng/gen.html, 1998.

Hausa

PRONUNCIATION: HOW-suh
LOCATION: Hausaland in West Africa (northwestern Nigeria and in adjoining southern Niger)
POPULATION: More than 20 million
LANGUAGE: Hausa; Arabic; French or English
RELIGION: Islam; native cults

1 ● INTRODUCTION

The Hausa, numbering more than 20 million, are the largest ethnic group in west Africa. They are widely distributed geographically and have intermingled with many different peoples.

Islam arrived in the area by the fourteenth century. By the fifteenth century, there were a number of independent Hausa city-states. They competed with each other for control of trade across the Sahara Desert, slaves, and natural resources. In the nineteenth century, the region was unified by a *jihad* (Islamic holy war) and became known as Hausaland. The British arrived and colonized the area in about 1900. Even during colonial times, the city-states and their leaders maintained some autonomy. Many Hausa traditions were preserved until late in the twentieth century.

2 ● LOCATION

The Hausa people are concentrated mainly in northwestern Nigeria and in adjoining southern Niger. This area is mostly semi-arid grassland or savanna, dotted with cities surrounded by farming communities. The cities of this region—Kano, Sokoto, Zari, and Katsina, for example—are among the greatest commercial centers of sub-Saharan Africa (Africa south of the Sahara Desert). Hausa people are also found living in other countries of west Africa like Cameroon, Togo, Chad, Benin, Burkina Faso, and Ghana.

3 ● LANGUAGE

Hausa is the most widely spoken language in west Africa. It is spoken by an estimated 22 million people. Another 17 million people speak Hausa as a second language. Hausa is written in Arabic characters, and about one-fourth of Hausa words come from Arabic. Many Hausa can read and write

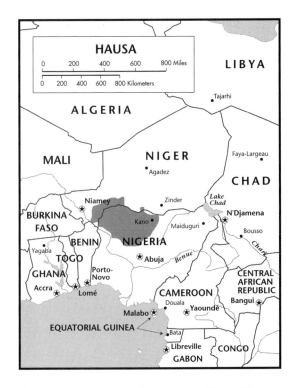

Arabic. Many can also speak either French or English.

4 ● FOLKLORE

According to tradition, Bayajidda, the mythical ancestor of the Hausa, migrated from Baghdad in the ninth or tenth century AD. After stopping at the kingdom of Bornu, he fled west and helped the king of Daura slay a dangerous snake. As a reward, he was given the Queen of Daura in marriage. Bayajidda's son, Bawo, founded the city of Biram. He had six sons who became the rulers of other Hausa city-states. Collectively, these are known as the *Hausa bakwai* (Hausa seven).

Hausa folklore includes *tatsunya*—stories that usually have a moral. They involve animals, young men and maidens, and heroes and villains. Many include proverbs and riddles.

5 ● RELIGION

Most Hausa are devout Muslims who believe in Allah and in Muhammad as his prophet. They pray five times each day, read the Koran (holy scriptures), fast during the month of Ramadan, give alms to the poor, and aspire to make the pilgrimage *(hajj)* to the Muslim holy land in Mecca. Islam affects nearly all aspects of Hausa behavior, including dress, art, housing, rites of passage, and laws. In the rural areas, there are communities of peoples who do not follow Islam. These people are called *Maguzawa.* They worship nature spirits known as *bori* or *iskoki.*

6 ● MAJOR HOLIDAYS

The Hausa observe the holy days of the Islamic calendar. *Eid* (Muslim feast days) celebrate the end of Ramadan (month of fasting), follow a *hajj* (pilgrimage to Mecca), and celebrate the birthday of the prophet Muhammad. On *Eid al-Adha,* Muslims sacrifice an animal to reenact the time Abraham was willing to sacrifice his son to God. Families also slaughter an animal in their own homes. This may be a male sheep or cow. People then celebrate with their relatives and friends and give each other gifts.

7 ● RITES OF PASSAGE

About a week after a child is born, it is given a name during an Islamic naming ceremony. Boys are usually circumcised at around the age of seven, but there is no special rite associated with this.

Jason Lauré

A Hausa father and son in their work clothes. Many Hausa men have more than one occupation. In rural areas, they farm and also engage in trade or craftsmanship. In the towns and cities, they may have formal jobs that they supplement with trade.

In their mid- to late teens, young men and women may become engaged. The marriage ceremony may take as long as several days. Celebrations begin among the bride and her family and friends as she is prepared for marriage. Male representatives of the bride's and the groom's families sign the marriage contract according to Islamic law, usually at the mosque. Shortly thereafter, the couple is brought together.

Following a death, Islamic burial principles are always followed. The deceased is washed, wrapped in a shroud, and buried facing eastward—toward the holy land of Mecca. Prayers are recited, and family members receive condolences. Wives mourn their deceased husbands for about three months.

8 ● RELATIONSHIPS

Hausa tend to be quiet and reserved. When they interact with outsiders, they generally do not show emotion. There are also some customs that govern interaction with one's relatives. For example, it is considered a sign of respect not to say the name of one's spouse or parents. By contrast, relaxed, playful relations are the norm with certain relatives, such as younger siblings, grandparents, and cousins.

From an early age, children develop friendships with their neighbors that may last a lifetime. In some towns, young people may form associations whose members socialize together until they marry.

9 ● LIVING CONDITIONS

In rural villages, Hausa usually live in large households *(gidaje)* that include a man, his wives, his sons, and their wives and children. In large cities, such as Kano or Katsina, Hausa live either in the old sections of town or in newer quarters built for civil servants. Hausa housing ranges from traditional family compounds in rural areas to modern, single-family houses in new sections of cities.

10 ● FAMILY LIFE

Relatives cooperate in activities such as farming and trade in rural areas, and business activities in urban areas. Relatives hope to live near each other to socialize and support each other. Families arrange marriages for their young people. Marriages between relatives, such as cousins, are preferred. Under Islamic law, a man may marry up to four wives.

Following Islamic custom, most married Hausa women live in seclusion. They stay in the home and only go out for ceremonies or to seek medical treatment. When they do leave their homes, women wear veils and are often escorted by their children.

11 ● CLOTHING

Hausa men are recognizable by their elaborate dress. Many wear large, flowing gowns *(gare, babban gida)* with elaborate embroi- dery around the neck. They also wear colorful embroidered caps *(huluna)*. Hausa women wear a wrap-around robe made of colorful cloth with a matching blouse, head tie, and shawl.

12 ● FOOD

Staple foods include grains (sorghum, millet, or rice) and maize, which are ground into flour for a variety of foods. Breakfast often consists of porridge. Sometimes it includes cakes made of fried beans *(kosai)* or wheat flour *(funkaso)*. Lunch and dinner usually include a heavy porridge *(tuwo)*. It is served with a soup or stew *(miya)*. Most soups are made with ground or chopped tomatoes, onions, and peppers. To this are added spices and other vegetables such as spinach, pumpkin, and okra. Small amounts of meat are eaten. Beans, peanuts, and milk also add protein to Hausa diets.

13 ● EDUCATION

From about the age of six, Hausa children attend Koranic schools (schools where teaching is based on the Islamic holy scripture, the Koran). They learn to recite the scriptures and learn about the practices, teachings, and morals of Islam. By the time they reach adulthood, many achieve high levels of Islamic scholarship.

Since Nigeria received its independence in 1960, the government has built many schools and universities. A majority of Hausa children, especially in urban areas, are now able to attend school, at least at the primary level.

14 ● CULTURAL HERITAGE

Music and art play are important in everyday life. From a young age, Hausa children participate in dances, which are held in meeting places such as the market. Work songs often accompany activities in the rural areas and in the markets. Praise-singers sing about community histories, leaders, and other prominent individuals. Storytelling, local dramas, and musical performances are also common forms of traditional entertainment.

15 ● EMPLOYMENT

Hausa society has a strong division of labor according to age and sex. The main activity in the towns is trade; in rural areas, it is agriculture. Many Hausa men have more than one occupation. In the towns and cities, they may have formal jobs, such as teaching or government work, and engage in trade on the side. In rural areas, they farm and also engage in trade or crafts. Some Hausa are full-time traders with shops or market stalls. Many Hausa are full-time Islamic scholars.

Hausa women earn money by processing, cooking, and selling food. They also sell cloth scraps, pots, medicines, vegetable oils, and other small items. Since women are generally secluded according to Islamic law, their children or servants go to other houses or the market on their behalf.

16 ● SPORTS

Both wrestling (koko) and boxing (dumb) are popular traditional sports among the Hausa. Matches take place in arenas or markets, often on religious holidays. Music, particularly drumming, accompanies the competition. Opponents wrestle until one is thrown to the ground. Boxers fight until one is either brought to his knees or falls flat on the ground.

Soccer is the most popular modern competitive sport, and is considered the national sport of Nigeria.

17 ● RECREATION

Musicians perform at weddings, naming ceremonies, and parties, as well as during Islamic holidays. Today, Western forms of entertainment are popular. Hausa listen to Western music, including rap and reggae, and view American and British television programs. Many have stereos, televisions, and VCRs in their homes.

18 ● CRAFTS AND HOBBIES

Hausa are well known for their craftsmanship. There are leather tanners and leatherworkers, weavers, carvers and sculptors, ironworkers and blacksmiths, silver workers, potters, dyers, tailors, and embroiderers. Their wares are sold in markets throughout west Africa.

19 ● SOCIAL PROBLEMS

Poverty is widespread among the Hausa. Poverty results in poor nutrition and diet, illness and inadequate health care, and lack of educational opportunities. Most of the region where the Hausa live is prone to drought. Hausa people suffer during harsh weather. Some Hausa have been unable to earn a living in rural areas, and have moved to the cities in search of work.

20 ● BIBLIOGRAPHY

Coles, Catherine, and Beverly Mack. *Hausa Women in the Twentieth Century*. Madison:

University of Wisconsin Press, 1991.

Koslow, Philip. *Hausaland: The Fortress Kingdoms.* Kingdoms of Africa. New York: Chelsea House Publishers, 1995.

Smith, Mary. *Baba of Karo: A Woman of the Muslim Hausa.* New Haven, Conn.: Yale University Press, 1981.

WEBSITES

World Travel Guide. Nigeria. [Online] Available http://www.wtgonline.com/country/ng/gen.html, 1998.

Igbo

PRONUNCIATION: EE-bo
ALTERNATE NAMES: Ibo
LOCATION: Southern Nigeria (Igboland)
POPULATION: 5.5 million
LANGUAGE: Igbo (Kwa subfamily of the Niger-Congo language family)
RELIGION: Tribal religion

1 ● INTRODUCTION

The Igbo are the second largest group of people living in southern Nigeria. They are socially and culturally diverse, consisting of many subgroups. Although they live in scattered groups of villages, they all speak one language.

The Igbo have no common traditional story of their origins. Historians have proposed two major theories of Igbo origins. One claims the existence of a core area, or "nuclear Igboland." The other claims that the Igbo are descended from waves of immigrants from the north and the west who arrived in the fourteenth or fifteenth century. Three of these are the Nri, Nzam, and Anam.

European contact with the Igbo began with the arrival of the Portuguese in the mid-fifteenth century. At first the Europeans confined themselves to slave trade on the Niger Coast. At this point, the main item of commerce provided by the Igbo was slaves, many of whom were sent to the New World. After the abolition of the slave trade in 1807, British companies pushed beyond the coastal areas and aggressively pursued control of the interior. The Protectorate of Southern Nigeria, created in 1900, included Igboland. Until 1960, Nigeria remained a British colony, and the Igbo were British subjects. On October 1, 1960, Nigeria became an independent nation structured as a federation of states.

2 ● LOCATION

Igboland is located in southeastern Nigeria, with a total land area of about 15,800 square miles (about 41,000 square kilometers). The Igbo country has four distinct areas. The low-lying deltas and riberbank areas are heavily inundated during the rainy season, and are very fertile. The central belt is a rather high plain. The Udi highlands are the only coal-mining area in West Africa.

It is difficult to obtain accurate census figures for either the Igbo or for Nigeria as a whole. The Igbo population is estimated to be between 5 and 6 million.

3 ● LANGUAGE

The Igbo language belongs to the Niger-Congo language family. It is part of the Kwa subfamily. A complicated system of high and low tones indicates differences in meaning and grammatical relationships. There are a wide range of dialects.

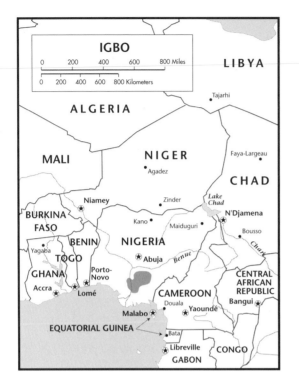

IGBO

| 0 | 200 | 400 | 600 | 800 Miles |
| 0 | 200 | 400 | 600 | 800 Kilometers |

Here are a few Igbo expressions:

English	Igbo
Hello, how are you?	Keku ka imelo?
What is your name?	Kedu ahagi?
Thank you	Ndewo

4 ● FOLKLORE

The Igbo have a system of folk beliefs that explains how everything in the world came into being. It explains what functions the heavenly and earthly bodies have and offers guidance on how to behave toward gods, spirits, and one's ancestors.

The Igbo believe the world is peopled by invisible and visible forces: by the living, the dead, and those yet to be born. Reincarnation is seen as a bridge between the living and the dead.

5 ● RELIGION

The major beliefs of the Igbo religion are shared by all Igbo-speaking people. However, many of its practices are locally organized, with the most effective unit of religious worship being the extended family. Periodic rituals and ceremonies may activate the lineage (larger kinship unit) or the village, which is the widest political community.

The Igbo believe in a supreme god who keeps watch over his creatures from a distance. He seldom interferes in the affairs of human beings. No sacrifices are made directly to him. However, he is seen as the ultimate receiver of sacrifices made to the minor gods. To distinguish him from the minor gods he is called Chukwu—the great or the high god. As the creator of everything, he is called Chukwu Abiama.

There are also minor gods, who are generally subject to human passions and weaknesses. They may be kind, hospitable, and industrious; at other times they are treacherous, unmerciful, and envious. These minor gods include Ala, the earth goddess. She is associated with fertility, both of human beings and of the land. Anyanwu is the sun god who makes crops and trees grow. Igwe is the sky god, the source of rain.

In addition to their gods, the Igbo believe in a variety of spirits whose good will depends on treating them well. Forests and rivers at the edge of cultivated land are said to be occupied by these spirits. Mbataku and Agwo are spirits of wealth. Others include Aha njoku (the yam spirit) and Ikoro (the drum spirit).

The Igbo attitude toward their deities and spirits is not one of fear but one of friendship.

6 ● MAJOR HOLIDAYS

The Igbo celebrate the major national holidays of Nigeria, including New Year's Day (January 1), Easter (March or April), Nigerian Independence Day (October 1), and Christmas (December 24 to 26) .

In addition, each town has its own local festivals. Those in the spring or summer are held to welcome the new agricultural cycle. In the fall, harvest festivals are held to mark the end of the cycle.

7 ● RITES OF PASSAGE

Circumcision takes place about eight days after the birth of a boy. At this time the umbilical cord is buried at the foot of a tree selected by the child's mother.

The name-giving ceremony is a formal occasion celebrated by feasting and drinking. A wide variety of names may be chosen. The name may be based on anything from the child's birthmarks to the opinion of the diviner, or seer. The name *Nwanyimeole*—"What can a woman do?"—means that a father desires a male child. *Onwubiko*—"May death forgive"—expresses the fact that parents have lost many of their children and pray that this child may survive.

The process of marrying a young Igbo woman is a long, elaborate one. It is rarely accomplished in less than a year and often takes several years. The process falls into four stages: asking the young woman's consent, negotiating through a middleman, testing the bride's character, and paying the bride wealth, a kind of dowry.

Death in old age is accepted as a blessing. After death, the body is clothed in the person's finest garments. The corpse is placed on a stool in a sitting posture. Old friends and relatives visit and pay their last respects. Young men wrap the corpse in grass mats, carry it out to the burial ground, and bury it. When the head of a family dies, he is buried beneath the floor of his house. Burial generally follows within twenty-four hours of death.

8 ● RELATIONSHIPS

Two criteria shape interpersonal relations: age and gender. Respect is given to males, and to older persons. Children are always required to offer the first greeting to their elders.

Social status is based on wealth, regardless of occupation. The Igbo distinguish between *obgenye* or *mbi* (the poor), *dinkpa* (the moderately prosperous), and *nnukwu madu* or *ogaranya* (the rich).

9 ● LIVING CONDITIONS

Village life has changed considerably since the discovery of oil in Nigeria. Houses, which used to have mud walls and thatched roofs, are now constructed of cement blocks with corrugated iron roofs. Electricity has been introduced; television sets and radios are now commonplace. Villages have running water, although it is not connected to every house.

10 ● FAMILY LIFE

Under the practice of polygyny, many Igbo men have more than one wife. A successful man marries as many wives as he can support. This involves providing farm plots to help the women and their dependents make a living. The polygynous family is made up of a man and his wives and all their children. Beyond that unit is the extended family, consisting of all the sons in a family and their parents, wives, and unmarried daughters. The extended family may have anywhere from five to thirty members. Ideally, all of the members of the extended family live in one large compound.

The Igbo family has changed in recent years. Christian marriage and civil marriage are important innovations. Among Igbo professional people, the trend is toward the nuclear family with its own residence.

11 ● CLOTHING

The everyday clothing in urban areas is not different from that of Westerners. Traditional clothing is still worn on important occasions in the cities and every day in rural areas. For everyday wear men wear a cotton wrap (robe), a shirt, and sandals. For formal occasions they wear a long shirt, often decorated with tucks and embroidery, over a dressy wrap, shoes, and a hat. Women wear wraps for both informal and formal occasions. The everyday wrapper is made from inexpensive cotton, dyed locally. For formal wear, the wrapper is either woven or batik-dyed, and often imported.

The blouse for formal wear is made of lace or embroidered. Women also wear a head tie, a rectangular piece of cloth that can be worn a number of different ways. The Igbo traditional dress is a *danshiki*, a long, loose-fitting top. Formerly Igbo women added pieces of cloth to show their marital status and number of children.

12 ● FOOD

The yam is the staple food of the Igbo. Traditionally, the yam was the food of choice for ceremonial occasions. Nowadays it has been replaced by rice. Other starchy foods include cassava, taro root, maize and plantains.

A typical meal includes a starch and a soup or stew, prepared with a vegetable to which pieces of fish, chicken, beef, or goat meat are added. Jollof rice of various types is popular throughout Nigeria. Among the Igbo who live near waterways it is often prepared with shrimp. The following recipe is very popular.

13 ● EDUCATION

Since gaining independence from Britain in 1960, Nigeria has set a priority on education. Universal primary education is the norm in southern Nigeria, where the Igbo live. Secondary education has also developed rapidly.

14 ● CULTURAL HERITAGE

The Igbo have number of wind and stringed musical instruments. The *ugene* is a whistle made of baked clay, round in form, and about the size of a billiard ball. Probably the most interesting of the Igbo instruments is the *ubaw-akwala,* a sort of guitar. It has a triangular body formed by three pieces of soft wood sewn together. It is played by strolling singers in the evenings. Igbo sing-

Recipe

Shrimp Jollof Rice

Ingredients

1 pound of shrimp, cooked, shelled, and deveined

2 or 3 fresh tomatoes, or 1 8-ounce can whole tomatoes

1 can tomato paste

1 onion, chopped

1 green pepper, chopped

½ teaspoon red pepper flakes

½ teaspoon ground black pepper

3 Tablespoons peanut oil

1 cup white rice cooked in chicken broth according to directions on the package

Directions

1. Heat the peanut oil in a large kettle.

2. Add the tomato, peppers, onion, and cook for about 3 minutes until the onions and peppers are softened.

3. Add the tomato paste, about 2 cups of water, and the red pepper flakes and black pepper. Simmer for about 15 minutes.

4. While this is simmering, cook the rice in another pot according to package directions.

5. Add the shrimp and simmer about 5 minutes longer.

6. Combine the shrimp sauce with the rice, and pour mixture into an ovenproof dish and cover.

7. Place in an oven set at 250°F. Bake until the liquid is absorbed completely.

8. Stir to loosen the rice grains and serve.

The flavors improve if this dish is made several hours in advance and allowed to rest in the oven with the door ajar.

ers improvise as the song proceeds and show great skill in fitting words to the song's rhythm and tune.

Dancing is a great Igbo pastime, practiced by everybody. There are special dances for boys, girls, men, women, and mixed groups. Group dancing is associated with religious observances and festivals.

15 ● EMPLOYMENT

The traditional Igbo economy depends on root-crop farming. Yams, cassava and taro are the chief root crops. There is a division of labor according to gender. Men clear the bush and plant the yams with the help of the women and the children. Following the planting of yams, plots are allocated to the women individually. Each woman plants other crops in the spaces between the yams and also on the slopes of hills.

Trading is an old occupation among the Igbo. The marketplace has become an important source of livelihood. An increasing number of Igbo are now engaged in wage labor. Growing cities, expanding road construction, new industries, and oil exploration are creating many job opportunities.

16 ● SPORTS

Wrestling is the most popular sport among boys and young men, with great annual contests in every part of Igbo country.

The other popular sport is soccer. Traditionally played only by boys, it has been introduced to girls through the school system.

17 ● RECREATION

Traditional entertainment includes storytelling, rituals, dancing, and music making. Modern forms of entertainment include watching television and going to movies and discos. Most households own radios, and there are several television sets in each village. The Igbo enjoy games, including card games and checkers. Among the younger people American youth culture is popular. Most enjoy listening to rap and rock music.

18 ● CRAFTS AND HOBBIES

The Igbo practice a number of crafts, some performed by men only and some by women. Carving is a skilled occupation practiced only by men. They produce doors and panels for houses, as well as stools, dancing masks, and boxes. Another valued craft is that of the blacksmith.

Women's crafts include pottery making, spinning, weaving, basketry, and grass plaiting.

19 ● SOCIAL PROBLEMS

The Igbo have been seriously affected by national problems ranging from civil war to military coups.

The crime rate in Nigeria is high. The problem is worst in larger urban centers, but rural areas are also affected. The crime wave was aggravated by the worsening economic conditions of the 1980s. Drug-related crime emerged as a major problem. Igboland has so far escaped the worst of this, although marijuana use among young people has been reported.

20 ● BIBLIOGRAPHY

Achebe, Chinua. *Things Fall Apart*. New York: Knopf, 1995.

Njoku, John E. Eberegbulam. *The Igbos of Nigeria: Ancient Rites, Changes, and Survival*. Lewiston, N.Y.: E. Mellen Press, 1990.

Ogbaa, Kalu. *Igbo*. Heritage Library of African Peoples. New York: Rosen Publishing Group, 1995.

WEBSITE

Igbo Homepage. [Online] Available http://www.lioness.cm.utexas.edu/igbo, 1998.

PrimaNet Communications. The Virtual Igbo Homesites. [Online] Available http://www.igbo.com, 1998.

World Travel Guide. [Online] Available http://www.wtgonline.com/country/ng/gen.html, 1998.

Yoruba

PRONUNCIATION: YAWR-uh-buh
LOCATION: West Africa (primarily Nigeria; also Benin and Togo)
POPULATION: 5.3 million
LANGUAGE: Yoruba
RELIGION: Ancestral religion; Islam; Christianity

1 ● INTRODUCTION

The Yoruba are one of the largest African ethnic groups south of the Sahara Desert. They are, in fact, not a single group, but rather a collection of diverse people bound together by a common language, history, and culture. Within Nigeria, the Yoruba dominate the western part of the country.

Yoruba mythology holds that all Yoruba people descended from a hero called Odua or Oduduwa. Today there are over fifty individuals who claim kingship as descendants of Odua.

During the four centuries of the slave trade, Yoruba territory was known as the Slave Coast. Uncounted numbers of Yoruba were carried to the Americas. Their descendants preserved Yoruba traditions. In several parts of the Caribbean and South America, Yoruba religion has been combined with Christianity. In 1893, the Yoruba kingdoms in Nigeria became part of the Protectorate of Great Britain. Until 1960 Nigeria was a British colony and the Yoruba were British subjects. On October 1, 1960, Nigeria became an independent nation structured as a federation of states.

2 ● LOCATION

The Yoruba homeland is located in west Africa. It stretches from a savanna (grassland) region in the north to a region of tropical rain forests in the south. Most Yoruba live in Nigeria. However there are also some scattered groups in Benin and Togo, small countries to the west of Nigeria. The occupations and living conditions of the Yoruba in the north and south differ sharply.

Current census figures are difficult to obtain. The Yoruba population is estimated to be 5.3 million.

3 ● LANGUAGE

The Yoruba language belongs to the Congo-Kordofanian language family. Yoruba has many dialects, but its speakers can all understand each other.

Yoruba is a tonal language. The same combination of vowels and consonants has different meanings depending on the pitch of the vowels (whether they are pronounced with a high voice or a low voice). For example, the same word, *aro*, can mean cymbal, indigo dye, lamentation, and granary, depending on intonation. *Pele o* is "Hello"; *Bawo ni?* is "How are you?"; and *Dada ni* is "Fine, thank you."

4 ● FOLKLORE

According to a Yoruba creation myth, the deities (gods) originally lived in the sky with only water below them. Olorun, the Sky God, gave to Orishala, the God of Whiteness, a chain, a bit of earth in a snail shell, and a five-toed chicken. He told Orishala to go down and create the earth. Orishala approached the gate of heaven. He saw some deities having a party and he stopped to greet them. They offered him palm wine and he drank too much and fell asleep. Odua, his younger brother, saw Orishala sleeping. He took the materials and went to the edge of heaven, accompanied by Chameleon. He let down the chain and they climbed down it. Odua threw the piece of earth on the water and placed the five-toed chicken upon it. The chicken began to scratch the earth, spreading it in all directions. After Chameleon had tested the firmness of the earth, Odua stepped down. A sacred grove is there today.

5 ● RELIGION

As many as 20 percent of the Yoruba still practice the traditional religions of their ancestors.

in times of trouble. Another god, Ogun (god of war, the hunt, and metalworking), is considered one of the most important. In Yoruba courts, people who follow traditional beliefs swear to give truthful testimony by kissing a machete sacred to Ogun.

Shango (also spelled Sango and Sagoe) is the deity that creates thunder. The Yoruba believe that when thunder and lightning strike, Shango has thrown a thunderstone to earth. After a thunderstorm, Yoruba religious leaders search the ground for the thunderstone, which is believed to have special powers. The stones are housed in shrines dedicated to Shango. Shango has four wives, each representing a river in Nigeria.

The Yoruba who practice other religious are divided about evenly between Muslims (followers of Islam) and Christians. Nearly all Yoruba still observe annual festivals and other traditional religious practices.

6 ● MAJOR HOLIDAYS

Local festivals are usually dedicated to individual deities. Yoruba may also celebrate the following holidays, depending on whether they are Christians or Muslims: New Year's Day, January; *Eid al-Adha* (Feast of Sacrifice), June or July; Easter, March or April; *Maulid an-Nabi* (Muhammad's birthday); Ramadan, followed by a three-day feast; Nigerian Independence Day (October); *Eid al-Fitr*; Christmas (December).

7 ● RITES OF PASSAGE

A newborn infant is sprinkled with water to make it cry. No word may be spoken until the infant cries. Also, no one younger than

The practice of traditional religion varies from community to community. For example, a deity (god) may be male in one village and female in another. Yoruba traditional religion holds that there is one supreme being and hundreds of *orisha,* or minor deities. The worshipers of a deity are referred to as his "children."

There are three gods who are available to all. Olorun (Sky God) is the high god, the Creator. One may call on him with prayers or by pouring water on kola nuts on the ground. Eshu (also called Legba by some) is the divine messenger who delivers sacrifices to Olorun after they are placed at his shrine. Everyone prays frequently to this deity. Ifa is the God of Divination, who interprets the wishes of Olorun to mankind. Believers in the Yoruba religion turn to Ifa

Yoruba girls in Lagos, Nigeria. Every Yoruba is born into a patrilineal clan whose members are descended from a remote common ancestor. The clan and sub-clan completely overshadow the immediate family in importance.

the mother should be present at the birth. The infant then is taken to the backyard. The umbilical cord is bound tightly with thread and then cut. The placenta is buried in the backyard. On the placenta burial spot, the child is bathed with a loofah sponge and rubbed with palm oil. The child is held by the feet and given three shakes to make it strong and brave. After a specified number of days, a naming ceremony is held. Relatives attend and bring small amounts of money. Male and female circumcision are usually performed in the first month.

Marriages are arranged. A man must negotiate with the girl's father. If he is approved he must bring the family a pay-ment called a bride wealth, paid in three installments. Wedding ceremonies begin at the bride's house after dark. There is a feast to which the groom contributes yams. The bride then is taken to the groom's house. There she is washed from foot to knee with an herbal mixture meant to bring her many children. For the first eight days after marriage she divides her time between her husband's and in her parents' compounds. On the ninth day she moves to her husband's home.

Burials are performed by the adult men who are not close relatives but belong to the clan of the deceased. The grave is dug in the floor of the room where the deceased lived.

After the burial there is a period of feasting. Many of the rituals associated with burial are intended to insure that the deceased will be reborn again.

8 ● RELATIONSHIPS

Kinship is the most important relationship for the Yorubas. Best friends are very important as well. A best friend is referred to as "friend not-see-not-sleep." This means that one does not go to sleep without having seen his best friend. When approaching death, a Yoruba shares his last wishes with his best friend.

Also important are clubs that grow out of childhood associations. When a group of young friends starts spending time together, they form a club. They choose a name and invite an older man and woman to serve as advisors. The clubs continue through adulthood. They hold monthly meetings, with the members serving as hosts in turn.

9 ● LIVING CONDITIONS

Traditional compounds (which house clans) in Yoruba villages are made up of rectangular courtyards, each with a single entrance. Around each courtyard is an open or a partly enclosed porch. Here the women sit, weave, and cook. Behind this are the rooms of each adult. Today the old compounds are rapidly being replaced by modern bungalows made of cement blocks with corrugated iron roofs. Most Yoruba towns, even small ones, have adequate basic services, including electricity, running water, and paved roads.

10 ● FAMILY LIFE

Every Yoruba is born into a clan whose members are descended from a common ancestor. Descent is patrilineal—both sons and daughters are born into the clan of their father. Clan members live in a large residential area called a compound. The males are born, married, and buried in it. Females live in the compound of their birth until they marry. Then they go to live with their husbands. The eldest male, or *Bale,* is the head of the compound. A husband is responsible for settling quarrels within his own family. However, if he is unsuccessful or if an argument involves members of two different families, it is referred to the Bale.

Within the compound, the immediate family consists of a man, his wives, and their children. The Yoruba practice polygyny (having more than one wife). Each wife and her children are considered a sub-family. They have a separate room within the husband's and they share possessions. Each mother cooks for her own children only. A man is expected to treat each wife equally. However, wives compete to gain additional favors for their own children. The father is strict and distant. Often, he sees little of his children. When they are young, children of co-wives play together. However, as they grow older, they usually grow apart because of quarrels over possessions.

11 ● CLOTHING

Western-style dress is worn in urban areas. Traditional clothing is still worn on important occasions and in rural areas. It is very colorful and elaborate. Traditional fabrics were block printed with geometric designs. Women wear a head tie made of a rectangu-

Recipe

Fufu (Pounded Yam)

Ingredients

Choose one of these:
3 or 4 white yams, preferably round and fat
3 or 4 orange yams
1 bunch plaintains
1 bunch green (unripe) bananas

Directions

1. Peel the vegetable or fruit of choice and cut into chunks or slices. Place the pieces into a pot and cover with water.

2. Cover the pot and heat until the water boils. Cook until the yams (plaintains or green bananas) can be pierced easily with a fork.

3. Drain well and place one or two pieces into a large mortar and pestle. Pound the pieces until a mass is formed that pulls away from the sides of the mortar. (This cannot be done with an electric mixer, because the pounded yams will be very stiff.)

Fufu is served with soups and stews at main meals. Diners pinch off a piece of fufu, make an indentation in it, and use it as a spoon to scoop up a mouthful of the main dish.

Chicken and Okra Soup

Ingredients

6 to 10 chicken legs or wings
1 small onion, chopped
18 large okra, chopped
1 teaspoon dry ground red pepper
1½ ounces (40 grams) dry crayfish, ground
2 medium fresh tomatoes
2 teaspoons tomato paste
Pinch of salt
½ teaspoon potash

Directions

1. Place the chicken in a pot with salt and pepper, cover with water and boil until tender. Drain, reserving broth for next step. Remove meat from bones and cut into bite-sized chunks.

2. Combine okra with reserved broth and remaining ingredients. Boil for 5 minutes. Add chicken and continue to cook for 5 minutes more. Serve with fufu.

lar piece of fabric. They carry babies or young children on their backs by tying another rectangular cloth around their the waists. A third cloth may be worn over the shoulder as a shawl over a loose-fitting, short-sleeved blouse. A larger cloth serves as a wrap-around skirt.

Men wear tailored cloth hats, gowns, and trousers. One popular type of gown is shaped like a poncho. It reaches to the fingertips, but is worn folded back on the shoulders. Trousers are usually very loose and baggy. All the cloth for traditional clothing is hand woven. Often it is elaborately embroidered.

12 ● FOOD

The Yoruba diet consists of starchy tubers, grains, and plantains. These are supplemented by vegetable oils, wild and culti-

The "talking drum" features an hourglass shape with laces that can be squeezed to tighten the goatskin head, altering the drum's pitch. Courtesy of Center for the Study of World Musics, Kent State University.

vated fruits and vegetables, meat, and fish. The daily family diet relies on cassava, taro, maize, beans, and plantains. One of the most popular foods is *fufu* (or *foo-foo*), similar to a dumpling, but made of cassava (white yams). Rice and yams are eaten on special occasions.

The recipes are very popular and are usually served together.

13 ● EDUCATION

Since attaining independence (1960), Nigeria has set a high priority on education. Uni-versal primary education has become the norm in southern Nigeria, where the Yoruba live. Secondary school (high school) education also became common. The first university in Nigeria was located in a Yoruba city. Originally called University College, it is now known as the University of Ibadan. The majority of students at Ibadan are Yoruba.

14 ● CULTURAL HERITAGE

The Yoruba oral tradition includes praise poems, tongue twisters, hundreds of prose narratives and riddles, and thousands of proverbs.

Yoruba music includes songs of ridicule and praise, as well as lullabies, religious songs, war songs, and work songs. These usually follow a "call and response" pattern between a leader and chorus. Rhythm is provided by drums, iron gongs, cymbals, rattles, and hand clapping. Other instruments include long brass trumpets, ivory trumpets, whistles, stringed instruments, and metallophones. Perhaps the most interesting musical instrument is the "talking drum." The "talking drum" features an hourglass shape with laces that can be squeezed to tighten the goatskin head, altering the drum's pitch.

15 ● EMPLOYMENT

About 75 percent of the Yoruba men are farmers, producing food crops for their domestic needs. Farming is considered men's work. Clearing or hoeing fields is done only by men. Wives help their husbands plant yams and harvest corn, beans, and cotton. They also help at the market, selling farm produce. Some Yoruba have large cocoa farms worked by hired labor.

The Yoruba enjoy trading. Huge markets with over a thousand sellers are common. Trade in foodstuffs and cloth is confined to women. Meat selling and produce buying are the province of men.

The new, educated generation is moving away from farming, and its members are looking for white-collar jobs.

16 ● SPORTS

Although there are few organized sports, Yoruba (like other Nigerians) in some areas participate in wrestling and soccer.

17 ● RECREATION

Traditional entertainment includes rituals, dancing, and music making. Modern forms of entertainment include watching television and going to movies and discos. Most households own televisions sets. The more religious households prohibit family members, especially women, from going to see films. Among urban teenagers, American youth culture is popular. Most young people listen to rap and rock music from the U.S. Ayo, a board game, is popular among people of all ages. It is a mancala game—a type of game popular in west Africa, that is played on a board with two rows of indentations or wells that are filled with small seeds or stones.

18 ● CRAFTS AND HOBBIES

Crafts include weaving, embroidering, pottery making, woodcarving, leather and bead working, and metalworking.

Both men and women weave, using different types of looms. Cloth is woven from wild silk and from locally grown cotton.

Men also do embroidery, particularly on men's gowns and caps, and work as tailors and dressmakers. Floor mats and mat storage bags are also made by men.

Women are the potters. In addition to palm oil lamps, they make over twenty kinds of pots and dishes for cooking, eating, and carrying and storing liquids.

EPD Photos

Traditional Yoruban fabrics were block printed with geometric designs.

Woodcarvers, all of whom are men, carve masks and figurines as well as mortars, pestles, and bowls. Some Yoruba woodcarvers also work in bone, ivory, and stone. Blacksmiths work both in iron and brass to create both useful and decorative objects.

19 ● SOCIAL PROBLEMS

There are vast differences in wealth among Yoruba of different social classes. Many urban occupations do not provide adequate wages to support a family.

Nigeria's human rights record is poor. A Yoruba, Olisa Agbakobe, led a group of lawyers that founded the human rights group, the Civil Liberties Organization (CLO).

The crime rate in Nigeria is high, particularly in Lagos, Ibadan, Abeokuta, and other urban areas. More than half the offenses are property crimes. Drug-related crime is a major problem. Young people are using both marijuana and cocaine in increasing numbers.

20 ● BIBLIOGRAPHY

Bascom, William. *The Yoruba of Southwestern Nigeria.* Prospect Heights, Ill.: Waveland Press, 1984.

Hetfield, Jamie. *The Yoruba of West Africa.* New York: Rosen Publishing Group, 1996.

Koslow, Philip. *Yorubaland: The Flowering of Genius.* Kingdoms of Africa. New York: Chelsea House, 1996.

WEBSITES

World Travel Guide. [Online] Available http://www.wtgonline.com/country/ng/gen.html, 1998.

Glossary

aboriginal: The first known inhabitants of a country.

adobe: A brick made from sun-dried heavy clay mixed with straw, used in building houses.

Altaic language family: A family of languages spoken in portions of northern and eastern Europe, and nearly the whole of northern and central Asia, together with some other regions.

Amerindian: A contraction of the two words, American Indian. It describes native peoples of North, South, or Central America.

Anglican: Pertaining to or connected with the Church of England.

animism: The belief that natural objects and phenomena have souls or innate spiritual powers.

apartheid: The past governmental policy in the Republic of South Africa of separating the races in society.

arable land: Land that can be cultivated by plowing and used for growing crops.

archipelago: Any body of water abounding with islands, or the islands themselves collectively.

Austronesian language: A family of languages which includes practically all the languages of the Pacific Islands—Indonesian, Melanesian, Polynesian, and Micronesian sub-families.

average life expectancy: In any given society, the average age attained by persons at the time of death.

Baha'i: The follower of a religious sect founded by Mirza Husayn Ali in Iran in 1863.

Baltic states: The three formerly communist countries of Estonia, Latvia, and Lithuania that border on the Baltic Sea.

Bantu language group: A name applied to the languages spoken in central and south Africa.

Baptist: A member of a Protestant denomination that practices adult baptism by complete immersion in water.

barren land: Unproductive land, partly or entirely treeless.

barter: Trade practice where merchandise is exchanged directly for other merchandise or services without use of money.

Berber: a member of one of the Afroasiatic peoples of northern Africa.

Brahman: A member (by heredity) of the highest caste among the Hindus, usually assigned to the priesthood.

bride wealth (bride price): Fee, in money or goods, paid by a prospective groom (and his family) to the bride's family.

Buddhism: A religious system common in India and eastern Asia. Founded by Siddhartha Gautama (c.563–c.483 BC), Buddhism asserts that suffering is an inescapable part of life. Deliverance can only be achieved through the practice of charity, temperance, justice, honesty, and truth.

Byzantine Empire: An empire centered in the city of Byzantium, now Istanbul in present-day Turkey.

cassava: The name of several species of stout herbs, extensively cultivated for food.

caste system: Heridtary social classes into which the Hindus are rigidly separated according to the religious law of Brahmanism. Privileges and limitations of each caste are passed down from parents to children.

Caucasian: The white race of human beings, as determined by genealogy and physical features.

census: An official counting of the inhabitants of a state or country with details of sex and age, family, occupation, possessions, etc.

Christianity: The religion founded by Jesus Christ, based on the Bible as holy scripture.

Church of England: The national and established church in England.

civil rights: The privileges of all individuals to be treated as equals under the laws of their country; specifically, the rights given by certain amendments to the U.S. Constitution.

coastal plain: A fairly level area of land along the coast of a land mass.

coca: A shrub native to South America, the leaves of which produce organic compounds that are used in the production of cocaine.

colonial period: The period of time when a country forms colonies in and extends control over a foreign area.

colonist: Any member of a colony or one who helps settle a new colony.

colony: A group of people who settle in a new area far from their original country, but still under the jurisdiction of that country. Also refers to the newly settled area itself.

commonwealth: A free association of sovereign independent states that has no charter, treaty, or constitution. The association promotes cooperation, consultation, and mutual assistance among members.

communism: A form of government whose system requires common ownership of property for the use of all citizens. Prices on goods and services are usually set by the government, and all profits are shared equally by everyone. Also, communism refers directly to the official doctrine of the former Soviet Union.

compulsory education: The mandatory requirement for children to attend school until they have reached a certain age or grade level.

GLOSSARY

Confucianism: The system of ethics and politics taught by the Chinese philosopher Confucius.

constitution: The written laws and basic rights of citizens of a country or members of an organized group.

copra: The dried meat of the coconut.

cordillera: A continuous ridge, range, or chain of mountains.

coup d'ètat (coup): A sudden, violent overthrow of a government or its leader.

cuisine: A particular style of preparing food, especially when referring to the cooking of a particular country or ethnic group.

Cushitic language group: A group of languages that are spoken in Ethiopia and other areas of eastern Africa.

Cyrillic alphabet: An alphabet invented by Cyril and Methodius in the ninth century as an alphabet that was easier for the copyist to write. The Russian alphabet is a slight modification of it.

deity: A being with the attributes, nature, and essence of a god; a divinity.

desegregation: The act of removing restrictions on people of a particular race that keep them socially, economically, and, sometimes, physically, separate from other groups.

desertification: The process of becoming a desert as a result of climatic changes, land mismanagement, or both.

Dewali (Deepavali, Divali): The Hindu Festival of Lights, when Lakshmi, goddess of good fortune, is said to visit the homes of humans. The four- or five-day festival occurs in October or November.

dialect: One of a number of regional or related modes of speech regarded as descending from a common origin.

dowry: The sum of the property or money that a bride brings to her groom at their marriage.

Druze: A member of a Muslim sect based in Syria, living chiefly in the mountain regions of Lebanon.

dynasty: A family line of sovereigns who rule in succession, and the time during which they reign.

Eastern Orthodox: The outgrowth of the original Eastern Church of the Eastern Roman Empire, consisting of eastern Europe, western Asia, and Egypt.

Eid al-Adha: The Muslim holiday that celebrates the end of the special pilgrimage season (hajj) to the city of Mecca in Saudi Arabia.

Eid al-Fitr: The Muslim holiday that begins just after the end of the month of Ramadan and is celebrated with three or four days of feasting.

emigration: Moving from one country or region to another for the purpose of residence.

empire: A group of territories ruled by one sovereign or supreme ruler. Also, the period of time under that rule.

Episcopal: Belonging to or vested in bishops or prelates; characteristic of or pertaining to a bishop or bishops.

exports: Goods sold to foreign buyers.

Finno-Ugric language group: A subfamily of languages spoken in northeastern Europe, including Finnish, Hungarian, Estonian, and Lapp.

fjord: A deep indentation of the land forming a comparatively narrow arm of the sea with more or less steep slopes or cliffs on each side.

folk religion: A religion with origins and traditions among the common people of a nation or region that is relevant to their particular life-style.

Former Soviet Union: Refers to the republics that were once part of a large nation called the Union of Soviet Socialists Republics (USSR). The USSR was commonly called the Soviet Union. It included the 12 republics: Russia, Ukraine, Belarus, Moldova, Armenia, Azerbaijan, Uzbekistan, Turkmenistan, Tajikistan, Kazakhstan, Kyrgizstan, and Georgia. Sometimes the Baltic republics of Estonia, Latvia, and Lithuania are also included.

fundamentalist: A person who holds religious beliefs based on the complete acceptance of the words of holy scriptures as the truth.

Germanic language group: A large branch of the Indo-European family of languages including German itself, the Scandinavian languages, Dutch, Yiddish, Modern English, Modern Scottish, Afrikaans, and others. The group also includes extinct languages such as Gothic, Old High German, Old Saxon, Old English, Middle English, and the like.

Greek Orthodox: The official church of Greece, a self-governing branch of the Orthodox Eastern Church.

guerrilla: A member of a small radical military organization that uses unconventional tactics to take their enemies by surprise.

hajj: A religious journey made by Muslims to the holy city of Mecca in Saudi Arabia.

Holi: A Hindu festival of processions and merriment lasting three to ten days that marks the end of the lunar year in February or March.

Holocaust: The mass slaughter of European civilians, the vast majority of whom were Jews, by the Nazis during World War II.

Holy Roman Empire: A kingdom consisting of a loose union of German and Italian territories that existed from around the ninth century until 1806.

homeland: A region or area set aside to be a state for a people of a particular national, cultural, or racial origin.

homogeneous: Of the same kind or nature, often used in reference to a whole.

Horn of Africa: The Horn of Africa comprises Djibouti, Eritrea, Ethiopia, Somalia, and Sudan.

human rights issues: Any matters involving people's basic rights which are in question or thought to be abused.

immigration: The act or process of passing or entering into another country for the purpose of permanent residence.

imports: Goods purchased from foreign suppliers.

indigenous: Born or originating in a particular place or country; native to a particular region or area.

Indo-Aryan language group: The group that includes the languages of India; also called Indo-European language group.

Indo-European language family: The group that includes the languages of India and much of Europe and southwestern Asia.

Islam: The religious system of Muhammad, practiced by Muslims and based on a belief in Allah as the supreme being and Muhammed as his prophet. Islam also refers to those nations in which it is the primary religion. There are two major sects: Sunni and Shia (or Shiite). The main difference between the two sects is in their belief in who follows Muhammad, founder of Islam, as the religious leader.

Judaism: The religious system of the Jews, based on the Old Testament as revealed to Moses and characterized by a belief in one God and adherence to the laws of scripture and rabbinic traditions.

khan: A sovereign, or ruler, in central Asia.

khanate: A kingdom ruled by a khan, or man of rank.

literacy: The ability to read and write.

Maghreb states: Refers to Algeria, Morocco, and Tunisia; sometimes includes Libya and Mauritania.

maize: Another name (Spanish or British) for corn or the color of ripe corn.

manioc: The cassava plant or its product. Manioc is a very important food-staple in tropical America.

matrilineal (descent): Descending from, or tracing descent through, the maternal, or mother's, family line.

Mayan language family: The languages of the Central American Indians, further divided into two subgroups: the Maya and the Huastek.

mean temperature: The air temperature unit measured by the National Weather Service by adding the maximum and minimum daily temperatures together and diving the sum by 2.

Mecca: A city in Saudi Arabia; a destination of Muslims in the Islamic world.

mestizo: The offspring of a person of mixed blood; especially, a person of mixed Spanish and American Indian parentage.

millet: A cereal grass whose small grain is used for food in Europe and Asia.

monarchy: Government by a sovereign, such as a king or queen.

Mongol: One of an Asiatic race chiefly resident in Mongolia, a region north of China proper and south of Siberia.

Moors: One of the Arab tribes that conquered Spain in the eighth century.

Moslem *see* **Muslim.**

mosque: An Islam place of worship and the organization with which it is connected.

Muhammad (or Muhammed or Mahomet): An Arabian prophet (AD 570–632), known as the "Prophet of Allah" who founded the religion of Islam in 622, and wrote the Koran, (also spelled Quran) the scripture of Islam.

mulatto: One who is the offspring of parents one of whom is white and the other is black.

Muslim: A follower of Muhammad in the religion of Islam.

Muslim New Year: A Muslim holiday also called Nawruz. In some countries Muharram 1, which is the first month of the Islamic year, is observed as a holiday, in other places the new year is observed on Sha'ban, the eighth month of the year. This practice apparently stems from pagan Arab times. Shab-i-Bharat, a national holiday in Bangladesh on this day, is held by many to be the occasion when God ordains all actions in the coming year.

mystic: Person who believes he or she can gain spiritual knowledge through processes like meditation that are not easily explained by reasoning or rational thinking.

nationalism: National spirit or aspirations; desire for national unity, independence, or prosperity.

oasis: Fertile spot in the midst of a desert or wasteland.

official language: The language in which the business of a country and its government is conducted.

Ottoman Empire: A Turkish empire that existed from about 1603 until 1918, and included lands around the Mediterranean, Black, and Caspian seas.

patriarchal system: A social system in which the head of the family or tribe is the father or oldest male. Ancestry is determined and traced through the male members of the tribe.

patrilineal (descent): Descending from, or tracing descent through, the paternal, or father's, family line.

pilgrimage: religious journey, usually to a holy place.

plantain: Tropical plant with fruit that looks like bananas, but that must be cooked before eating.

Protestant: A member of one of the Christian bodies that descended from the Reformation of the sixteenth century.

pulses: Beans, peas, or lentils.

Ramadan: The ninth month of the Muslim calender. The entire month commemorates the period in which the Prophet Muhammad is said to have recieved divine revelation and is observed by a strict fast from sunrise to sundown.

Rastafarian: A member of a Jamaican cult begun in 1930 that is partly religious and partly political.

refugee: Person who, in times of persecution or political commotion, flees to a foreign country for safety.

revolution: A complete change in a government or society, such as in an overthrow of the government by the people.

Roman alphabet: Alphabet of the ancient Romans from which alphabets of most modern European languages, including English, are derived.

Roman Catholic Church: Christian church headed by the pope or Bishop of Rome.

Russian Orthodox: The arm of the Eastern Orthodox Church that was the official church of Russia under the tsars.

Sahelian zone: Eight countries make up this dry desert zone in Africa: Burkina Faso, Chad, Gambia, Mali, Mauritania, Niger, Senegal, and the Cape Verde Islands.

savanna: A treeless or near treeless grassland or plain.

segregation: The enforced separation of a racial or religious group from other groups, compelling them to live and go to school separately from the rest of society.

Seventh-day Adventist: One who believes in the second coming of Christ to establish a personal reign upon the earth.

shamanism: A religion in which shamans (priests or medicine men) are believed to influence spirits.

shantytown: An urban settlement of people in inadequate houses.

Shia Muslim see Islam.

Shiites see Islam.

Shintoism: The system of nature- and hero-worship that forms the native religion of Japan.

sierra: A chain of hills or mountains.

Sikh: A member of a community of India, founded around 1500 and based on the principles of monotheism (belief in one god) and human brotherhood.

Sino-Tibetan language family: The family of languages spoken in eastern Asia, including China, Thailand, Tibet, and Myanmar.

slash-and-burn agriculture: A hasty and sometimes temporary way of clearing land to make it available for agriculture by cutting down trees and burning them; also known as swidden agriculture.

slave trade: The transportation of black Africans beginning in the 1700s to other countries to be sold as slaves—people owned as property and compelled to work for their owners at no pay.

Slavic languages: A major subgroup of the Indo-European language family. It is further subdivided into West Slavic (including Polish, Czech, Slovak and Serbian), South Slavic (including Bulgarian, Serbo-Croatian, Slovene, and Old Church Slavonic), and East Slavic (including Russian Ukrainian and Byelorussian).

sorghum: Plant grown for its valuable uses, such as for grain, syrup, or fodder.

Southeast Asia: The region in Asia that consists of the Malay Archipelago, the Malay Peninsula, and Indochina.

Soviet Union see **Former Soviet Union.**

subcontinent: A large subdivision of a continent.

subsistence farming: Farming that provides only the minimum food goods necessary for the continuation of the farm family.

Sudanic language group: A related group of languages spoken in various areas of northern Africa, including Yoruba, Mandingo, and Tshi.

Sufi: A Muslim mystic who believes that God alone exists, there can be no real difference between good and evil, that the soul exists within the body as in a cage, so death should be the chief object of desire.

sultan: A king of a Muslim state.

Sunni Muslim see Islam.

Taoism: The doctrine of Lao-Tzu, an ancient Chinese philosopher (c.500 **BC**) as laid down by him in the *Tao-te-ching.*

Third World: A term used to describe less developed countries; as of the mid-1990s, it is being replaced by the United Nations designation Less Developed Countries, or LDC.

treaty: A negotiated agreement between two governments.

tribal system: A social community in which people are organized into groups or clans descended from common ancestors and sharing customs and languages.

tundra: A nearly level treeless area whose climate and vegetation are characteristically arctic due to its northern position; the subsoil is permanently frozen.

untouchables: In India, members of the lowest caste in the caste system, a hereditary social class system. They were considered unworthy to touch members of higher castes.

Union of the Soviet Socialist Republics see Former Soviet Union.

veldt: A grassland in South Africa.

Western nations: General term used to describe democratic, capitalist countries, including the United States, Canada, and western European countries.

Zoroastrianism: The system of religious doctrine taught by Zoroaster and his followers in the Avesta; the religion prevalent in Persia until its overthrow by the Muslims in the seventh century.

Index

All culture groups and countries included in this encyclopedia are included in this index. Selected regions, alternate groups names, and historical country names are cross-referenced. Country chapter titles are in boldface; volume numbers appear in brackets, with page number following.